Make the Night Hideous
Four English-Canadian Charivaris, 1881–1940

The charivari is a loud, late-night surprise house visit usually made on a newly wed couple by members of their community, accompanied by a quête (a request for a treat or money in exchange for the noisy performance) and/or pranks. Up to the first decades of the twentieth century, charivaris were for the most part enacted to express disapproval of the relationship that was their focus, such as those between individuals of different ages, races, or religions. While later charivaris maintained the same rituals, their meaning changed to herald a welcoming of the marriage.

Make the Night Hideous explores this mysterious transformation using four detailed case studies from different time periods and locations across English Canada, as well as first-person accounts of more recent charivari participants. Pauline Greenhill's unique and fascinating work explores the malleability of a tradition, its continuing value, and its contestation in a variety of discourses.

PAULINE GREENHILL is a professor in the Department of Women's and Gender Studies at the University of Winnipeg.

Make the Night Hideous

Four English-Canadian Charivaris, 1881–1940

Pauline Greenhill

UNIVERSITY OF TORONTO PRESS

Toronto   Buffalo   London

© University of Toronto Press Incorporated 2010
Toronto Buffalo London
www.utppublishing.com
Printed in Canada

ISBN 978-1-4426-4077-1 (cloth)
ISBN 978-1-4426-1015-6 (paper)

Printed on acid-free and 100% post-consumer recycled paper
with vegetable-based inks

Library and Archives Canada Cataloguing in Publication

Greenhill, Pauline, 1955–
Make the night hideous : four English-Canadian charivaris, 1881–1940 /
Pauline Greenhill.

(Canadian social history series)
Includes bibliographical references and index.
ISBN 978-1-4426-4077-1 (bound)
ISBN 978-1-4426-1015-6 (pbk.)

1. Shivaree – Canada – History.   2. Marriage customs and rites – Canada
– History.   I. Title.   II. Series: Canadian social history series.

GT2713.A2G74 2010   392.50971   C2010-904000-7

University of Toronto Press acknowledges the financial assistance to its publishing program of the Canada Council for the Arts and the Ontario Arts
Council.

 Canada Council   Conseil des Arts   ONTARIO ARTS COUNCIL
for the Arts   du Canada   CONSEIL DES ARTS DE L'ONTARIO

University of Toronto Press acknowledges the financial support of the
Government of Canada through the Canada Book Fund for its publishing
activities.

This book has been published with the help of a grant from the Canadian
Federation for the Humanities and Social Sciences, through the Aid to Scholarly Publications Programme, using funds provided by the Social Sciences
and Humanities Research Council of Canada.

Contents

List of Illustrations

Acknowledgments

I conducted this research thanks to a Social Sciences and Humanities Research Council of Canada (SSHRC) Standard Research Grant 2004–2008, 'Charivari and the Sexual Regulation of Women in Formal and Folk Law.' Without the support of SSHRC, little Canadian research in the social sciences and humanities would be possible.

There are always many people and institutions who make possible a study like this one. I remember and thank the following people for all the assistance, both extensive and specific, that they rendered on this work. I apologize if I've inadvertently left someone out. To start most locally, where I live in Manitoba, archive and museum staff at the Beautiful Plains Museum in Neepawa, the Brandon University Archives, the Carberry Plains Archives, the Manitoba Archives, and the United Church Archives were most helpful, including Diane Haglund, Don McGillivray, Tom Mitchell, Don Murray, Penny Shaw, Paula Warsaba, and Tannis Young. John Dobson of the University of Winnipeg Library started me on my search through genealogical sources and generously offered a great deal of help with census and related searches. He also did the index. Heather Mathieson and Lynn Schultz in Document Delivery endured endless requests for obscure and not-so-obscure materials. Ian MacKenzie was a careful, patient, and diligent copy editor. Harriette Fried at the City of Ottawa Archives was extremely helpful, Brian Silcoff in the Ottawa Room at the Ottawa Public Library also gave assistance, and Steve Dezort of the Bytown Museum directed me to these institutions. Illustrations for chapter 2 are thanks to Leah Claire Allen and to the City of Ottawa Archives.

Individuals who shared their knowledge of the Manitoba charivari were Elizabeth Ames, Bill Dunn, Don Murray, Cecil Pittman, Charlie

Simpson, Eleanor Swanson, Kathleen Swanson, and Donna Walker. I can't express the depth of my gratitude to them. My article on one event, 'Make the Night Hideous: Death at a Manitoba Charivari, 1909,' from which I draw extensively here, was originally published in *Manitoba History* 52 (June 2006): 3–17. I thank the editor, Bob Coutts, for his support of my work. The detail from the Neepawa Methodist Church register was provided thanks to the United Church Archives, the United Church of Canada, Conference of Manitoba and Ontario.

In Nova Scotia, my thanks to all those whose help with this research was invaluable, especially Sarah Carswell, Margaret McKean, Wayne Morgan, Rosemary Rafuse, Bernard Spurr, Brian Varner, Ella and Fletcher Varner, and Debbie Vermeulen. Barry Cahill, then of the Nova Scotia Archives, located a great deal of material on the case; his knowledge of the area was invaluable. I owe a particular debt of gratitude to Lloyd Varner, who made the connections with the Varner family, genealogists, and local historians, and who also provided some excellent insights into the individual and community dynamics. Because the Nova Scotia case I discuss was appealed, it was reported and published, and thus forms part of official Canadian case law and legal history. For that I must thank both the plaintiff, Irene Varner, for pressing her case in the first place, and the losing defendants for pressing theirs on appeal!

In Saskatchewan, the Archives staff in Regina assisted me in finding local history work. But the three photographs that provide the focus for my Avonlea shivaree discussion were drawn to my attention by photo archivist Tim Novak, whom I thank for this. Special thanks also to Gertrude Bircher, William Dumur, Dorothy Dunn, Jean Kincaid, Sandra Kochie, Mavis Leakey, Marian New, Carl Richter, Archie and Berenice Sanderson, Cora and Darryl Seghers, George Taylor, Patricia Thompson, Otto Ulrich, and the Saskatchewan questionnaire respondents who chose to remain anonymous. Thanks to the Saskatchewan Archives Board for permission to use the three photographs.

For the final chapter, I'm grateful to Joe Grant and Steve Ritchie for giving permission for me to quote their lyrics for 'Sullivan's Shivaree,' to Verna Stephenson for drawing 'Murphy's Shivaree' to my attention and Lori McCormick for information about it, as well as to all the respondents whose commentaries I surveyed, including Evelyn Adams, Wanda Allaby, David Barrett, Norma M. Chisholm, Marlene Chornie, Sandra Densmore, Eunice Dietrich, Marilyn Doughty, Grant Ketcheson, Ruby Kewachuk, Antonette Lane, Elizabeth McKinlay, Chester McMackin, William McMillan, Marion Schweitzer, Lucille Stuckless, William Sweezey, Wanda Taylor, Kathy Wells, and Cathy Young. In addition, I'd like to thank John Carley, Clair Corbin, and Tony Reader.

Several research assistants worked with me during this project. Leah Claire Allen, Angela Schippers Armstrong, Leigh Anne Caron, Sandra Klowak, Juliette Loewen, Natasha Pinterics, Alex Pustogorodsky, and Lisa Vivian, all in their own way, contributed to my information and thinking. Elysia DeLaurentis gave me several helpful leads. Lorna Turnbull was an invaluable consultant on legal matters relating to the work. I also thank Greg Kealey and Len Husband for their support of this work, two anonymous social historians who read an earlier draft, which assisted me particularly in knowing what I could and could not take for granted, and what I needed to be clear about that might be simply understood in the disciplines of my own background: feminism, gender studies, cultural studies, and folkloristics/ethnology. Two other readers for the press gave gratifyingly positive readings, but also pushed me to do more with the material.

Thanks to John Junson for supporting my ideas for nearly thirty years. This book is dedicated to the memory of my aunt Pauline Whitehouse, and to the memory of John's friend and mine, Evan Godt. Each in her or his own way, profoundly understood, but also critiqued, tradition.

Make the Night Hideous

1

Introduction

Throughout this research, I have had tremendous luck. I've been in the right place at the right time to get information that would not have been available otherwise. I've encountered individuals specially qualified to assist me. Friends and colleagues have offered brilliant insights. I hope the results adequately reflect how much I have enjoyed this work, and how much I appreciate the help I have received, not just all that I learned. I would, however, like to begin with a personal note about my own attitudes to charivari. (Charivari is the original and most correct spelling. I use it except when a writer spelled it otherwise, such as *shivaree*.)

Survey respondents and interviewees often questioned me about how I felt about the practice. Research in the human sciences is often presumed to aim at ferreting out the secrets behind individuals' ideas and knowledges – usually ones that are detrimental to those people, their reputations, and/or their self-images. Some folks were concerned that as an academic I would be speaking negatively about events they had enjoyed and appreciated. On the other hand, one potential respondent refused to do my survey because I was perceived as supporting charivari, a practice about which the respondent felt extremely negative, even accusing me of trying to revive it. Indeed, a reader of this manuscript similarly presumed that I was a charivari supporter, and that surprised me, considering that two of the three legal cases I deal with ended in deaths, and I make no secret of my admiration for the plaintiff in the third, a woman who successfully fought back against her charivariers using the legal system.

I suppose my background as a folklorist/ethnologist leads to the presumption that I adore everything about the practices I study, that I think them quaint and cute, and indeed that I want to revive them. But my feelings about charivari are ambivalent. I don't think I can be described as either a charivari supporter or a detractor – any more than I am a supporter or detractor of any traditional genre per se. Sometimes charivaris were fun for everyone involved. At other times, as is arguably the case in the three charivari legal cases I discuss, they were more like an act of terrorism than they were like a party. Indeed, both extremes of charivari practice – the fun and the horrible – are found within the tradition. Each one, and all of the forms in between, comprise the traditional genre. I'm not studying charivari because I think it's fabulous and want to revive it; nor am I labouring under the misconception that all charivaris were or are simply horrible. I look at charivaris, as others look at fairy traditions (e.g., Bourke 1999) or witch practices (Rieti 2008), among many other possibilities, as a route to understanding everyday lives and experiences, now and in the past.

Everyday Life

Charivari is usually a loud, late night, surprise, house-visiting custom, accompanied by a *quête* (request for a treat or money) and/or pranks. Those I discuss in detail here concern marriages or hetero-social (possibly sexual) relationships. Generally, the earlier charivaris, in the nineteenth and early twentieth century, expressed disapproval of the relationship that was their focus – between older folks, those of different ages, involving a widow and/or widower, interracial couples, or inter-religious couples. While later charivaris maintained the same ritual means – noise, surprise, trickery, and *quête*[1] in some form – their meaning changed to a welcome of the marriage and the couple. I discuss this mysterious transformation and some of the reasons for it, throughout this work.

Charivaris form part of everyday life for those communities in which they are and were found. That is not to say that they were necessarily regular or frequent occurrences, any more than are celebratory parties, or, for that matter, the weddings that engendered most of the charivaris themselves. They are among the many other special events that punctuate daily experience. The individual elements, similarly, are by no means uniquely associated with charivaris. In rural areas, people may bang on pots and pans or blow conch shells to call folks in from the field for dinner; they may shoot a volley into the air at New Year's. Surprise parties can be associated with birthdays, housewarmings, or other notable occasions. Tricks are part of hazing of newcomers to university residences, or played on marked occasions like Halloween or Gate Night (the night before or after Halloween). Even the *quête* is part of contemporary life, as is well known by anyone who dares to answer a telephone call from an unknown number or who works at any large Canadian institution in October during the United Way campaign. And as I will argue, even the same congeries of practices, with the same combination of ritual means – noise, surprise, *quête* or tricks, and sociability – with an identical or cognate name – charivari, shivaree, and so on – can be used for a variety of different purposes. This work, then, is not about a single practice with a common intent. It is about the malleability of a tradition, its continuing value, and its contestation in a variety of discourses.

In writing *Make the Night Hideous*, I have been inspired by three exemplary works in social history and cultural studies. Lisa Duggan's *Sapphic Slashers: Sex, Violence, and American Modernity* (2000) is an account of a murder in Memphis, Tennessee, in 1892. Alice Mitchell cut the throat of her friend and lover Freda Ward, probably because Ward had declined to run away with her to marry her and had announced her engagement to a man. Like the charivari examples I detail here, the subject concerns a personal connection normally seen as private. The case did not result from actions by famous individuals, though the protagonists became infamous in consequence. A relationship like Alice Mitchell and Freda Ward's was by no means unheard of at the time (see, for example, Smith-Rosenberg 1975). Nothing about their friendship or love would necessarily or usually lead to extreme actions such as murder. Like three of the four charivaris I detail, everyday events became extraordinary because of their particular circumstances.

Further, Mitchell's murder of Ward became the subject of a variety of discourses from the journalistic to the fictitious – as did (and do) charivaris in Canada. Duggan weaves newspaper accounts of the events with those of other media sensations, including notorious female murderers Lizzie Borden and the cases of those who would, at the time, be called 'female husbands' and 'male impersonators,' but might now be understood as transgender.[2] Because those newspaper discourses are intrinsically compelling but not readily available, and are a central focus for her work, Duggan quotes them at considerable length, as I do for the charivari cases, for the same reasons. She also works with racist discourses actively resisted by

Mitchell and Ward's local contemporary, African-American newspaper editor and anti-lynching campaigner Ida B. Wells. Duggan uses the medical discourses of the time about sex and race that attempted to explain what were then considered the perversions involved in same-sex love and racial mixing. Similarly, I use contemporary discourses to illuminate understandings of the charivaris at the times they occurred. *Sapphic Slashers* exemplifies the central role of newspapers in the construction of accounts of such events, and offers a model for connecting – as well as separating – a series of discourses from different sources that address the same ostensible topic.

Another exemplar for my work, Reinhold Kramer and Tom Mitchell's *Walk towards the Gallows: The Tragedy of Hilda Blake, Hanged 1899* (2002) also deals with a series of discourses, but, more than Duggan's, it draws on multiple popular cultural genres of the time, especially those with which convicted murderer Hilda Blake herself engaged, such as 'coon songs,' novels, and sentimental poetry. I similarly offer examples of traditional culture that illuminate the charivari events, though my focus is directly trained upon that practice itself, and on each individual case. As with *Sapphic Slashers*, newspaper reportage forms a major source for *Walk towards the Gallows*. Centring on Blake's crime and its aftermath, this book sketches in detail the sociocultural surround of late-nineteenth-century Manitoba, the situation of English workhouse orphans sent to Canada (as were Blake and her brother Tommy), and the expectations for relations between employers (as the victim was) and servants (as Blake was). Likewise, the sociocultural context – particularly relations of gender, family, and community – offer for me an account that elucidates the practice of charivari.

Finally, Angela Bourke's *The Burning of Bridget Cleary* (1999), like this work, focuses on a folkloric subject – the alleged fairy-abduction of Cleary, actually killed by her husband and other family members who claimed they thought she had been replaced by a fairy changeling. Once the changeling was driven off, Bridget herself could be rescued at midnight at the top of a certain hill, while she rode by with the fairies. Bourke trenchantly discusses the politics of the day, and offers a convincing presentation of the multiple viewpoints on what actually happened to the victim. Further, she intimates that traditional culture can sometimes provide a justification or even an alibi for more personal motivations. Just as charivari, being a collective censure or celebration of a marriage or other relationship, may sometimes be prompted by personal opinions and evaluations about the specific individuals being charivaried, Bourke suggests that Bridget Cleary's husband Michael and other members of her family charged with the death may have been jealous of Bridget's social and economic success, and angered by her apparent disregard for a woman's expected role as submissive wife.

These three studies happen to be approximately contemporaneous with the three earlier charivari cases I examine. The three books concern American, Canadian, and Irish examples, where mine are all Canadian, but they have in common with my work a concern for discourse and genre as well as for history. All deal with the extraordinary results of very everyday events – a love affair and friendship gone wrong, conflict between an employer and employee, and family struggles. All are at least equally concerned with the mundane aspects of the cases they refer to and with the unusual; the writers of all three attend to the often overlooked quotidian aspects of life. As with the charivari cases, though the remarkable and unusual result – a homicide or other criminal and/or civil charge – brings the individuals involved to public attention, the particular value of the extensive discursive material generated as a result – primarily newspaper accounts and court records – is its illumination of everyday life.

The focus on murder in the three model books is not entirely coincidental, as of all crimes it is perhaps most likely to be subjected to extensive public and private discussion. In fact, two charivari case studies I discuss also concern deaths, though only one was arguably a murder (despite the fact that the apparent perpetrators were not convicted) and the other seemingly accidental (and thus potentially only manslaughter, though the admitted culprit was not found guilty or even tried by a regular jury).

As a folklorist, ethnologist, and anthropologist by training, I'm accustomed to seeking information from oral tradition, but the first case, from 1881, is perhaps too early to have knowledge maintained from that source in Euro North America.[3] In addition, the surnames of those involved (with the exception of the victim, who apparently had no male heirs) are common ones, and thus I have been unable to trace them and their descendants. Given common surnames and inconsistent spellings, I also had considerable difficulty locating most of the principals in the manuscript census, and ultimately could find neither the murder victim nor one of the four men charged with his death. Finally, the event's urban location – in what is now the city of Ottawa – has meant that the likelihood of those involved (and their descendants) remaining together within the community has attenuated. My sources for that study were mainly the (incomplete) legal case files and the Ottawa newspaper records located in the Ontario Archives.

In contrast, the kinds of conditions that sustain oral history are well demonstrated in my second example, from 1909, which took place in tiny Brookdale, near Neepawa, Manitoba.[4] Family of those involved still live in the area or nearby, and many former community members who have moved away retain strong connections. In addition to newspaper accounts and the case file, this charivari still has a fairly extensive oral tradition, ranging from memories of the simple fact that someone was killed at a charivari, to a family story about the event and its consequences, to a personal experience account. The manuscript census combined with local histories and genealogies offered considerable personal information about the participants.

I located the first two charivaris through the word-searchable archives of the *Toronto Globe* and *Toronto Star*.[5] As more databases of Canadian newspaper records are developed, locating specific charivaris will become easier.[6] A third case, wherein a woman sued her charivariers for defamation, conspiracy, and personal injury, generated very little newspaper discourse other than reports that the trial and appeal cases were being heard, and the outcome. Further, even though it was later (1917) than the Brookdale charivari, and implicated the similarly small and close communities of Springfield and New Germany, Nova Scotia, my contacts with family members as well as community historians suggest that it was actively and successfully suppressed. Everyone I located was surprised to learn what I had found out – mainly from the reported appeal case and the archival law case record – about their family and area. They had never heard of the lawsuit or the event that started it all. I was extraordinarily fortunate that their interest in the case matched my own, and they helped me enormously with information about genealogy and local history, and with interpreting surnames in the manuscript census.

The fourth charivari case was not implicated in the legal system. Like most such events of its time outside Quebec and Acadia, it was a celebration of a union the community approved of, not a condemnation of the marriage. My information about this 1940 'shivaree' in Avonlea, Saskatchewan, began with three remarkable photographs in the collection of the Saskatchewan Archives in Regina, drawn to my attention by its photo archivist. Taken by professional photographers and cinematographers Dick and Ada Bird, they record the celebration following the marriage of Ada's sister Edna Bovee to Les Babcock.

The visual information is supported by interview and oral history material on the participants from their community, family, and friends, as well as by information from my interviews and survey on shivarees in the area, as will be discussed below.

The final chapter draws upon a few of the hundreds of responses to the requests for interviews and mailed surveys on charivari and related practices from across Canada that I gathered continuously from spring 2004 to spring 2008. Most respondents contacted me after seeing my request for information in local, regional, and national newspapers and periodicals. I also did guest spots on programs on CBC radio (broadcast in various locations across Canada) and worked with historical and genealogical societies, both of which turned up more participants. One focus of this chapter is a song by the Ontario folk revival group Tanglefoot, entitled 'Sullivan's Shivaree,' but I also draw attention to the various forms of tricks, elucidating how they express the tradition's highly gendered qualities.

The four events I discuss, as well as the myriad referred to in my closing, concern individuals who are almost exclusively white, rural or urban but primarily middle class, and with names indicating British origins. I have argued elsewhere (e.g., Greenhill 1989a and 1994) that those of us raised in white, Euro North American, middle-class society tend to presume that we unproblematically understand everyday life and that we are simply normal people, not the 'others' who bear culture in an anthropological sense. Indeed, some of the greatest contributions of cultural studies as a research focus and emerging (inter)discipline have been to show how whiteness, Euro North American-ness, and middle-class-ness are anything but transparent, and that they do not confer ordinariness upon anyone. Further, feminist studies have trenchantly shown how gender permeates our lives in what may retroactively seem to be obvious ways, but were, at the time they were first discussed, absolutely groundbreaking.[7] One of the lessons that emerges from the three exemplary studies – as well as, I hope, from my own work – is how much more compelling everyday life may be than we may usually think.

Similarly, we little understand how everyday life can sometimes morph into something very unusual. As such, the three histories and my charivari studies instantiate Karl Marx's famous comment that 'men [*sic*] make their own history, but they do not make it as they please; they do not make it under self-selected circumstances, but under circumstances existing already, given and transmitted from the past. The tradition of all dead generations weighs like a nightmare on the brains of the living' (1852). Much historiography focuses on the conditions and circumstances to which Marx himself particularly attends, but my concerns for gender and cultural studies incline me more to the choices and traditions – and on how individuals' and groups' traditions and choices influence each other. Hence my interest remains with the everyday, and my attention focuses where possible upon what people said about what they and others were doing.

Why, then, is this work relevant for a social history series, particularly since I am a cultural and gender studies scholar, rather than a social historian? My understanding of the kind of micro-history I'm crafting here probably differs from what most social historians would expect. The result may be what Clifford Geertz called a 'blurred genre' (1980), one that draws on and combines disciplinary perspectives in ways that may seem sometimes unmindful and even disrespectful of the originals. But no such ignorance or contempt is intended here. I may vary from some social historians in that I am crucially interested in the most apparently mundane social relations – between families, and even between individuals – as they manifest in small communities. I am not interested in family and individual experiences primarily as exemplars of wider social relations, though they certainly are; I see them as part of the necessary construction of everyday life, which is itself my focus. I am concerned with how a specific tradition, particularly because of its multiple possibilities in the quotidian, can refer to a variety of different geographic, historic, and sociocultural situations.

Such understandings are increasingly valuable to historiography, not only for their intrinsic contributions, but also as the interpretation of daily life in the past becomes a visible and public part of historiographic praxis. I use here the example of the representation of taverns, as they are relevant to some of my discussions of charivari, but others could have been chosen. With respect to museum interpretation, studies of building construction can correct misinterpretations such as at Etobicoke's Montgomery's Inn, where a restoration removing the pebble dashing to expose the original river stones underneath 'that local press described as "a real Cinderella story" was historically inauthentic: Montgomery had had the exterior covered with "pebble dashing" in 1838, less than a decade after the building was constructed' (Bonnell 2008, 133).

But in addition, work that attends to everyday life may be better able to illuminate the realities behind matters related to the interpretation of taverns as apparently diverse as a female museum interpreter dressing in male clothing[8] and the selective erasure of religious conflict, family strife, litigiousness, crime, illness, and early mortality in favour of 'a positive and harmonious vision of the past' (ibid., 139). A historical awareness, for example, of biological women dressing as men may open interpretive possibilities. And knowledge about actual interactions may mitigate the presumed absenting of women from certain crucial spaces like barrooms, and men from other equally critical locations like kitchens. As historian Julia Roberts observes, 'Although the tavern was a predominantly male world, it was never exclusively so. Women often kept taverns ... usually under licenses held by their husbands, or as widows licensed in their own right. The daughters of tavern-keeping families routinely worked about the house. Men with their wives, sisters, mothers, and courting partners came together to the taverns on excursions' (2003, 15; see also Roberts 2004, 607–8). Historical presumptions that foster inaccurate views of gender prevent a consideration of actual 'experiences of friendship, sexuality, and marriage' (Bonnell 2008, 143). All these are very much the stuff of the everyday.

But I am attentive to the fact that I have no direct route to understanding everyday life. Instead, I can locate it only as it is discursively constructed – in these cases, through legal documents and the press, and sometimes in more local and individual community discourses as well. Thus discourse itself must be a central element in the analyses I construct. The materials familiar to social historians ground my work – primarily legal records, newspapers, the manuscript census, and vital statistics documents – but I also bring a more personalized, community-based perspective in the interview and survey results discussed, as well as by using the community's own folk histories, constructed for local consumption. By using the sources to speak to one other, I learn quite a bit about the discourses' formations and the intentions behind them. Through them, I can construct a more nuanced account.

I note that where they are available, I privilege the commentaries made by community members. I don't think they can be understood, any more than any other discourse, without interpretation, but I am most compelled by their understandings of what is going on. Undoubtedly, my conclusions and aspects of my methods differ from those of many social historians. But to me that's the point. Social historians may in fact draw different results from identical data. But that does not make my conclusions and perspectives irrelevant to social history. It means only that I must try to be as explicit as possible about my own presumptions so they may be transparent to readers.

Until fairly recently, historians rejected oral traditions as lacking the factual bases and objectivity of written forms (see, for example,

Allen 1979). However, since at least the 1980s, historians have been looking at oral history not only as material to be gathered from living individuals now for future historians, as a source of information about the disenfranchised and disempowered, and as a mode of developing museum and archive collections, but also as part of the process and interdisciplinary application of historiography (see Dunaway and Baum 1984). Various writers, most famously Jan Vansina (1961), put to rest the notion that oral sources could not be factual or accurate.[9]

At around the same time, Hayden White argued that in telling stories, history itself employs different forms of plot – romance, satire, comedy, and tragedy – as well as different tropes – metaphor, synecdoche, metonymy, and irony (1973). The notion that there could be a single, truthful version of history was further critiqued by James Clifford. For example, he discussed divergent narratives that emerged in the context of an American First Nations land claims case: 'The case against the Mashpee plaintiffs was based on a reading of Cape Cod history. Documents were gathered, interpreted, and arranged in a coherent sequence. The story emerged of a small mixed community fighting for equality and citizenship while abandoning, by choice or coercion, most of its aboriginal heritage. But a different, also coherent, story was constructed by the plaintiffs, drawing on the same documentary record. In this account the residents of Mashpee had managed to keep alive a core of Indian identity over three centuries against enormous odds. They had done so in supple, sometimes surreptitious ways, always attempting to control, not reject, outside influences' (1988, 302).

That a single body of evidence could produce divergent kinds of stories, as White suggests, or that they could produce mutually contradictory ones, as Clifford offers, leads to a kind of necessary scepticism about history that is consistent with the perspectives of many feminist and cultural studies scholars, who argue that there is not one single truth (or one single history). Such work asks that scholars identify their locations and allegiances, to assist readers in understanding their perspectives (e.g., Collins 2000). That different versions of a story could be equally useful in narrating different perspectives (e.g., Schely-Newman 1993) has been taken up quite extensively in the disciplines of anthropology and folkloristics.

Even in written cultural forms, different genres express different sorts of ideas. For example, poetry works to convey emotion and impression. It's nonsensical to say of a poem's assertions, 'But that's not literally true.' Literal truth is not poetry's purpose. For example, in a local newspaper that published poems and letters to the editor on the same topic, the two genres worked to varying ends. The same writer used a letter to the editor to polemically address a local and personal concern, and a poem to signal its resolution (see Greenhill 1989a, 58–61, 83–92, 102–4). There's no generic law that says those forms must be used in those particular ways. A poem could be polemical and a letter to the editor resolving. But as individuals raised with basic Euro Canadian cultural knowledge, we understand that we should approach the meanings of these two genres differently.

Similar processes apply to other cultures and forms. Ruth Finnegan argues that in some kinds of Limba storytelling, 'even though the events depicted were clearly imaginative rather than "factual" there was also something true and abiding about them ... [I]t lay in the observation of the *kinds* of things people do and say – human even in fantastic settings or animal guises – and in the recurrent patterns of human intercourse depicted through the storyteller's art and performance' (1994, 8). Like other material and verbal forms, oral traditional culture employs different genres to impart its messages. Problems can arise interculturally when misrecognition of a genre or its purpose gets in the way of understanding. For example, Madronna Holden demonstrates that problem in her discussion of an early-twentieth-century encounter between Coast Salish people and a white visiting anthropologist: 'The white visitor was treated to the tale of the native war-making venture of the century – or so it would appear ... From the way in which this tale was enjoyed, one might well envision a culture whose military exploits were of paramount importance to it ... if the whole thing had not been a joke. That violent story of battle was no more and no less than a native joke ... crafted in terms of that which our own culture treats with utmost delicacy: the tale ... was in fact a native euphemism for the finding of an adequate toilet. And the "great battle," the journey of the war canoes along those waters from the North, referred in fact to the elimination of one's body wastes' (1976, 271).[10]

Understanding genres, and their content, can aid in interpreting actual practice. For example, folklorist Bill Ellis convincingly links contemporary legend with various acts including murder. He suggests that contemporary legend can provide a kind of alibi that influences actions, such as the possibility that individuals will use legendary information about satanic rituals to structure specific acts to hide a more personal motivation and fool the authorities. But he also suggests that some action can actually be suggested or inspired by traditional culture, such as that 'the current popularity of real-life food and drug tampering may derive from a tradition of stories involving booby-trapped trick-or-treat candy' (1989, 202).

Thus, in many oral traditions as well as written forms, interplay between the personal and the collective means that tellers as well as writers interpret information or texts. But the verbatim re-representation of their raw material is rarely the desideratum. Generally, all these forms offer an opportunity to learn about individual as well as group understandings. And in Euro North American culture, one of the fundamentals of both personal and communal understandings is gender. Thus, with Judith Butler (1993, 1999), I see gender created and recreated in discourse, including that of the charivari.

Make the Night Hideous

'Make the night hideous' is a journalistic convention for referring to charivari (e.g., *Globe*, 2 May 1877, 2; *Toronto Star*, 5 January 1899, 1).[11] Charivaris almost always involve late-night house visits accompanied by an unmusical racket as well as traditional pranks or a demand for money. The ritual means – the actual tools and/or methods used to construct the practice – are consistent, despite the fact that earlier forms of charivari expressed disapproval and later ones approval of those they targeted. Never linked with formal governmental actions or modernity, charivaris make what many understand as private activities – marriages and/or sexual relationships – into public affairs. Historically, the marriages at issue were those that involved partners of disparate ages, older couples, widows and/or widowers, different racialized groups, and rarely, different religions. I'll discuss in detail throughout this work what made those kinds of unions problematic for their communities. More recent charivaris are for those whose marriages the community approves of, expressed as a 'welcome' to the newlyweds. Again, I problematize throughout the issue of why such marriages should call for this particular form of traditional marking.

The study of charivaris has been part of examinations of folklore, ethnology, and anthropology since the beginnings of those disciplines in the nineteenth century. In addition, historians as distinguished as E.P. Thompson (1993) and Natalie Zemon Davis (1975, 1984) on Europe, and Allan Greer (1990, 1993) and Bryan Palmer (1978) on Canada, have looked at the topic in English. Charivari has received extensive attention in France from ethnologists including Christian Desplat (1982) and Henri Rey-Flaud (1985), and in Quebec and Acadia from Jean-Claude Dupont (1977), Lauraine Léger (1979, 1980,

2000), Edouard-Zotique Massicotte (1976), and many others. The tradition has made its way into television drama (an episode of *The Waltons*), musical comedy (*Oklahoma*), novels (including *The Mayor of Casterbridge* by Thomas Hardy), and in Canada, an opera (Reaney 1978). Academic research on English-Canadian charivaris, however, has not been extensive.

In English Canada, charivari is currently known most often as 'shivaree' or 'chivaree,' though in Nova Scotia it may instead be called 'banjo,' 'saluting,' or 'serenade,' with the last term sporadically distributed across the Maritime provinces. 'Shivaree''s obvious connection to the French 'charivari' suggests much about the origins of the practice in Canada. Cognate forms have been recorded in other European locations, and an especially broad range in England, including 'skimmington' (Baker 2002, 446), 'riding the stang,' and 'rough music,' some of which were also known in early colonial America (Gilje 1996, 47). The primary use in Canada of a word based on the French suggests that French culture is its source. 'Shivaree' is also well known in the United States, its etymology 'satisfactorily established' as being from the French, since 'although raucous celebrations are common in rural England following unpopular or atypical weddings or as a form of social censure, the French term does not seem to be part of the British folk vocabulary' (Davis and McDavid 1949, 250).[12]

My own arrival at the topic came from a chance comment by a colleague at lunch in the late 1980s. She was moving from her farmhouse in a rural area north of London, Ontario, to the city, and mentioned that she had planned to bring the bell from the schoolhouse that was on her property, but that she was leaving it because her neighbours wanted it for shivarees. As an urban Ontarian, raised in Toronto, I had presumed (with many others) that the tradition had died out in the nineteenth century, so I was more than somewhat surprised to learn charivaris were still taking place. When I began asking around, I found that not only my colleague's rural friends and neighbours, but also several students in the University of Waterloo residence where I then worked, had participated in them. Furthermore, the students particularly were surprised that a folklorist was interested in something that, as one put it, 'wasn't folklore, just a wild and crazy thing that Junior Farmers do.'[13] Another colleague to whom I described my fieldwork concurred, saying, 'That's not folklore, that's just people being obnoxious.' Knowing well that a traditional practice that *wasn't* seen as folklore was a healthy, active one, and thus recognizing charivaris as folk events par excellence, I interviewed several participants and wrote an article on the topic (Greenhill 1989b). I did not imagine at the time that I would ever return to it.

But more than ten years later, I spent two years doing half-time law studies at the University of Manitoba. During my second term, I signed up for a course in Canadian legal history.[14] As a Canadianist, who had taught for five years in a Canadian studies program at the University of Waterloo, the area seemed appropriate.

For the essay requirement, I wanted to produce something that I could later rework for a publication that would count for me professionally, so I looked around for a topic that would allow me to do original research, but that I was already familiar with. Having studied two traditions that sometimes led to deaths – charivari and mumming – and knowing that deaths under such circumstances and court cases often went together, I conducted a word search of the Canadian law databases to see if I could find any cases relating to these practices.[15] I was unable to find any mumming cases. But I found three references to charivari – two relatively unpromising, and the other to the *Varner v. Morton et al.* defamation, conspiracy, and personal injury case that is the subject of my fourth chapter.[16] That summer, after finding the case file in the Nova Scotia Archives, I proposed a research program to the Social Sciences and Humanities Research Council of Canada that would allow me to pursue the topic of charivari in English Canada further. That successful application formed the basis of the work I discuss here.[17]

Background: Charivari and Shivaree

Charivari comprises a cross-cultural range of originally European practices, symbolic means, and purposes. At their most extreme, charivaris approach or even achieve riot status; when benign they are simply playful gatherings. They include noisemaking, house visiting – usually unexpected and late at night – and often pranks. Most are associated with weddings – demonstrating approval of matches the community deemed suitable, or the converse, showing or stirring up disapproval of old/old, old/young, interracial, or inter-religious ones. Still others provide overt negative commentary on individuals' behaviour, particularly in the political and sexual realms (see Alford 1959; Amussen 1985; Atwood 1964; Burke 1978; Davis 1975, 1984; Desplat 1982; DeVoto 1947; Dobash and Dobash 1981, 1992; Dufresne 2000; Greer 1993; Ingram 1984, 1985; Jones 1990; Kent

1983; Le Goff and Schmitt 1981; Pettitt 1999; Rey-Flaud 1985; Thompson 1992, 1993; Underdown 1985, 1987; Ziff 2002).

There has long been a range of wedding-associated practices usually gathered by academics under the heading of *charivari* (LeGoff and Schmidt 1981). In English Canada, charivaris were probably historically associated most often with heterosexual marriages considered in some way problematic by the communities in which they took place. In that form, charivari can be understood as an extra-legal mode of social control,[18] 'to publicly ridicule an object of communal scorn' (Gilje 1996, 47). Historian Natalie Zemon Davis argues, 'At best, a charivari in its boisterous mixture of playfulness and cruelty tries to set things right in a community' (1984, 42). According to sociologists Russell P. Dobash and R. Emerson Dobash in their discussion of historic charivaris, 'Public shamings were attempts to make unspeakable community grievances and private disputes into matters of community concern' (1981, 565). At their worst, charivaris were a kind of local terrorism – directed to specifically punish a wrongdoer, but also making an example for the rest of the community to show what would happen if they were to do likewise – culminating, particularly in the case of interracial marriages, in murder (e.g., Moodie 1997; Roberts 2002).[19] However, even negative charivaris by no means always led to bad outcomes; usually the recipients simply paid the charivariers to go away, because 'accepting to make the payment demanded by the crowd brought charivaris and community disapproval to an end' (Noël 2003, 61).

Canadian historian Bryan Palmer notes, 'In nineteenth-century Upper Canada ... the charivari was often a force undermining social authority, resolutely opposed by magistrate and police' (1978, 24–5). Specifically, for example, 'Three Kingston, Upper Canada, charivaris of the mid-1830s, all directed against remarriage, forced the hand of the local authorities, one leading to two arrests, another necessitating the calling into action of the Summary Punishment Act, the third leading to the creation of a special force of constables, 40 strong, to enforce the peace' (ibid., 26). Just because it opposed formal legal structures, however, does not mean that charivari was not in its own way a quasi-legal form – enforcing good behaviour by negative example (this is what happens when you step outside the bounds of community morality) as well as punishing specific culprits. Well into the twentieth century, charivaris certainly provided a context for both criminal and civil charges. The combination of guns (used as noisemakers) and alcohol (lubricating the participants) made bodily harm and even homicide a rare but nevertheless predictable outcome. Recipients of charivaris sometimes brought trespass charges, and other illegal acts such as disturbing the peace and public drunkenness also occasioned court cases.

The significance of the *quête* manifests the charivari's quasi-legal form. Reciprocity and mutual obligation were significant in working-class culture in the nineteenth century, as evidenced by the practice of the tavern 'treat': 'Commensurate with early tavern culture was the practice of treating or the buying of rounds of liquor for all men present. Those on the receiving end were obliged to drink and to reciprocate at a later date, and those treating others were obligated by expenditure. Such obligatory expressions of manhood and economic exchange exhibited character and reputation that invoked a certain fraternity among drinking men' (Wamsley and Kossuth 2000, 417).

The 1881 Ottawa charivari discussed in chapter 2 shows that the wedding of two older people (including the further problematic aspects of differing ages, widow- and widowerhood of the parties, and divorce) called for a payment in recompense to young men. That payment was also clearly part of the culture of reciprocity among those young men themselves, as the first set of charivariers went to a tavern to drink together. In some ways, the charivari treat money was a fine paid by the couple for their contravention of expectation. As Allan Greer argues, 'More was involved than a simple clearing of the air; charivari was also ... a punitive procedure. Victims were punished through both humiliation and monetary extraction' (1993, 77). That fine, however, needed to be redistributed in a specific way, just as legal fines are paid to the court, not to a wronged individual.

But the notion of reciprocity and sharing of wealth is equally significant in rural cultures, as the examples of early- to mid-twentieth-century western Canadian charivaris show. Individuals and communities survived the rigours of farming, economic depression, and wartime (among many others) primarily by working together, and the reciprocity of the treat echoed and cemented the relations involved. However, as the charivari changed from disapproval to a more positive statement, the *quête* as a collection of money – mere exchange value – was replaced by a treat in the form of specific commodities marking special occasions, such as alcohol, candy, and cigarettes, or, alternatively, as a full-blown party with sociability as well as consumption. Crucially, though it did not involve money, and sometimes not even the sharing of alcohol (though in the alternative, ritual tea and coffee would be served) that often marks a social occasion, this part of the charivari was frequently still called a 'treat.' The common nomenclature of charivari/shivaree is not surprising, however, especially considering that it retained the form of a special kind of sharing and reciprocity among community members.

The culture of the rural 'good sport' underlines these ideas of redistribution. Good sports are quintessential community participants, who endure hardships together but who also celebrate together. The quality of being able to take a joke, to laugh at oneself as well as at others, extensively comprises the male bonding experience of rural western Canadian good sports (Taft 1997). The development of solidarity means that no one must be consistently elevated or, conversely, debased.[20] This notion of equality persists across the contemporary charivari. Reciprocity employs the notion that no individual should be markedly wealthier than another; similarly, no individual should be ritually raised above others – as happens during a wedding, when the bride and groom are the centre of attention – without experiencing some parallel ritual debasement (often seen in sexualized humiliation in charivari tricks).

The links between the earlier (disapproval) and later (approval) charivari are underlined further by the fact that just because a charivari was intended as a celebration of the wedding did not necessarily preclude damage or harm. Often such events came to the attention of the authorities because of problems that arose. According to folklorist Monica Morrison, who studied New Brunswick serenades, 'General questioning also brought [this] response, especially from women. "I don't like that kind of thing, it can go too far," followed by a sort of cautionary tale ... "This guy he was drunk and he put a fire extinguisher – a fire hose – he put the stuff in it in the groom's drink ... And he drank it and that poor guy was unconscious for two days ... and that guy his kidneys were shot and they had to take them out and he died within a week. And that guy who did it, he didn't know that the chemical was poison, he probably thought it was just water. But that's where that sort of thing goes' (1974, 295).

Morrison seems sceptical about how realistic accounts like the above might be.[21] However, a 2003 search through the American law database Westlaw uncovered forty-nine pre-1944 appeal cases in the United States directly or indirectly related to charivari and seventeen post-1944. While a number of the latter series referred to the New York / Japan fashion boutique 'Charivari,' and some concerned anti-choice demonstrations against clinics providing reproductive services to women, most referred to events like those discussed here. They include a 1964 Missouri appeal case, *State v. Parker* (378 S.W.2d. 274), which dealt with a celebratory charivari in the Ozarks (see Greenhill forthcoming [b]). Many of the charivaris that resulted in these legal actions did not appear to have been explicitly negative in origin, and yet eight resulted in homicide,[22] eight in assault and battery, weapons, and injury-related cases short of homicide,[23] six in riot or disorderly conduct,[24] four in property crimes,[25] and one in an employers' liability case (for a charivari during a last-night theatre performance).[26]

Morrison had to admit that not everyone was thrilled about being charivaried, though most of those she describes were celebratory.[27] 'Everybody gets a shivaree, everybody gets tricks played on them. There are two exceptions in the earlier accounts: the mean (in the sense of stingy or crotchety) person and the couple that is too old.' One of her informants told her, '"Well this old maid and this old bachelor got married and did they ever shivaree them. He was too mean to give a treat anyway – he had a store. But finally they did come out and they did pass around a treat. And they went back inside and they wouldn't come out again"' (1974, 292). In another example, '"This here Marvin Phillips got married, and this was his fourth wife he had, we went over the shivaree and we couldn't get them out – guess they was old and sulky and they wouldn't come out"' (ibid., 294). Nova Scotian Clair Corbin noted, 'Depends on who the people were, too. Sometimes you had to be careful because that trick might be taken not as in fun. And there could have been a retaliation, possibly' (interview PG2005, 9–10).[28] Positive or negative, the wedding charivari is by no means a universally welcomed or approved practice.

An early account with extensive description and discussion is found in Susanna Moodie's *Roughing It in the Bush*, from 1833. It begins, 'I was startled one night, just before retiring to rest, by the sudden firing of guns in our near vicinity, accompanied by shouts and yells, the braying of horns, the beating of drums, and the barking of all the dogs in the neighbourhood. I never heard a more stunning uproar of discordant and hideous sounds' (1997, 151). Mrs Moodie fears an invasion by Yankees, but instead finds out from her neighbour Mrs O—— that 'a set of wild fellows have met to charivari Old Satan, who has married his fourth wife to-night, a young gal of sixteen. I should not wonder if some mischief happens among them, for they are a bad set, made up of all the idle loafers about Port H—— and C——' (ibid., 150–1). The neighbour explains that 'when an old man marries a young wife, or an old woman a young husband, or two old people, who ought to be thinking of their graves, enter for the second or third time into the holy estate of wedlock ... all the idle young fellows in the neighbourhood meet together to charivari them' (ibid., 151). She goes on to talk about the charivariers' disguises and demands for drink or money 'to treat the band at the nearest tavern' (ibid.). The discordant noise begins if the bride or groom fails to treat or pay.[29]

Mrs Moodie's neighbour then goes on to describe other charivaris. At one, a rich storekeeper who has married his third wife bargains with the charivariers and eventually pays them half of the amount they originally demanded. In another, an African-American man, 'a runaway nigger from the States' (ibid., 154), marries an Irish woman and is murdered by the mob.[10] Yet another charivari also leads to a death – one charivarier is killed and two others wounded by the bridegroom, who apparently finds the assault on his property and person threatening (ibid., 154–5).

Mrs Moodie, unimpressed by the practice of charivari in principle, notes her 'truly British indignation at such a lawless infringement upon the natural rights of man' (ibid., 152). Her neighbour's view is more forgiving. She explains, 'A charivari would seldom be attended with bad consequences if people would take it as a joke, and join in the spree' (ibid., 155). Clearly, even in the nineteenth century, the community was by no means in complete accord about the value of charivari or the morality or lack thereof in the practices that precipitated it.

The charivari as expression of disapproval against a contentious marriage continued well into the twentieth century. Most English-Canadian charivaris in the nineteenth and early twentieth century involved late-night house visiting, noise-making (as the contemporary newspapers frequently put it, 'making the night hideous'), and usually also a request for money (to be spent on drink for the revellers). For charivaris in rural Canada, the reasons for this practice probably relate to the particular socio-economic significance of the husband/wife/children family, which was fundamental to the economic and social base of nineteenth- and early-twentieth-century farming communities. As historian Cecilia Danysk notes, 'The economic contribution of a family was proportionally much greater than their mere numbers, since the costs of their labour and provisions were hidden in their production. Politically and socially, individual farm ownership meant conservative values, while the predominance of families ensured the entrenchment of institutions and fostered social stability' (1995, 70). Women were crucial to the household (see, e.g., Comacchio 1999, 43–5). As Rouleau, Saskatchewan, poet Edith Gordon put it in her 1955 composition,[31]

We had those pioneer women then, God rest them one and all,
Who mothered all the bachelors and were always at beck and
  call.
They helped bring all the babies in and helped the old depart ...
There were no teenage problems then, each child had work to
  do –
From Henry farming with his dad, right down to baby Sue ...
Johnny to the pasture would ride and bring the cows,
And feed the calves and slop the pigs and pitch down hay from
  the mows;
Get the kindling and bring in the coal and take the lantern out,
And help harness the horses when he heard his father shout.
Mary would feed the chickens and gather the eggs ...
She would also wash the dishes and lamps must be cleaned and
  filled,
And make the beds and wipe the floor where water had been
  spilled.
While mother was busy kneading the bread she had set the night
  before,
With potato water and homemade yeast, it was almost a daily
  chore.
She would make some pies and some cinnamon rolls as well as
  cookies and cake ...
When Mom was shut in for the winters, she made all the chil-
  dren's clothes,
Crocheted and tatted and pieced a quilt, knit their mittens and
  hose ...
Mom braided rugs from coats and pants that could be worn no
  more,
And hooked rugs on a gunny sack base to spread before the door.
  (1971, 16–17)

In early-twentieth-century western Canada, for example, where the
disapproval charivari survived well into the first quarter-century, the
proportion of men to women was skewed. Charivari underlined the
family's importance. Women were in such a minority that there was
no social stigma on bachelorhood, though bachelors were to an extent
figures of fun.[32] As Gordon noted,

Bachelors and mosquitoes were the chief inhabitants then,
And hunting season was open to any girls looking for men.
A bachelor with a rubber tired rig and a speedy little driver,

Quite likely in the race of love would be the soul [*sic*] survivor ...
The married folks held open house, their doors were open wide;
When bachelors came from far and near to share the feast inside.
For during the week they had been living on prunes, dried apples,
    and beans,
And sight of a woman's cooking recalled their boyhood scenes.
Biscuits made by the bachelors were the hardest things in the
    world,
And many a gopher bit the dust from a biscuit neatly hurled. (1971,
    16–17)

Given their difficult social position, bachelors felt that they had a right to ask for money from someone who married beyond the community's conventional ideas.

But the inadequate resource argument – the scarcity of young women makes charivari a reasonable treatment for a man who takes more than one – doesn't explain charivaris against older widowers or especially widows, or between older, interracial, or inter-religious partners. With respect to remarriages, Davis offers, 'Why then the charivaris? First there was the dead spouse to be placated ... Then there were the children from the first marriage to be thought about, psychologically and economically ... And last and most fundamental, there was resentment when someone had been inappropriately removed by an older widow or widower from the pool of young eligibles' (1975, 106). Davis, then, sees the charivari mainly as recompense. Allan Greer, discussing French Canada, argues, 'To marry for money or out of mere sexual appetite was not just morally reprehensible: it was sacrilegious' (1993, 75).

However, it seems likely that in rural Canada, the problem in historic negative charivaris was not the individual identities of the participants, but the fertility issues that might be raised by particular matches. Then as now, marriage is all about reproduction in small communities, to ensure their continuation via the passing of land from fathers to sons. Marriages between racially and religiously different partners would not produce offspring who could be easily incorporated into racially and religiously divided communities. Marriages of older individuals are less likely to be fertile, and, as Davis notes, younger/older marriages would be more apt to raise concerns about inheritance, especially when bride, groom, or both bring children from a previous marriage into the relationship.

Thus, people of colour marrying white folks presented a social problem for community membership from the perspective of white members. Individuals who would be tolerated in, even at times wel-comed into, other parts of white society would meet the strongest resistance, to the point of murder, if they attempted to marry outside their racially/ethnically defined grouping. Historian Julia Roberts argues, 'There was a strange contradiction between white settlers' marginalization of black and First Nations peoples and the sometimes easy accommodation afforded them in the public houses' (2002, 1). She offers example after example of Black and First Nations peoples being given accommodation, food, and drink in taverns. But when James Ferinson, 'a black man, a private in the 67th regiment' went to a tavern in St Catharines in 1841, he was accosted on the road and apparently murdered. 'The company at Stinson's had gathered on Saturday night, "perhaps 10 o'c," to make a charivari of "a servant girl who was to marry the Black Man." Enraged by the rumour of interracial marriage, the company at Stinson's seized on Ferinson as he made his way to the tavern ... Stinson's brutal charivari crowd built its collective identity around the violent exclusion of "others"' (ibid., 25). It seems unclear from the account whether Ferinson was even the groom-to-be. As in other forms of lynching, the alleged provocation had little to do with any kind of legally or rationally based infraction (see, e.g., Wells-Barnett 2005). But the intended les-son is clear: interracial marriage is potentially deadly, especially for the partner of colour. And the consequences for charivari perpetrators and participants aren't always commensurate. For example, in the two charivaris I discuss in which deaths resulted, the killers were not convicted.

Yet an explanation based on rural community concepts does not apparently fit the more urban situation of the first charivari I discuss, from Ottawa, 1881. Though the fact that the majority of the chari-variers seem to have come from the same census division as the loca-tion where the charivari was held suggests a strong community link, it is clear that individuals from across the border of Rochesterville and Mount Sherwood (Nepean), and folks from Wellington Ward of Ottawa, also attended. It is not at all clear that the four individuals from that location, eventually charged with murdering the bride-groom, were even aware of the reason for the charivari – that the sixty-five-year-old James Wetherill, rumoured to be an American twice-divorced widower, was marrying forty-five-year-old Margaret Dougherty. They may simply have been drawn to the noise. But I will argue that the concern for appropriate family relations combined with a wish to get money from a reputedly wealthy man probably precip-itated that event.

Celebratory Charivari

Nevertheless, as already indicated, charivaris changed from being commentaries directed against inappropriate marriages to ones that celebrated unions that the community appreciated, which are the vast majority of those I heard about during my research.[33] Surprisingly, the two types of marriage charivaris – punishment and celebration – appear to have coexisted for quite some time in Canada and the United States. I will argue that the forms share not only the ritual means of noise and surprise, but also a concern for fertility. But contemporary shivaree noise is mostly male, produced by objects that men own and work with (car horns and chainsaws) or even by instruments that they may manufacture themselves, such as the horse fiddle.[34] The discordant sound that used to be produced by the female-associated objects of pots and pans is drowned out now by these more decibel-producing male objects. Specifically, the negative and positive charivari both concern the maintenance of the community through biological succession.

With increasing rural depopulation as younger community members moved to cities to seek work potentially more remunerative and less inconsistent than farming, the biggest challenge to communities became those who moved away or failed to reproduce promptly and often, thus keeping them tied to the land. As religious and racial tolerance became more common, and the support of the existing community became tied more to keeping families in the area than to policing particular types of relationships, the positive charivari became the norm. That sociability and support from family, friends, and neighbours was the primary point of the later charivari form is underlined by the fact that it did not usually include a *quête* in its formal mode of a request/demand for money. As already indicated, the money to treat the charivariers was almost invariably replaced with collective socializing with their victims. I will further detail this change and its symbolic logic in the fifth and sixth chapters of this work.

The earliest Canadian note I have of a charivari that appears *not* to be associated with community disapproval of a mismatched, interracial, or inter-religious couple was from the *Globe* (Toronto), 1865. 'A Fatal Charivari' noted, 'There was nothing at all peculiar in the match – not even the usual excuse of silly charivarists, that a blooming damsel should not be allowed to link herself to hoary-headed age without due celebration … where extremes of age meet or there is some other striking want of fitness' (8 June, 1).[35] Of course, newspapers can be wrong about the ages of newlyweds (or other details), as they were for a Snowflake, Manitoba, charivari of 1906. As will be discussed further in chapter 3, one paper described the couple as 'young' though both bride and groom were in their early forties. However, the transition certainly happened, and the 1865 account may well be accurate, particularly since the lack of age difference was made its specific point, as it was not in the 1906 article. The apparent detachment of charivari from an age-mismatched or otherwise unconventional couple was also evident in 'Heavy Fines,' from 1879: 'On the 1st of September a *young* man named Harry C. Gully married a Copetown woman and in the evening the *young couple* were made the subjects of a charivari' (*Globe*, 11 September, 8; my emphases). Though 'shivarees' in early- to mid-twentieth-century Saskatchewan seem to have been given mainly to those who didn't invite the entire community to celebrate their wedding,[36] very few outside Acadian New Brunswick and the province of Quebec, from the late 1920s to the present, were about money or involved older, interracial, or inter-religious couples or couples of different ages.

Thus, according to an Ontario account of shivaree from 1931, 'When a countryman, farmer, owner, tenant, or laborer, "hired man," on land got married, it was the custom for many of the neighbouring men and boys approaching manhood – in my country, young lads being rigidly excluded – to congregate early in the night and serenade the bridal couple in the house in which they were spending the nuptial night' (Riddell 1931, 522). According to William Riddell, the original shivaree form indicated disapproval, but in his boyhood and youth it was considered 'a compliment and a form of public congratulations' (ibid).

Those about to be shivareed prepared with doughnuts and cider; 'The cider was not infrequently "hard," and substitution or reinforcement of Canadian whiskey was not unknown' (ibid., 523). Evidently, the element of eliciting a treat remained part of the charivari for some time. Nevertheless, 'satisfaction in being Shivareed was not universally felt: sometimes, instead of doughnuts and hard cider, the groom provided a loaded shot-gun; and a hail of snipe-shot sometimes greeted the crowd – it was bad form to use buck-shot for the purpose … I have never known, personally, of any fatality at a "Shivaree"; but some were reported in other parts of the Province' (ibid.).

Nevertheless, it may be tempting to see the more recent forms of charivari as fundamentally different from their predecessors. But apart from their common ritual means and naming, both forms of charivari address concerns that would be outside the formal legal system of their times, but would be absolutely pressing issues to those involved. The shared interest in the continuation of community in its appropriate form to a great extent links the events. The extra-legal authority of charivaris, no matter what form they take, comes from shared community notions about appropriate behaviour, proper relationships, and laudable (or not-so-laudable) unions.

Why Charivari?

There is no law that says that a man must not accumulate wealth, and that if he does so, he must not be miserly with it, or hide it from others, unless he pays a fine,[37] or that an older, widowed, divorced man may not marry a younger but still post-reproductive-aged widow unless he pays a fine. And yet the Wetherill case shows that young men in the Ottawa region in 1881 felt they had a right to ask for money from a man who had done both, and were willing to press those rights firmly with noise, disorder, and even violence.

There is no law that says a man can't marry a much younger woman, less than eight months after his first wife has died in childbirth, and steal a friend's girlfriend, unless he pays a fine. And yet that man's age mates, as well as much younger men, felt they had a right to ask for money from William McLaughlin for doing just that in rural Manitoba in 1909.

There is no law that says a woman can't walk arm in arm with a young man in front of the general store, or pick flowers along the railway line, or go driving with a much older man to visit her in-laws, without enduring public ridicule. And yet in 1917 six upstanding members of the Nova Scotia community of Springfield felt they had a right to draw public attention to the alleged moral infractions of Irene Varner and to ridicule her in front of her neighbours and family. So strongly did they feel that when she won her defamation and conspiracy case at trial, they appealed (unsuccessfully) to the Supreme Court of Nova Scotia.

The involvement of the first three charivari cases with law is their epiphenomenon. From that time period in Canada, at least, charivari never enforced the formal legal system. Instead, it maintained ideas of proper behaviour, appropriate action, and community membership. And the same can be said of the more recent, approval charivari. There is no law that says a couple who marry must stay in the community, produce children, never be elevated, even symbolically, above their peers, and/or invite everybody to a party to celebrate their wedding, or be punished with noise and tricks – and treat or feed anyone who is willing to attend the charivari. And yet from the beginning of the twentieth century even to the present day in some places, relatives, friends, neighbours, and the community as a whole may demand exactly that.

Elements of charivari are highly gendered. It's not coincidental that all the participants in the first three charivari were men, or that their wives supported the actions of the Varner charivariers, or that women disapprove of charivari more often than men, or that women are usually the ones expected to provide the treat in the contemporary charivari. These issues will form part of the explanation of each charivari case.

Clearly, the charivari is a pliable practice, surviving with extensive commonalities besides its name from the beginnings of European settlement in Canada to the present day. The four examples demonstrate its uses in city, industrial village, rural village, and farm; by groups of young men, groups of peers and young men, groups of adult men, and a mixed groups of children and adolescents as well as the present day's mixed sex and age groups; and to indicate disapproval and approval. Indeed, that's one of the problems of this grouping. Despite clearly recognizable similarities, each case is most telling for its specific manifestations. They resist a common theme or perspective. Though all are strongly gendered, relate to community morality, and implicate ideas of reciprocity, each says something different – slightly or radically – about these issues.

Perhaps because of its distance from formal systems, and its emphasis on aspects that many Canadians would now see as primarily personal, charivari research may not be exactly in the academic mainstream, but it has elements of intrinsic interest. First, it directly relates to aspects of community life that become the object of talk (and gossip) – interpersonal relationships, both sanctioned and illicit. Second, the contents of discourses around charivari include elements of humour for the twenty-first-century reader – as they sometimes did for these events' contemporaries. Finally, its manifestations have been overlooked by academics and – at least in Canada – detailed analyses of particular events are missing from the record. With respect to the last, as already suggested, most scholars think charivari died out in the nineteenth century. E.P. Thompson observes that 'the forms of rough music and of charivari are part of the expressive symbolic vocabulary of a certain kind of society – a vocabulary available to all and in which many different sentences may be pronounced. It is a discourse which (while often coincident with literacy) derives its resources from oral transmission, within a society which regulates many of its occasions – of authority and moral conduct – through such theatrical forms as the solemn procession, the pageant, the public exhibition of justice or of charity, public punishment, the display of emblems and favours, etc.' (1993, 479).

One may doubt that current Canadian society shows those kinds of characteristics, but it is certain that charivari persists in some locations in Canada, and that its current suspension in some areas happened as recently as the 1980s and 1990s.[38] Canadian historian Bryan Palmer is wisely cautious about the tradition's demise, saying, 'It is impossible to date the decline of the ritual; indeed numerous colleagues have witnessed forms of the charivari in Canadian villages and towns as late as 1963' (1978, 38). Charivari, like other forms of traditional culture, has long been suspected of dying out – in fact, it's almost axiomatic that whatever is popularly understood as folkloric is also moribund, which was exactly why I was so fascinated by the practice in Ontario in the late 1980s – clearly a thriving tradition and thus not seen by its participants as 'folklore.' The folkloric is also too often associated with 'others,' at least by those who consider themselves urbane and sophisticated. As early as 1838, a New York newspaper asserted, 'The only portions of this continent, we believe, in which the evil custom of the Charivari is kept up are the Canadas and New Orleans ... [It is] practiced when matrimony is committed between persons whose age exhibit a strong disparity ... [and] performed nightly ... until the demands of the musicians are complied with ... for money to be given for some charitable society or sometimes it is expended for jollification ... It is a wrongful custom and ought to be abolished' (qtd in Haywood 1957, 279).

John T. Flanagan notes the difficulty of getting *shiveree* into the 1872 Webster's American lexicon, and writes, 'Perhaps by the time the custom which it denotes has become obsolete even in the backwoods, the word will become part of standard English' (1940, 110). In fact, charivari endures today in parts of New Brunswick, Ontario, and Alberta, and among devoted communities and interested families elsewhere in southern Canada – with the almost certain exception of Newfoundland.

My original work placed charivaris in the context of conventional house-visiting within Ontario's rural communities, marked in the local newspaper columns by notice of who went to see whom both from within and outside the community. Charivaris are arguably close relatives of another more rowdy type of traditional house visit, Christmas mumm(er)ing or janneying, found primarily in Newfoundland (Halpert and Story 1969), but also with cognate seasonal and ethnically marked forms in other locations such as Nova Scotia German *belsnickling* (Bauman 1972a) and prairie Ukrainian *Malanka* (Klymasz 1985). There are no charivari traditions per se in Newfoundland and Labrador; that province's rambunctious house-visiting customs are normally associated with Christmas rather than with matrimony. As a life-cycle event, rather than what folklorists and ethnologists would call a 'calendar custom' – one associated, usually annually, with a particular day or season – charivari has its differences, but it is still a boisterous, ritualized house visit.

In Newfoundland, the cognate house-visiting custom of Christmas mumming (also known as mummering and janneying) may have taken up some of the symbolic space occupied by charivari. Mumming, too, was sometimes used to express political disapproval and the tense relationship between the family fishery and merchant capitalism (see Sider 1986), though it was primarily a sociable custom. Associated with the transitions of the Christmas season (from one year to another) rather than with those of the life cycle (from unmarried to married states), mumming uses similar ritual means, particularly noise, surprise, and sociability. It would be telling to determine if other locations with Christmas house-visiting customs (e.g., Bauman 1972a; Goodwin 1975; White 1981) also include events similar to the charivari or, like Newfoundland, include only one form. But charivari continues in other parts of Canada, and the four cases I detail here have not hitherto been explored by other scholars.[39]

With respect to the charivari as diversion, while the murder of James Wetherill[40] near Ottawa, Ontario, in 1881, and the manslaughter of Harry Bosnell near Neepawa, Manitoba, in 1909 may lack that quality, the defamation, conspiracy, and personal injury case *Varner v. Morton et al* from Springfield, Nova Scotia, in 1917 has many amusing aspects. Now, if not then, the idea that a woman and a man driving around together would so shock a community as to lead the two to be suspected of having an affair seems laughable. The shivaree of Les and Edna Babcock in Avonlea, Saskatchewan, in 1940 was an entirely good-tempered event, intended to celebrate the long-awaited marriage of a couple known and loved within their community. The photographs taken by Edna (Bovee)'s sister Ada Bird and her husband Dick show that the children and adolescents who created this shivaree obviously enjoyed themselves enormously, beating on a garbage can and a washtub with sticks, and banging pots and pans. The honoured couple stand among them, perhaps examining a gift the visitors have brought.

Interpersonal and community discourse are extensive in the accounts of all four events – particularly community and newspaper gossip. Gossip tends to be an under-appreciated genre of traditional expression (see Jones 1990). Though in some communities the information passed between men is usually seen as news and that between women as gossip (Szwed 1966), the actual content can be identical. Both women and men in Springfield, Nova Scotia, were gossiping about Irene Varner and Lambert McNayr in 1917. Gossip, in fact, is the essence of the case in *Varner v. Morton et al.* Defendant Elwood Mailman testified, 'I heard rumors that McNayr had told Mrs Conn the plaintiff and he were married.' Defendant Isaac B. Saunders said, 'I came home one morning and the boys said he has introduced her to old Mrs Conn as his wife in the road. We thought if we gave him a little serenade he would take the hint and go home and act like a man.' And not all the gossip material was received second hand. Henry A. Oakes, station master at Springfield, testified, 'There is a ditch near Station House about 200 yards below station and about 3 or 4 feet below level of road. I frequently saw plaintiff around station. I saw her go into the ditch one day with a commercial traveller by the name of Purney. I could see Mr Purney greater part of time. They were down 10 or 15 minutes. They then went down trunk together.'[41]

Scurrilous talk also surrounded the charivari near Ottawa, 1881, resulting in the murder of James Wetherill. On the morning Wetherill's body was discovered, immediately following the night of the charivari, the *Toronto Globe* reported, 'THE MARRIAGE appears to have been one of convenience.' Wetherill 'wanted a housekeeper and Mrs Dougherty [the bride] a house ... A near neighbour told ... that the deceased said he had a wife in Kingston and some children. But owing to his improper conduct he was divorced from her, and that he would not have married again but that his daughter would not come to keep house for him but preferred living with her mother ... Notwithstanding that the deceased appears to have borne a good name generally, it is also said that he had another wife from whom he was divorced in Racine, Wisconsin' (12 August 1881). The *Globe* also noted that Wetherill 'has lived for a good while in Rochesterville and speculated in [illegible]. He was a thrifty man, made and saved some money and in addition to a house and lot in Rochesterville had informed Mrs Dougherty that he owned two lots in Chicago, a large farm at Sherwood Lake, and some Montreal bank stock' (ibid.). The lawyer for one of the defendants, apparently moved by the accounts of Wetherill's wealth, was reported to say, 'Old [Wetherill] had been too tenacious of his rights and if he had given way a little and yielded to the demand made on him for money, he would not have brought this affair on himself. He was, however, very obstinate and whatever had happened he had brought on himself' (Ottawa *Daily Citizen*, 15 October 1881).[42]

Indeed, it is the variety of discourses that surround the charivari – including gossip, oral history, family and community narrative, newspaper reporting, legal testimony, and photographic record – that focus my attention upon the four specific examples here. These discourses often vary widely in their actual content as well as in the attitudes they display toward the practice of charivari. But where nineteenth- and early-twentieth-century newspapers were almost univocal in their condemnation, community-based discourses tend to be more sympathetic.

The four cases I discuss here do not represent the run-of-the-mill charivari. In fact, each is in its own way quite atypical. Now as then, the vast majority of charivaris do not lead to legal actions, as they did in the first three cases. As I've suggested, the tradition, even in its nineteenth-century manifestations, was probably more often given in a spirit of mischief and received at worst in resignation, if not exactly welcomed. The charivaris that made their way into the kinds of documents that historians examine – including newspapers and court records – were usually those that ended badly. Unfortunately it is impossible to know how frequent were the more good natured ones.

But that statistic is not particularly relevant to this discussion. Just because these particular events had problematic outcomes does not mean that they were necessarily atypical otherwise. Further, the law case examples and newspaper reportage have the considerable advantage over some of the accounts I gathered in that they were noted hours, days, or weeks after the event, not years afterwards. I sometimes liken asking people to recall a charivari to asking someone to remember what she did on a particular Halloween night twenty or more years ago. A few outstanding aspects may be remembered with great specificity, but for most of us the recollections are very much homogenized, the details lost, and it's difficult to distinguish one Halloween from another. Nevertheless, there are always a few remarkable individuals who can provide specific details and elaborated memories.

In any case, it is clear that many couples did welcome their neighbours and community coming to charivari, even if the event was apparently directed against their marriage. Bernard Spurr of Bridgetown, Nova Scotia, who attended salutings – the local name for charivari – when he was a boy in the 1920s, explained that at the time they marked what he called 'unique' marriages. When an older, relatively wealthy widower married a younger, physically challenged woman, they obviously expected to be saluted; at the first sounds of bells and rifles, the groom came out with plates full of tailor-made cigarettes, and the bride invited the saluters in for food and drink. In another example, Mr Spurr's uncle, who had vowed never to marry, fell for a young woman from out of town. They too were saluted, and they too invited the revellers in for a treat.[43]

Even the 1940 Saskatchewan shivaree is somewhat unusual. It's remarkable because it was recorded by professional photographers, who were careful enough to also note the date and location. But it's also uncommon because most shivarees of the time recalled by those who lived in the community of Avonlea, where the shivaree took place, were not afternoon celebrations by children and adolescents, but the more usual late-night visitations by the honoured couple's peers and family. I offer this example, nevertheless, because it clearly shows the kind of welcome charivari that the vast majority of those who recalled the events in response to my research queries remember. Ironically, especially given its relative recency, it has been difficult to find out many of the details of this event. Its run-of-the-mill character, and the fact that no legal problems resulted that required more immediate testimony, work against my learning a great deal about it. The photographs remain, to a large extent, all-too-tantalizing evidence that something compelling was happening, without providing much other information.

The legal case examples, then, to an extent perpetuate a scholarly misconception about charivaris – that they were invariably negative in tone and often ended in violence of some kind. In my defence, though, I'm not just perpetuating an error, because these examples are invaluable for providing the kind of details that form the substance of ethnographic description, and they are the ones about which information survives. The four cases, however, are not entirely lacking in representative qualities. From Nova Scotia, to Ontario, to Manitoba, to Saskatchewan, like the practice of charivari itself, they traverse the country. They also range in time – from 1881, to 1909, to 1917, and finally to 1940. And they move (in chronological order) from murder to manslaughter to tort (defamation, conspiracy, and personal injury) to an event entirely beyond the concern of the legal system. This series should not be taken to indicate a progression or evolution as such, from the most violent possible to the entirely innocuous. However, it's not entirely untrue that generally the charivari over time became a less fraught activity, as my final chapter will show.

The first case I consider in this volume was no good-natured, pranking party, but an example of exactly how bad such events could get. Culminating in a murder, this 1881 charivari from the Ottawa area is among the most violent such examples in the legal case files and newspaper reports in Canada or elsewhere.

2

'Murder Most Foul': The Wetherill Charivari, Near Ottawa, 1881

By any standard, the charivari of Margaret and James Wetherill[1] was a bad one. Lasting more than four hours, and taking the form of a near-riot, it ended in a brutal homicide that was reported as far away as New York only a day after the event ('An Aged Bridegroom Murdered,' *New York Times*, 12 August 1881).[2] Discussed in the *Toronto Globe* – 'MARRIED AND MURDERED / An Old Man at Ottawa Killed on His Wedding Night / ONE MORE 'CHARIVARI' VICTIM / Disgraceful Conduct of Roughs in a City Suburb / BEATEN TO DEATH WITH STICKS' (12 August) – with opinions reported in the *London Free Press*, the *London Advertiser*, the *Brockville Recorder*, the *Hamilton Spectator*, the *Toronto Evening Telegram*, the *Toronto Evening News*, the *Brantford Telegram*, the *Montreal Herald*, the *Montreal Witness*, and the *Montreal Evening Post*, it became notorious (see also Dubinsky 1993).[3]

Here, as elsewhere, specific facts in the newspaper vary from other sources. For example, nowhere else are sticks mentioned as weapons; other sources agree that Wetherill was killed by a rock thrown at his head. Note, of course, the arguably greater brutality of being cudgelled to death over a possibly accidental homicide by a rock thrown from a distance. But as Robert Darnton points out, 'News is not what happened – yesterday, or last week – but rather stories about what happened. It is a kind of narrative, transmitted by special kinds of media' (2000, 1).[4] The gruesome details – often embellished or speculated on to elicit horror, disgust, and outrage received extensive newspaper coverage in Ottawa throughout the August aftermath, and again in October when the four suspects were brought to trial for

TABLE 2.1 List of protagonists

The wedding party (in order of appearance):
James Wetherill (65), the groom, killed by charivariers
Margaret Dougherty Wetherill (45), the bride
Catherine Cooper (36), owned house where Margaret had lived and where
the wedding and charivari took place
George Fowler (31), messenger, wedding witness, pays first group of chari-
variers to go away

The first group of charivariers (in order of appearance):
Ruggles Bonnell, Jr. (19), returns to the second charivari, where he goes to
the house and asks for money, then claims he was 'nearly murdered,' testifies
that he saw the four accused at the charivari
J.L. Foss (14), newsboy, returns to second charivari
Archer H. Murphy (14), mill worker, returns to second charivari
Robert J. Garvin (14), mill worker
Joseph Arneau(lt) (18), 'the boy who received the dollar from Mr. Fowler,'
fined $10

The second group of charivariers (selected, in order of appearance):
Hugh McMillan (22), grocer, goes to the house and asks for money,
    fined $15
Ruggles Bonnell, Sr. (48)
William McGrath (23), stone-cutter, returning from playing baseball
Edward Edwards (21), mill hand, returning from playing baseball
John H. Slack (20), journeyman cabinet maker, returning from playing
    baseball
Patrick Darcy (D'Arcy? Darcey?) (16), horse team driver, returning
    from the opera house, testifies that he saw 'four boys' at the charivari
Fred Colvin (Frederick Colville?) (14), driver, testifies that he saw
    the four accused, the last ones there, when he left the charivari

The final four, charged with murder:
Christopher Berry (14), father dead
James Kelly (19), labourer, father dead
Robert McLaren (18 or 20), sawmill and shanty worker
James O'Brien (18), labourer, parents separated, father 'given to drink'

Charivari witnesses:
Mary (31) and John (29) Courtman, testify they saw four men being
    chased by a man with a 'white hat'
Edward O'Neill, Dominion Police Superintendent, testifies that upon arrest,
    despite being cautioned, McLaren said Kelly and O'Brien had committed
    the murder, and Kelly, also cautioned, blamed McLaren and Berry.

murder. A jury acquitted the four, but as the *New York Times* reported, 'The verdict surprised the Judge, who charged strongly against the prisoners' (16 October). (See table 2.1 for a list of protagonists.)

Most of the discourses I draw on for this chapter come from two Ottawa newspapers – the *Free Press*[5] and the *Citizen*.[6] The Information of Witnesses – taken at the Coroner's Inquest – survives in the Archives of Ontario, but that document may be incomplete; several witnesses noted and discussed in the papers do not appear in it. None of the rest of the trial material seems extant. The census records unfortunately have no evidence of either James or Margaret (Dougherty) Wetherill. They do offer some material suggesting the linkages between some of the charivariers. But the census has not been a particularly fruitful source for this case, especially since the bride and groom, as well as one of the accused, can't be located.[7]

Fortunately, the newspapers of the day gave incredibly detailed though sometimes varying descriptions of the events and proceedings. For their material, they also tapped into community and individual gossip,[8] and the results instantiate contemporary concepts of sources of criminality as well as urban mainstream ideas about traditional culture. In societies like that of late-nineteenth-century Ottawa and its suburbs, in which communication face to face retains significance, the community receives gossip, rumour, and scandal as legitimate sources of information. Filtered through the newspaper, the charivariers' views also come through. Whatever the truth of the Wetherills' individual and collective situations might have been, it is clear that the charivari was occasioned by beliefs that James Wetherill was not only a misanthropic recluse, but also a widower and possibly a twice-divorced American; that he was considerably older than his widowed bride; and that he was wealthy.[9] Thus, the discursive form of the daily papers provides a rich source.

To a large extent, then, this chapter is about the charivari as a news story, and I follow the leads its discourse suggests, particularly about leisure activities and drink. Because of the material's richness, and because it is not readily available in publication, I employ lengthy quotations from the newspaper accounts. As a foundational history of Canadian journalism put it, in nineteenth-century newspapers 'local events were not ... reported in the objective fashion of the modern news story. Even accounts of fires, drownings, and other disasters were heavily interlarded with opinion and comment' (Kesterton 1967, 15). An 1894 comment from businessperson and writer J. Macdonald Oxley echoed the newspapers' own hyperbole: '[The newspaper] reaches a wider audience than the pulpit; it uses more effective arguments than the platform; it smites harder and more enduring blows than the sword' (qtd in Rutherford 1982, 4).

While some might question the actual objectivity of current news reportage,[10] the distanced style now employed by daily newspapers – though not necessarily by local community newspapers (see Greenhill 1989a) – is absent from these accounts of the charivari. Historian Paul Rutherford argues, 'Popular journalism was committed to accuracy, getting all the facts right, but not to the ideal of objectivity. Editors had few scruples about slanting the news to favour some particular point of view or provoke some kind of response' (1982, 139). This partisanship was as true of the news reporting as of the editorial content per se. Media social effects included 'agenda-setting (ordering the priority of issues or values in the public domain), mobilization (calling the people to arms), stereotyping (fixing images of particular ideas, events, or occupations), conferring of status (the creation of heroes and villains), manipulation of mood (emphasizing some collective emotion ...), and socialization (the education of people in the "proper" ways of thinking and behaving)' (ibid., 7–8). All these can be seen in newspaper content about the Wetherill charivari.

The format in which most of the charivari reports are found is what Rutherford calls 'the story,' which 'strove to reach the reader's "heart" as well as "mind," indeed to involve the reader in whatever joyful or tragic item the newspaper was serving up' (ibid., 142). If moral lessons could be drawn from stories about events resulting from accidents and forces of nature, like fires and drownings, the charivari – as a complex, already impassioned, and deliberate interaction between humans – formed a particularly rich subject. The moral lessons indicated in the papers are on the evils of drink, but they are also about how young men spend (and misspend) their time. Further, 'the nineteenth-century editor was guilty of circumlocutions, discursiveness and occasionally, pretentiousness' (Kesterton 1967, 18) – qualities amply present in the examples that follow.

Yet clearly 'the popular newspaper ... can exercise a great deal of ideological power' (Rutherford 1982, 8). Specifically, 'the big-city daily empowered the forces of progress in the modernizing community ... [T]he very bias of popular journalism, its emphasis on mass literacy, made newspapers leading antagonists of the force of custom which buttressed old ways' (ibid.). The values newspapers created and maintained focused on notions of modernity, a 'dogma ... built upon apparent certitudes ... The idea of progress was the most hallowed maxim of the age' (ibid., 156–7). In such a world, the charivari was a throwback, a relic, an outdated practice, and – in the Wetherill case – a grim reminder that progress had been neither uniform nor complete.

Rutherford argues that at the middle of the nineteenth century, 'the publisher or editor could indulge his own idiosyncrasies. What news to feature, which causes should be served, whether or not to entertain readers were the prerogatives of the journalist' (ibid., 118). He suggests that the contents were thus variable from newspaper to newspaper. And yet, the coverage of the Wetherill charivari in the *Daily Citizen* and the *Free Press* is notable less for its differences than for its similarities.

An alternative view suggests that journalism may work within two sometimes congruent, sometime contradictory models – that of information and conversation. Their purpose, then, was not simply to report what was going on, but to stimulate public and community debate on the issues at hand (see, e.g., Nord 2001). Evidently, the newspapers were an integral part of the contemporary discourse on the charivari. Interactions between oral testimonies and local talk, on the one hand, and reportage, on the other, appear periodically in both newspaper and legal discourse. Their contents suggest a mutual productiveness between the oral texts and the written newspaper accounts. Of course, the translation of traditional practice and oral testimony to written form often includes semantic as well as structural alteration of content.[11]

Indeed, the papers were at times implicated in the development of their own stories, and their reportage obviously had an effect upon those involved. The *Ottawa Daily Free Press* (henceforth *FP* in citations) reported that at the Coroner's Inquest, Margaret Wetherill commented that her friend Hugh McMillan (born 1859 Quebec, grocer, Scottish Catholic),[12] who had been present during the charivari, 'spoke to me to-day about the report in the *Free Press*, and complained that it stated that he did more than he did [the *Daily Citizen* said 'misrepresented,' 12 August], and said that he had only acted out of friendliness. I told him the paper did not seem to condemn him as much as he thought' (*FP*, 12 August).[13]

On the same day, the *Free Press* reported, 'We have been requested to state that there is no truth in the statement made by the *Citizen* to-day, to the effect that a wake was to be held over the body of the deceased, James Wetherill, who was a Protestant as well as his wife' (*FP*, 12 August). The following day, the *Daily Citizen* (henceforth

DC in citations) shot back, 'The *Free Press* says it is authorised to state that the statement in the *Citizen* about the wake at the dead man's house is not correct. It may be that his friends had no such intention, but it was stated after the inquest that a wake would take place, and Mr N. Favreau said that if such was the case he would not be responsible for the key of the house as coroner's constable. The rumour may have been false but it bore every appearance of authenticity' (*DC*, 13 August). Clearly, people were concerned about how they were represented, and at times successfully deployed one newspaper against the other in order to ensure that their perspective prevailed.

Similar effects can be seen in the final summation on behalf of one of the accused by his lawyer. Ironically, as reported in the papers, he charged the news media with prejudging the guilt of his client and the others:

> He regretted that the local press had given currency to … outside rumors. A number of irresponsible and incompetent persons of very limited capacity, who were utterly incapable of judging what was evidence and what was not, had freely discussed this case and had picked up every idle tale they could find, not for the purpose of furthering the ends of justice, but merely for the purposes of furnishing sensational articles for their newspapers, careless as to whether they injured the cases of the accused or not … Referring to charivaris he said that one of the newspapers which had been the strongest in condemning this charivari had had columns of commendatory notice of charivaris which had taken place in days gone by, merely because the people who took part in them were friends of the papers. He contended that this had the effect of encouraging charivaris. (*FP*, 14 October)

The newspapers' influence is constructed here in terms of inaccurate representation of the charivari, self-serving rather than responsible reportage, inappropriate judgment of legalities (and illegalities), and duplicitous and/or inconsistent representation. A reader of today might find much to agree with in these criticisms. Indeed, it is frequently difficult to separate the reports' rhetorical flourishes from coverage of the actual events. Where there is substantial agreement in content between the two papers, I assume *some* accuracy in the reporting. Yet the discursive form strongly influences the information provided.

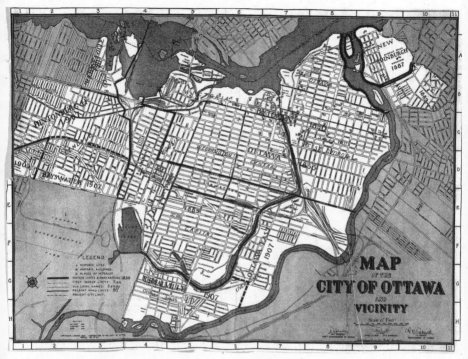

2.1 Map of the City of Ottawa (City of Ottawa Archives C. 1–35)

'Give It to Him, Boys': Reporting the Charivari

The *Free Press* reported on 11 August under the headline 'MURDER MOST FOUL' that James Wetherill had been 'married in the evening and killed in the morning.' Wetherill had 'resided in Rochesterville where he has been engaged in business as a speculator in cattle and farm produce.' (See figures 2.1, 2.2.) His body was found on Emily Street, near the corner of Lisgar Street, just outside the city limits of Ottawa (see figure 2.3).[14] The dead man's pockets held 'a leather pouch containing nineteen dollars in notes and $1.70 in silver; a cotton pocket handkerchief, and a brass key' (*FP*, 11 August).

Wetherill was described on his marriage registration as a fifty-year-old widower and stock dealer, born in Rothwell, Yorkshire, England, son of John and Martha [Allandale]. His age as recorded was

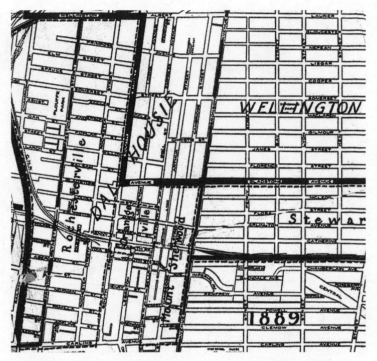

2.2   Detail, Rochesterville and Mount Sherwood (City of Ottawa Archives C. 1–35)

inaccurate, however, since he was christened on 6 July 1817; the newspapers reporting him as sixty-five were – at least this time – more correct. He had been married on 10 August, before a Methodist clergyman, to the widow Margaret Dougherty, forty-five years of age, born in Port Stewart, near Colraine, Ireland,[15] daughter of James and Sarah [Wilson] Taylor. The witnesses were George Fowler (born 1850 England, married messenger, Wesleyan Methodist) of Mount Sherwood and Mrs George Payne (Lidia, born 1831 England, Church of England, husband labourer) of Rochesterville. Margaret Dougherty had once kept a grocery store at the corner of Lisgar and Emily streets, and at the time of her marriage was boarding with Catherine Cooper (born 1845 Ontario, English Wesleyan Methodist),[16] whose husband Thomas (born 1838 Ontario, Irish Wesleyan Methodist), a stone-cutter, was in Chicago on business on the

2.3   Bell and Gladstone streets, Ottawa (formerly Lisgar and Emily streets) (Photo Leah Claire Allen)

day of the wedding and charivari (see figure 2.4.) The wedding was performed at the Cooper residence.

Around dark on the evening of the wedding, about eight o'clock according to the very clear testimony of Catherine Cooper, 'a number of boys gathered around the house and organized a charivari, hooting, yelling, and in various other ways annoying the inmates. Wetherill came to the door and offered the boys a dollar if they would leave. They accepted the offer, were paid the money, and at once left, returning no more' (*FP*, 11 August). Later testimony and reports suggest that it was not Wetherill himself, but wedding witness George

2.4   Grocery store interior, Ottawa, 1875 (City of Ottawa
Archives CA 2800)

Fowler, who had paid this group to go away. These sources also
demonstrated that several individuals from the first set of charivariers did indeed return later – an act that, as will be discussed later, is
somewhat unusual in the tradition. Hugh McMillan, the proprietor of
the shop formerly owned by Margaret Wetherill, testified at the
Inquest, 'About half past eight a crowd of little boys gathered. They
beat tins, one had bells, they were about Cooper's door … One asked

whether there were any old tins around [my] place. Told them there were in the yard and he could get them if not afraid of dog. He went. Some old stovepipes of mine were taken for the charivari' (*FP*, 19 August).

Later, estimated by various witnesses as happening between eight p.m. and midnight (Catherine Cooper says around ten), a second group, 'a large gang of men' (*FP*, 11 August), began the same procedure. Catherine Cooper testified at the Coroner's Inquest, 'They made more noise than the first. They shouted and asked for five dollars.'[17] Accounts suggest that at least some of this group were intoxicated. They threw stones, breaking two panes of glass and knocking plaster off the walls inside the house, 'cursed and swore, and vowed they would have Wetherill outside the house' (ibid.).

Ruggles Bonell Jr (John Bonell, born 1862 Ontario, English Church of England)[18] from the second set of charivariers, and Hugh McMillan, intending to serve as an intermediary, went to negotiate with James Wetherill for money. McMillan claimed, 'I was sitting on Ald Scott's[19] verandah at that time. Mrs Scott told me I had better go over and try to settle things' (*FP*, 13 October). At first Catherine Cooper tried to persuade the two that the Wetherills had left, but Bonell and McMillan discovered them in an upstairs room. McMillan 'says he went into the house to try and arrange matters by getting Mr Wetherill to pay the men two dollars, as he understood that they would go away for that amount. When he made this proposition to the deceased he struck him and refused to comply with the request. Mr McMillan says that he then told Mr Wetherill that he was a mean man, and left the house' (*FP*, 11 August). Margaret had offered to recompense them in the morning, but 'according to her statement [McMillan] refused to do so unless [James] authorized him to' (ibid.).

At the Coroner's Inquest, Margaret Wetherill testified to similar details: 'Mr McMillan ... said ... "if you give two dollars to the boys they will go away" – My husband said no he would not encourage any blaguards[20] like what they were. My husband was very angry ... and hit him a slap in side of the face when McMillan said again that he had plenty of money and ought to give the two dollars.' McMillan himself attested, 'I said the best thing they could do was to settle it or go down to their own place. I mean by "settle it" to give the charivari party the two dollars as they were young men and not children, and would not go away except they got two dollars for they said they would come back every night until they would get it.' He was probably correct that the charivari would have continued night after night until payment or halting by the authorities.

He added, however, that Bonell 'rushed out shouting to the crowd that he was nearly murdered, [which] was to the best of my opinion false and for the purpose of exciting the crowd.' He also indicated that James Wetherill thought that the Coopers' neighbour, Peter Potvin (born 1836, labourer, French Catholic), was involved in the charivari: 'He lifted a stick to them when they shouted "It's not me It's not me" Mr Wetherill said "You ought to be shot for harboring them you damned whores."' Wetherill's presumption that someone who was apparently sitting on his porch with his family watching the proceedings was responsible for the charivari may be an example of his reported 'misanthropy.'

It seems evident that 'There were three parties, small boys, larger boys, and a party of four or five who came after the others ... Stone throwing had not commenced till the last party of four or five arrived' (McMillan, qtd in *FP*, 19 August). Catherine Cooper apparently did not simply accept the situation. At the trial Hugh McMillan testified, "I heard one of the crowd say Mrs Cooper had thrown water on them, and then at another time, she struck them with tins' (*FP*, 13 October). Margaret Wetherill also tried to end the charivari. At around midnight, she left the Cooper residence to summon the police. When she returned and told the second set of charivariers that the police were on their way, most left. Eventually James also left the house, apparently concerned for the safety of his wife, Catherine Cooper, and her four children, as well as about the damage to the Cooper property. Margaret reported that James had a verbal altercation with Peter Potvin, accusing him of being part of the charivari, to which she said Potvin answered. "'I'll give him a beating that he won't get over in a hurry for insulting my family" or words to that effect.'

James Wetherill's body was found around five o'clock the following morning 'by a cow boy' (*FP*, 11 August). As the *New York Times* reported, 'At daylight this morning his dead body was found lying by the roadside with his head crushed in' (12 August). Though both Catherine Cooper and Margaret Wetherill 'have resided in the neighbourhood for some years they say that they were both unable to recognise any of the men who made the attack on the house notwithstanding that the moon was shining brightly' (*FP*, 11 August).[21]

Margaret Wetherill initially suspected, as her husband had, that the Coopers' neighbour, Peter Potvin, was the perpetrator. (He was kept in custody during the inquest.) However, tellingly of the four youths who would later be charged, she also testified, 'When my husband went out to chase the boys away they all left but four or five who remained on Emily street. My husband went down Emily street after these boys.' Witness Mary Courtman (born 1850 Ontario, English Catholic) also saw four men being chased by another she thought was a police officer because of his white head[22] but later surmised must have been Wetherill. Her husband John (born 1852 England, Catholic) told the *Free Press*, 'When they had got about a hundred and fifty yards above his dwelling, the fellows stopped, and one was heard to say, "Give it to him, boys." They were there together just a short time when he saw four persons making toward the city. He wondered what had become of the policeman as he saw no more of him after the gang halted. There was not a groan, moan or cry to intimate that a frightful tragedy had been committed. In the morning the old man Wetherill was found at the place where the roughs had halted while being chased' (*FP*, 15 August).

Wetherill's funeral was held on 13 August. Something of the personal unpopularity that would have furthered such a fraught charivari is evident in his description. The *Citizen* reported, 'If in life he had been excluded and had lived by himself, the manner of his death evoked warm sympathy from many who had before only thought of him as a misanthropic recluse ... The scene when the mournful procession moved off was most affecting. The newly-made wife of the murdered man made the air ring with her shrieks, and all who heard her fully sympathised with her heartrending cries. The poor woman seemed to feel that but for her matrimonial alliance with the dead man he would, in all human probability, be then alive and well' (15 August).

The *Globe* (12 August) reported that 'THE MARRIAGE APPEARS TO HAVE BEEN ONE OF CONVENIENCE. Earl wanted a housekeeper and Mrs Dougherty a house.' If these decidedly nasty commentaries came from his neighbours, it suggests that Wetherill was not a popular man.

'A Foolish Love of Company': The Arrests

By 15 August, the Dominion Police had made some twenty arrests. Initially Ruggles Bonell, William Fraser,[23] and Wickliff Robinson were arrested and charged with 'riotous and tumultuous conduct' (or 'disorderly and tumultuous conduct'). But the police next abandoned their 'lesser game' (*FP*, 15 August) and arrested four men – Christopher Berry (born 1867 Ontario, Irish Church of England), James Kelly (born 1862 Ontario, labourer, Irish Catholic), Robert McLaren,[24] and James O'Brien (probably James O'Brian, born 1863 Ontario, labourer, Irish Catholic)[25] – who were initially charged with manslaughter. The three identified in the 1881 census lived in Wellington Ward of Ottawa (as did Bonell, McMillan, and charivarier William McGrath). Their neighbours in the same ward were carpenters, masons, servants, labourers, engineers, tailors, sailors, school teachers, clerks, butchers, bookkeepers, smiths, merchants, gardeners, grooms, farmers, and messengers.

On 16 August, the Dominion Police made further arrests on the conduct charges. The newspaper reports indicate something of the nature and quality of charivari involvement, as well as the bases for their immediate presumptions of guilt or innocence – appearance and demeanour. Those accused included Ruggles Bonell (Sr), thirty-six (census says born 1833, which makes him forty-eight, Church of England), Canadian born, English descent, carpenter: 'Considerable importance has been attached to his appearance in court, not so much from [illegible] that he would wilfully have injured the old man, but because he knows the parties who are most active in organizing the charivari party' (*FP*, 16 August). His son Ruggles Bonell Jr was also charged. William McGrath, twenty-one (twenty-four *FP*; born 1858, Catholic), Canadian born, Irish descent, stone-cutter, was 'not fully allied to the serious nature of the crime of which he was accused … spoke openly and fearlessly of his conduct being free from any criminal intent' (*DC*, 16 August). He 'is a baseball player and was at the ball until ten o'clock when he went with others down to the place where the crowd had congregated. Took no hand whatever in the charivari. He says that there was a crowd of thirty or forty at the place at that time. He stood on the opposite side of the street and came to his home in the city soon after eleven o'clock' (*FP*, 16 August). McMillan was also arrested, and Alderman Scott paid his $500 bail.

Most of the charivariers charged who could be identified in the census came from the same division as the Cooper household. The occupations listed for their neighbours include boat captain, engineer, sash factory worker, foreman, commercial traveller, teacher, shipping clerk, trader, manufacturer, carter, plasterer, bookkeeper, messenger, agent, baker, lumberer, butcher, carpenters, farmers, many gardeners, many labourers, and a washerwoman. The area, then, appears to be primarily middle class – many professions and skilled trades are represented. Indeed, there is not a great deal to distinguish this area, Nepean, from Wellington Ward.

The charivariers include Edward Edwards, twenty-one, Canadian born, English descent (census says Irish), Church of England, millhand,[26] who 'came quietly along and showed no disposition to shirk the unpleasant position in which he found himself placed … and from

his demeanour it was plain that he did not consider that anything serious could result from his supposed misconduct' (*DC*, 16 August). He
'had been playing ball, too. He states that he took no hand in the
charivari, went home soon after eleven o'clock, lives below Mrs
Cooper's place' (*FP*, 16 August). His brother, James (Joseph *FP* and
census) Edwards, fifteen, Canadian born, Irish descent, student,
Church of England, 'a bright looking lad of decidedly prepossessing
appearance, and from his conduct a young fellow of more than usual
intelligence' (*DC*, 16 August), 'says that he was not around the locality where the charivari was at all that night' (*FP*, 16 August). Of
Frank (Frederick *FP* and census) J.L. Foss, fourteen, (born England)
newsboy, Church of England, the papers said, 'Shrewd and honest, he
did not seem at first to understand that he had been engaged in anything likely to lead him into trouble and admitted without contention
to his detention. This boy, with [John] Ross, who works at Brouse's
confectionary, young James Dunn, and one or two more are examples
of the trouble folly will get boys into who are in general well-
behaved' (*DC*, 16 August). He 'was there between seven and eight,
returned again about ten and remained until near twelve when his
father took him home. The father stated that there were twenty-five
or thirty in the crowd at that time' (*FP*, 16 August).

Living adjacent to wedding witness George Fowler were two boys
from the family of the widow Susana Slack. William Slack, sixteen,
Canadian born, English descent (census says Irish Wesleyan
Methodist), carriage-maker's apprentice, was 'neatly dressed and
spoke in a quiet manner … The lad appears to have the makings of a
respectable mechanic and his share in the row was probably that of a
foolish youth who went in for the fun of the thing without considering how serious the ultimate results might be' (*DC*, 16 August). He
'went to the charivari at the same hour as his brother. Rattled a tin for
a short time and went home at about a quarter past eleven. Saw no
stone throwing while he was there' (*FP*, 16 August). Of his brother,
John H. Slack, twenty, journeyman cabinetmaker, Methodist (Irish,
Wesleyan Methodist according to the census), 'there was certainly
nothing in his appearance or style of conversation to lead anyone to
suppose that he would have a hand in a dastardly midnight attack on
old men and women and young children. But his complicity in the
unfortunate affair was more than likely the result of foolish love of
company … He did not appear callous to the circumstances in which
he found himself, but at the same time did not act as though he felt
any serious responsibility in regard to the matter' (*DC*, 16 August).
He 'had been attending a baseball meeting, having been playing in

the early evening and at the close, about ten o'clock, went down with some others to where the charivari was. Talked to some girls on the walk until eleven o'clock. Went around a little after that and then proceeded home' (*FP*, 16 August).

Adjacent to the Slacks lived Archer H. Murphy,[27] fourteen, Canadian born, Irish descent (census says English, Church of England), mill worker, who was 'perhaps the brightest looking of the whole squad taken up' (*DC*, 16 August). He was living with his schoolteacher father James J. Murphy (born 1836 Ireland, Church of England), mother Zenobia, and eight siblings. He 'states that he was there with the first crowd and went back the second time but was home before eleven o'clock' (*FP*, 16 August). An 'Edward Morphy'[28] was also charged. Probably he is Edmund Murphy (born 1865, Ontario, English, Church of England), Archer's brother. A few houses away Robert J. Garvin, fourteen, Irish Canadian, mill worker (census says Ontario born, Scottish, Presbyterian) lived. He was 'from outward appearance, anything but a hard one. The lad was well-spoken and intelligent' (*DC*, 16 August). He 'says that he went home between seven and eight o'clock and was not back there at all that night' (*FP*, 16 August). John Ross, sixteen (born 1866, Ontario, Scottish Presbyterian), 'acted like a man when he understood that the police wanted him … He said he been around on the night and had been looking at the fun, also that he had been playing crackers there. The open speech of the lad bore such an impress of truth that no one who heard him could doubt him. He works at Mr Rouse's confectionary and spoke with confidence as to being able to get a good character from his employer' (*DC*, 16 August). He 'says that he was on his way home about half past eight when he discovered the crowd. He played the bones he had in his pockets, but did not know who they were charivaring. Soon got tired and went home before eleven o'clock (*FP*, 16 August).

Charles Blunt, thirty-three (thirty-five *FP*, census born 1845, married), butcher, Church of England, 'went down to the locality where the charivari was in progress about ten o'clock at night … was just at Alderman Scott's place and remained there for an hour or a little more, being merely a spectator of proceedings. There was no stone throwing up to that time, nothing more than tin pan beating and such like' (ibid.). Joseph Arneau(lt), eighteen, Irish Canadian, Roman Catholic,[29] was 'the boy who received the dollar from Mr Fowler, which was given by Mr Wetherill for the boys … Arneau stated that after getting the money they went and spent it for liquor. There was not a great crowd as they had two treats, but he had to add ten cents to square accounts so that only a dozen had drinks' (ibid.).

I could not locate the rest of the charivariers with any certainty in the census. They may have been itinerant workers, and thus not domiciled in Carleton county in April 1881. They included James Dunn, nineteen, Canadian born, Irish descent, carpenter's apprentice:[30] 'His relations are well known in the city as people of good standing and he seemed to feel, more than most of the others, the awkward fix in which his folly had placed him. He did not speak as if ... he felt himself guilty of any crime. The disgrace of being placed under arrest at all was what troubled him. Dunn is a good-looking, intelligent young fellow and it seems strange that he should have been mixed up with such a rowdy crew' (*DC*, 16 August). Fred Colvin (Frederick Colville?), fourteen, Canadian born, Irish descent, driver, Roman Catholic: 'He lives with his parents and his education would seem to be almost nothing' (ibid.). He 'was down where the noise was at half past ten o'clock, but only stopped a few minutes and then went home and to bed, being under the clothes when it struck eleven' (*FP*, 16 August). Patrick Darcy (Darcey *FP*), sixteen, Canadian born, Irish descent, horse-team driver, Roman Catholic: 'His only request was that he might put his horses away and that was complied with' (*DC*, 16 August). He 'was returning home from the opera house at half-past ten, and after remaining about twenty minutes proceeded to his home in Mount Sherwood; did nothing' (*FP*, 16 August).

Adolphe Desormeau, fifteen, labourer, 'did not look "hard" but rather the victim of circumstances. He made no pretensions to be able to read or write' (*DC*, 16 August). He 'says that he was not at the charivari at all and wondered why he had been arrested. He works at Mr Cochrane's, at the Chaudière, and on Wednesday night last went straight to his home at the Flats when his work was done' (*FP*, 16 August). Robert Palen, seventeen, Canadian born, Irish descent, driver, 'except as one of the rowdy lot out that night, not really wanted' (*DC*, 16 August), 'states that he was not at the charivari at all, that he was at home at half past nine in the evening' (*FP*, 16 August). A William Palen, possibly a relative, was also charged, as were William Howlett, W. Robertson, and John Corville. Of the arrested, the *Free Press* commented obliquely, 'It is quite evident that what some of them don't know about religion is more than they know' (ibid.). Each was given bail at $500.

The *Daily Citizen* noted in the later appearance of the 'minor offenders' before the county magistrates,

When arrested, the parties were certainly not in a position to be too favourably judged by outsiders. Most ... were in their working clothes, dirty after the usual day's labour and exhibiting the nervousness which was natural to all persons, whether innocent or guilty, suddenly taken in charge on suspicion as most of them thought of what might cost them their lives, while in several cases the feeling was increased by the weeping of the female members of the families from which they were so suddenly snatched. The courtroom yesterday was crowded and until called upon to answer to their names the accused were mixed up with the general crowd. The crowd was one more cleanly and intelligent in appearance than usually fills the courtroom, and the keenest observer would have found it a futile undertaking to pick out the alleged rioters from the spectators. Even when gathered in a bunch inside the railings, no unprejudiced person would set them down as a bad lot. There is hardly one of those races on which vice can be said to have placed its mark. Some of the younger ones are as bright looking fellows as any parent would want to see about a home. (20 August)

The charivariers appeared in Police Court, charged that they 'did unlawfully, riotously and tumultuously assemble and gather together, and ... demand and extort from one James Wetherill a certain sum of money, to wit to the amount of two dollars, against the peace of Our Lady the Queen, her Crown and dignity' (*FP*, 31 August). Most were fined five dollars or two weeks' hard labour, or three dollars or one week. Some were discharged for lack of anyone to identify them as having been at the charivari. One who didn't appear had a warrant issued for his arrest.

McMillan was fined fifteen dollars. The penalty assessed indicates that the magistrate saw his actions as particularly heinous. As a respectable citizen, presumably his only option would have been to have tried to persuade the charivariers to leave. Instead, however well-meaning, he acted in concert with them. Further, as a twenty-two-year-old storekeeper, his age and respectability may have counted against him. The younger men who had participated were not considered as blameworthy. Even Joseph Arneau, who accepted money from Fowler, and was arguably more implicated in the events, was fined less than McMillan: ten dollars or three weeks. 'Mr Langrell [the magistrate] advised them to stay home of nights and take no part in charivaris' (ibid.).

Interlude: Things to Do on a Wednesday Night in Ottawa, 1881

The charivariers had in common age, sex, and working-class occupations. Clearly, the majority of those who participated in the charivari were in their early teens and unmarried. Even Hugh McMillan was only twenty-two and unmarried. Only Ruggles Bonell Sr and Charles Blunt (both married) were over thirty. Few women or girls seem to have been involved – John Slack is reported to have 'talked to some girls on the walk until eleven o'clock' (*FP*, 16 August). But females who were present during the proceedings apparently were not considered participants by the authorities. The arrested were apparently all white (not from 'races on which vice can be said to have placed its mark' [*DC*, 20 August]). Of the eight whose religions were noted by the papers, four were Church of England, three Roman Catholic, and one Methodist. The census indicates twelve Protestant and seven Catholic participants; the possibility that religious difference drove the charivaris is discounted by the fact that the Wetherills were also Protestant. The majority worked in the industries around Ottawa – millhands, stone-cutters, drivers, carpenters, and cabinetmakers. Despite the young ages of the accused, only one was a student. Most lived with their parents, and most had no occupation listed in the census.

Both newspapers commented on the psychosocial tendencies of the arrested, almost exclusively on the basis of their physical appearance (see Chevalier 1973, 408–17). They provided evaluations of the characters of those involved, sometimes developing extended expositions upon qualities not now usually taken as deducible from an individual's looks, including mechanical ability, foolhardiness, intelligence, sense of guilt or lack thereof, honesty, and truthfulness (ibid., 419–33). It does seem evident, however, that most if not all those charged were surprised that going to, watching, or making noise at a charivari could be illegal. Further, those who came only to watch the proceedings (and did not make noise or demand money) did not consider themselves actual participants – a distinction not made, as it turned out, by the magistrate.

The charivariers' other activities that night that were reported in the newspapers give a good idea of what would be the usual diversions available for young men of their class and age at the time. Specifically mentioned are baseball and going to the opera house – amusements generally understood as more worthy pursuits than charivari (see figure 2.5). For example, 'Social reformers saw ama-

2.5   Ottawa Amateur Athletic Club Baseball Team, 1892 (City of Ottawa Archives CA 15266)

teur team sports bearing the stamp of muscular Christianity and rational recreation as a way to project images of respectability to themselves and to those outside their towns. To them, sports could also deal with the ills that plagued urban life – keeping kids away from street corners while defining what it meant to be masculine … revitalizing the bodies of sedentary workers, and providing entertainment for city dwellers' (Bouchier 2003, 5–6).

Three men – William McGrath, Edward Edwards, and John Slack – told reporters they were playing baseball. 'In the years between Confederation and the First World War, baseball established itself as Canada's summer sport of choice, pushing aside cricket and lacrosse'

(Howell 2001, 39). The games that McGrath, Edwards, and Slack played were almost certainly fairly informal, since Ottawa did not have an organized baseball team until 1895 (Humber 1995, 207). Apart from indicating how they came to be out and hearing the charivari – McGrath lived in a different census division, the other two the same as the Coopers – this activity would help to construct them for the authorities as men engaged in benign, perhaps even actively positive, activities.

'It was believed that sports and games promoted gentlemanly behaviour, individualism, social responsibility, imperial allegiance, and respect for private property' (Howell 2001, 30). As historian Nancy Bouchier indicates, 'Sport reformers believed that amateur sport helped all manner of fellow man … [They] praised the sense of camaraderie and appropriate social behaviour they believed club membership engendered, even holding these things up as a model for the rest of the community to emulate' (2003, 78). Informal team sports were 'eminently respectable activities … for men' (Marks 1996, 121). For example, the Queen's Birthday was celebrated in Toronto in 1881 with cricket and baseball matches (*Globe*, 25 May, 3) (see also Bouchier 2003, 31–59). The *Globe* also reported that lawyers and bankers of Fergus played the medical profession 'on Thursday last,' with the latter winning 13–7 (*Globe*, 19 July, 10). In City News, the paper notes, 'On Richmond-Street West yesterday afternoon some boys were engaged at baseball' (*Globe*, 2 April, 14). Baseball was newsworthy as part of the everyday life of the cities and towns in which it was played.

Nineteenth-century baseball had not yet become standardized and professionalized, as it would be in the twentieth century. Baseball clubs originated in Hamilton in 1854,[31] in London, Ontario, in 1856, in Woodstock and Ingersoll both in 1860, as well as later in Dundas, Guelph, Stratford, and St Marys (Barney 1993, 155). An article by a former resident of Beachville in southwestern Ontario, regarding a baseball game there in 1838, discussed the technicalities but unfortunately little of the social surround of the game. However, 'regarding the [players] mentioned … a study of genealogical, obituary and tombstone evidence confirms that most of them … were between 15 and 24 years old at the time' (Bouchier and Barney 1988, 80). This is almost precisely the age range of the Ottawa charivariers over forty years later. Similarly, a source from 1841 links baseball with the activities of the St Mary's Total Abstinence Society of Halifax, where 'between 700 and 800 met, and at which "Quadrille and Contra dances were got up on the

green, and games of ball and bat, and such sports proceeded"'
(Humber 2005, n.p.).

In 1830s Brighton, Ontario, 'Baseball was an evening practice of
the young men after the day's work. The game was popular, matches
were frequent with the villagers on the court house green, and the
play exciting' (quoted in Humber 1995, 20). The players, described
as British emigrants, were mainly English Episcopalians and
Methodists (fourteen of twenty-one families). 'They were former
military officers, carpenters, shoemakers and labourers' (ibid.). Fifty
years, later, a similar demographic is evident in the Ottawa charivari's baseballers: McGrath was Irish; Edwards, Church of England;
and Slack, Methodist. Their occupations and evident working-class
backgrounds were also similar.

Historian William Humber argues that baseball underwent a transition after the middle of the nineteenth century 'from an informal
folk game to one characterized by the adoption of semi-formalized
though regionally differentiated rules and play, largely within one's
own club' (ibid.). He contends that baseball was well adapted to its
time and place. Players 'wanted to play a game that could be completed in several hours to conform to their busy work schedules ...
Baseball was as well a game that still welcomed the unskilled' (ibid.).
Undoubtedly, the Wetherill charivari baseball players were amateurs;
McGrath was a stone-cutter, Edwards a millhand, and Slack a journeyman cabinetmaker by trade. But tellingly, baseball, like the charivari, was not entirely divorced from violence and rowdyism. Bouchier discusses 'vast contradictions ... between the notion of the
respectability presumed by promoters of representative sport and the
deeper messages that at times accompanied crowd unruliness' (2003,
107). Bryan Palmer argues that in Hamilton, the sport expressed
working-class solidarity and showed class inequities (1979).[32] Thus,
it may be that baseball's resistant undercurrent supported the Wetherill charivari's obvious sense that the rich middle class owed the
worker something more than mere wages.

Charivarier Patrick Darcy was coming back from 'the opera
house.' Opera houses were then venues for performances of all kinds.
They 'were used not only for music but also for political rallies, balls,
plays, lectures, minstrel shows, vaudeville, and, on occasion, even
operetta and opera ... Although opera was rare ... the name stood for
the ultimate in elegant entertainment, and many opera houses in
which opera would never be heard were erected. The name thus was
a deliberate euphemism' (Kallman et al. 1992, n.p.). The Ottawa
Grand Opera House on Albert Street was built in 1874 (ibid.) and

opened the following year with a seating capacity of 1,400 (Edwards 1968, 181). A recent newspaper article notes,

> Ottawa wasn't always 'the city that fun forgot.' By the time Bytown became Ottawa in 1855, it already had a reputation for being a prosperous, sophisticated urban centre that was a little rough around the edges. In those early days, every growing city had to have four essentials: An alehouse, prostitutes, a church and at least one opera house. The Victorians called them opera houses rather than theatres, which they associated with the low-brow burlesque venues that offered intoxicated ticket buyers cheap thrills ... [T]he ornate [1,000 seat] Grand Opera House, later called The Colonial, located on Albert St at O'Connor ... drew such celebrated actors as Thomas Keane and Edwin Booth, brother to Lincoln's assassin, John Wilkes Booth. (Armstrong 2005, n.p.)[33]

A year after the Wetherill charivari, 'Oscar Wilde spoke in Ottawa's "Grand Opera House" (then at 134 Albert St) during a visit in 1882' (Sibbald 2004, n.p.).

Opera houses at the time were multipurpose buildings. One example, the Palace Grand in Dawson City, Yukon, showcased 'comedy, melodrama, musical concerts and sporting exhibitions ... housed a saloon and theatre at street level, two apartments and a row of private boxes on the second floor, and another row of boxes and four smaller apartments on the upper level' (Coutts 1982, 41). There drink and hetero-sociality were central to the entertainment. Historian Lynne Marks points out that not all such presentations were equally respectable (e.g. 1996, 130–3). However, it appears that Ontario opera houses were generally sedate and temperate. Windsor's Hall Opera House was constructed in 1875: 'At first only the ground floor was completed and it housed the commercial establishments of Hiram's Grocery and Peddies Silk House ... In 1882 ... renamed ... the Windsor Opera House[,] it was officially opened by the Brown Theatrical Company with *Ten Nights in a Bar Room* and *Hazel Kirk* ... As with many other opera houses, the Windsor Opera House existed primarily for non-musical functions ... In its early years, [it] ... presented the usual touring theatrical companies and such entertainment as a series of revival meetings presented by the evangelists Crossley and Hunter in the winter of 1887' (Hall 1974, 86).

Both baseball and the opera house were considered more useful, educational, and healthy forms of entertainment than the charivari. Yet each, in its way, would have offered diversion and entertainment primarily for young men. However the latter two amusements would be considered by the papers and their middle- and upper-class audiences as primarily improving diversions, in contrast with the charivari and some of its attendant practices. For example, as will be discussed later, *Ten Nights in a Barroom* was a temperance play, dramatizing the immorality of drink – one of the social evils alleged to have resulted in the charivari and murder. Indeed, drinking was an integral part of the socializing of the charivari, as well as an entertainment in itself. Those subjects will be addressed specifically below.

'A Justifiable Verdict of Wilful Murder': The Inquest

Several of those charged with assembly, including Colvin and Darcy, testified that they saw Berry, Kelly, McLaren, and O'Brien at the end of the charivari. Ruggles Bonell Jr, however, appeared to be the main inquest witness identifying all four. Superintendent Edward O'Neill of the Dominion Police, who headed the investigation, also testified at the inquest that upon arrest, despite being cautioned, McLaren told him that Kelly and O'Brien had committed the murder, and that Kelly, also cautioned, had blamed McLaren and Berry.

On 23 August, when all the evidence had been presented, Coroner Robillard addressed the Coroner's Jury, with a good summary of known events:

> On the night of the 10th inst. the deceased Wetherill was married and … he came to his death the same night. On the evening the marriage ceremony was performed a few boys gathered and started what is known as a charivari near the house where the wedding took place. They were given the sum of one dollar, after which they dispersed … [S]hortly after this a crowd of larger boys and young men were gathered and made a great noise about the house. They continued their riotous conduct till a pretty late hour, but they did not get what they wanted – money. They appeared to have dispersed, or the greater number of them had, when a third party appeared on the scene. This party consisted of four men who acted in a very riotous manner and continued to for so long that the deceased, who appeared to have been unable to stand their riotous conduct any longer, ran out in the direction of where they were congregated. That was the last time he was seen alive. Those four men … have been identified by one of the witnesses who was at

the charivari; and from the evidence of that witness as well as other evidence before you, and also the confessions of the four made at the time of their arrest before witnesses, I think you will have little difficulty in arriving at the conclusion that they committed the deed ... [U]nder the circumstances it will not be difficult for you to arrive at a justifiable verdict ... .of 'wilful murder' against those four men. (*FP*, 24 August)

The Coroner's Jury found that the four 'did unlawfully and feloniously kill and slay James Wetherill on the 11th inst' and the four suspects were held in jail until the next assizes. The jury also 'passed a strong vote of censure on the Carleton County Council for their neglect to appoint constables' (*FP*, 14 August). Though the Coroner's Inquest cites the lack of officials to shut down the event, Allan Greer's research on Quebec charivaris around 1837 suggests that police interference might indeed have had quite another effect: 'When victims ... called on "the forces of order" to stop the demonstration, the invariable result was that the charivari intensified. From the crowd's point of view the offence was then compounded since, in addition to soiling the wedding rites, the subjects had also challenged its authority to right the wrong' (1993, 79–80).

Greer discusses earlier Quebec charivaris, but much of his description also applies to the Wetherills. Yet he argues, 'As soon as a fine had changed hands, the harassment stopped. The money ... placed the [crowd] under an obligation to drop hostilities. There may have been some hard feelings in the wake of a charivari, but there is no indication that under normal circumstances they would have been long-lasting' (ibid., 80). Since it appears that some charivariers did return, and indeed that there was more than one charivaring group on the same night, the notion of consensus on the fine and the reciprocal obligation seems absent in the Wetherill event. Perhaps, as Greer suggests for later Quebec charivaris, this was 'an all-purpose weapon for chastising more transgressions and punishing non-conformists ... Moreover, the attacks were much more vicious than they had been ... earlier' (ibid., 362).

'Hardened, Reckless Youths': Constructing Criminals

The *Free Press* stated, 'On Sunday many score of people visited Emily and Lisgar Streets, viewing Mrs Cooper's house and locating the spot where the poor old man fell by the wayside, killed with

stones thrown by hardened, reckless youths, whose moral sensibili-
ties were dull through lack of home training and discipline, and who
little thought of results. All the four parties now under arrest on the
charge of complicity in the crime admit to have been drinking some
during the evening but none of them were drunk – in their own opinion. It would be far better for them even though they could have had
such a poor excuse as being drunk to offer for their lawless and murderous conduct' (*FP*, 16 August).

Notions of criminality expounded here and below by the press
draw upon notions such as the fundamental animality and savagery
of those who perpetrate crime,[34] and the concept that criminals can
be identified on the basis of their physical characteristics (see, e.g.,
Chevalier 1973, 409–33). Reportage on the four accused exemplifies
how the newspaper used contemporary concepts of criminality as a
descriptive frame. The *Daily Citizen* reported, 'Christopher Berry
lives in that part of the By estate known as Bully's Acre, (so christened from the number of roughs who for years past have
congregated there and committed all kinds of depredations)' (15
August). Berry admitted to being at the charivari, and to having 'had
a glass on board,' but claimed that he and Bob McLaren had been
bystanders: 'When O'Brien and Kelly were beating the old man with
stones we went away and called them away also, and told them to let
him alone … Kelly came up to us and said "by God, we have killed
him," and immediately O'Brien came up and says, "the old man was
as dead as a nail," at the same time laughing' (ibid.).

Conversely, Kelly laid the blame on McLaren: 'McLaren, who
had stones in his possession, immediately began to treat the old man
with them. We heard him moan and saw him fall down, and we knew
he was dead. McLaren may tell what he likes, but that is God's truth'
(ibid.). When O'Brien was arrested, he was reported as saying,
'"You may lecture me if you like, but it is not a neck-snapping
affair"' (ibid.). The *Daily Citizen* noted, 'He is a hardened young
character, and has only been out of jail a few days' (ibid.). The
arresting constable, Edward John O'Neill, testified that O'Brien had
told him, '"McLaren and Berry are the lads that done it and now they
want to put it on us."' Ruggles Bonell testified that he had seen
Berry and McLaren at the charivari. He didn't know the names of
the other two men also present when he had left, but those at the
Police Court were the ones he had seen at the charivari. He had
attended both the first charivari, with the 'little boys and men
amongst them,' and the second.

Robert McLaren

Robert McLaren 'is the son of a respectable gardener, is about 20 years of age, strong, active and somewhat prepossessing. He has a sandy complexion, and could hardly be suspected of conspiring to commit murder' (ibid.). The *Free Press* described 'a well built, and rather good-looking young fellow eighteen years old. So far from being a bad looking boy, his countenance is rather prepossessing. His face is sun-burned and entirely devoid of hair ... His parents are of Irish decent; notwithstanding their Scotch name, and are known to be very respectable people. In the summer he works in sawmills, and generally goes to the shanties in the winter' (15 August). The same paper reported that McLaren volunteered the following story:

'Look here, now, I'll tell you all about the whole thing from first to last. About eleven o'clock on Wednesday night me and Berry were sitting on the grass on Bay street just a little piece off of Lisgar street. We had a box of sardines or a can of lobsters – I don't just rightly remember which it was now – when Johnnie Hennessy and Matty McMahon came along and sat down with us. Presently up comes O'Brien and Kelly with a bottle of whiskey. They asked us to have a drink and Hennessy and I each took a pull. They coaxed me to come with them up to the charivari and I started off with them. One of them said "Come back and give them some more whiskey, and we'll get them all to come." I wouldn't take any more whiskey but the rest did. Hennessy and McMahon could not be coaxed to go to the charivari so I and Berry started off with Kelly and O'Brien. When we got up to Cooper's house I stood across the street by the fence while O'Brien and Kelly pegged stones at the house. I don't know whether Berry fired any or not, but I know I didn't. We staid there quite a time, and then I said "Boys, come, let us go home." Berry and I started around the corner of Potvin's house and Kelly and O'Brien came after a little piece behind us. When they got down far enough past Potvin's house to see Cooper's house they commenced pegging stones at it again. I shouted "Boys come on. Go home and leave the house alone." They walked about ten or fifteen feet and then threw another shower of stones. Some glass broke that time and the old man came out of the house and ran round the corner. Me and Berry was then a good piece down the platform. We went ahead and Kelly and O'Brien followed and shouted "Boys, don't run." I called to them to come along and let the old man alone. When I turned around to look behind me and see what they were doing, I seen the old fellow drop. O'Brien and Kelly then caught up to me and Kelly said "We have the man dead." O'Brien came up laughing and said, "Yes, he's dead." One of them – I don't remember which one – said, "we'll clear out in the morning." We separated then and I went home and went to bed. Now that's the whole story from first to last.' (ibid.)

McLaren assured the reporter, '"I had some liquor in me, but I wasn't anyways tight,"' and finally offered, '"I've been home every night and around town every day. I could easily have got away if I wanted to, but I never dreamed of it, because I had nothing to do with killing the old man, and never expected to be arrested. I think I ought to get off; but I don't know about that though. It ain't alwas [*sic*] the innocent that gets clear"' (*FP*, August 15).

Christopher Berry

The *Daily Citizen* described Christopher Berry as 'a young man about 16 years of age, and his manner indicates that his early training has been sadly neglected' (15 August). The same source noted that he had 'wept bitterly since being arrested' and that 'so far as your reporter is aware, he has never before been under arrest' (ibid.). According to the *Free Press*,

Berry is a quiet looking boy, of some fifteen years of age and light in build, complexion dark. In disposition he does not appear to be viciously inclined, but the authorities say that he is rather a bad one. He is of Irish parentage, and was born in Canada, at this city. His father has been dead a good number of years, as he does not recollect much about him. He has five sisters and two brothers, all at home but a brother and sister, who are in the States. The lad seems to feel the position in which he is placed somewhat keenly, but was quite willing to tell what he knew about the fatal affair ... Berry's father belonged to a rather aristocratic family in Ireland, it is said, but he went to the dogs on coming to Canada and his death quite a number of winters ago, was a result of having his feet frozen. (15 August)

Berry's story was essentially the same as McLaren's. He noted, 'There was quite a crowd there when we arrived. They were beating tin pans and throwing sticks and stones at the house,' and recalled, 'This was after the demand for two dollars has been made' (ibid.). He asserted that he and McLaren never threw stones. Both newspapers seemed to believe Berry and McLaren's story. They constructed the two as perhaps misguided, uneducated, even lacking appropriate parental influence, but not 'viciously inclined.' In contrast, the *Free Press* imputed guilt in the other two, even from the outset. 'Kelly and O'Brien occupied a cell together. When asked "if they wished to say anything in regard to the matter for which they were under arrest," they hesitated, but when told that they need not say anything that would criminate themselves they were not so reticent' (ibid.). Kelly and O'Brien were depicted and named as prisoners, using images strategically locating them in their cell as well as implying guilty consciences: "Kelly had taken hold of a bar of the iron door, while O'Brien continued to pace the floor of his cell uneasily' (ibid.).

James Kelly

'Kelly, aged 20 years, is a sallow-complexioned individual, and looks like a man who had seen considerable of the rough side of life. His manner is very gruff, and his countenance indicates that he is very passionate and revengeful' (*DC*, 15 August). The *Free Press* was a bit more measured: 'James Kelly is a young man of 19 years of age; an Irish Canadian, having been born in the city. His father was a laborer, but is now dead. The widowed mother is living, and the prisoner has two brothers who are married ... Kelly is a light, wiry-built young fellow, rather dark in complexion, stands five feet four inches in height. He is quite downcast but told his story of the matter willingly' (*FP*, 15 August). When asked about employment, 'the prisoner' said, '"I was working lately around the mills. Eddy's was the last place, and on Wednesday last Kelly and myself[35] were out as far as the DesChenes mills to get work, but failed, so we came back to town"' (*DC*, 15 August). According to him, '"When we got there we found a crowd drumming on tin pans and yelling. They wanted some money. Our party did not join in with them. We staid on the opposite side of the road watching the others"' (ibid.). 'He denied taking any part in the charivari, but said that when Wetherill left the house: first he chased the other crowd away, and then made after us ... The old man overhauled us when we were about halfway up the block and hit O'Brien on the shoulder with a piece of board or slab. McLaren yelled, "Stand your ground, boys," and fired a stone at the old man. I had no stone, but tried to find one on the roadway. I had to go quite a distance before I got one, and just as I did I saw the old man fall down. McLaren threw the first and last stone; saw O'Brien throw a stone. Berry and McLaren had stones in their pockets when we went to the charivari (ibid.).

Kelly said that he and O'Brien immediately went to Aylmer to seek farm work.

James O'Brien

'O'Brien is, perhaps, the coolest and most bloodthirsty looking little rascal one could find in a week's walk. He is short in stature, about 5 feet 4 inches in height, strongly built, square shoulders, and very muscular. Both his father and mother are, however, honest and industrious people, and are respected by all who know them' (*DC*, 15 August). The *Free Press* said, 'O'Brien is a chunky fellow, about the same height as Kelly, but considerably heavier. He was quite reserved in manner, and somewhat dogged in disposition. As he paced the cell uneasily he would take an occasional look through the grated door, as though he longed to be outside again' (15 August). Note again the description of O'Brien as a caged animal. The reporter also remarked upon his reticence to speak: 'The prisoner addressed replied, "It will be time enough for me to say something when the right time comes" And he continued to walk in the cell.' Also his claim was noted: '"It was Berry and McLaren who did it so they needn't try to blame it on us"' (ibid.). The *Free Press* also described O'Brien as 'very anxious,' asking the reporter, 'What do you think will be done with us? ... Will we be hung for murder?' (ibid.), implying a sense of guilt. Indeed, 'Of the quartette under arrest, O'Brien seems to be the hardest one of the lot. While the other three appear to take the matter a good deal to heart and are willing to unbosom themselves, O'Brien is more reticent, and while anxious as to the final result refuses to say much, making an unfavourable impression on those who speak to him. The father and mother of O'Brien do not live together. Mrs O'Brien resides on Nepean Street; she is well spoken of by her neighbors as a hard-working, industrious woman. She quit living with her husband about two years ago owing to his being given to drink' (ibid.).

The papers note that Berry's and Kelly's mothers are widowed, and O'Brien's mother is separated. The descriptions, however, point the direction of guilt as the papers see it. McLaren is good looking, comes from a good family, and speaks openly; therefore he cannot be guilty of murder. Berry, although 'the authorities say he is a bad one,' weeps, has never before been under arrest, and is willing to talk; therefore, although possibly implicated in the events, he is unlikely to be one of the murderers. Both Kelly and O'Brien, on the other hand, are constructed in the mode of guilt (both are Catholic, Berry is Church of England). Kelly is 'passionate and revengeful' and rough. O'Brien, however, again only on appearance, is constructed as the most guilty. Though from 'honest people,' he is cool, bloodthirsty, and goes out of his way to blame others (a kind of reverse evidence that he is himself guilty).

Character, appearance, family background, and employment were just some of the aspects used in the newspapers to direct their readers toward presumptions of guilt or innocence of the four accused. Their influence and success in this process is suggested by the fact that lawyers for the four men alluded to the press accounts in their addresses to the jury on behalf of their clients. Perhaps because it underlined their own influence, these interventions, too, were reported in the papers.

A Verdict on the Practice of Charivari: The Trial

It appears that the four were together charged with murder. Assize Court Chief Justice Wilson notes,

> The offence of murder was very well described in the language of the indictment when it is spoken of as killing with malice aforethought. What the law meant by malice was that the person who committed the deed had not any justification for it ... It was not necessary that there should be any actual ill will. A person might take the life of a man and be guilty of murder although he had never seen him before and did not even see him at the time the act was committed. If a man were to fire into a crowd of strangers and kill one of them, that would be murder. If a person were to throw stones without regarding the danger to life and were to kill anybody, he would be guilty of murder ... With regard to the charge against the four prisoners, it was one of a very serious kind although arising from a comparatively trivial matter ... When a person kills another there was prima facie evidence of murder and it rested with the accused to show that the offence was less than murder or no offence at all. Unless the evidence clearly showed that the crime was less than murder, the grand jury must bring in a bill of murder against them. (*FP*, 4 October)

O'Brien's lawyer was Gibb; Kelly's and McLaren's was Mosgrove (an unusual pairing perhaps, because at least initially they accused each other); Berry's was Ward. R.W. Scott and County Crown Attorney Lees appeared for the prosecution. The Crown's witnesses included Margaret Wetherill, Catherine Cooper, and Hugh McMillan. Superintendent O'Neill testified on 'the correctness of a plan of the scene of the tragedy' (*FP*, 13 October). Frederick Colville testified that when he left the charivari the four – Kelly, O'Brien, McLaren, and Berry – were the only ones still there. Patrick D'Arcy testified, "'I do not know that I saw the prisoners there ... I can only say I saw four boys'" (*FP*, 13 October). Ruggles Bonell also testified that he saw the four at the charivari. Margaret Courtman and her husband reprised their Coroner's Inquest evidence of seeing four men running away from where Wetherill's body was found.

Given the lack of eyewitnesses linking the four Margaret Courtman saw running from the scene and the four who were left at the charivari, Superintendent O'Neill's evidence was crucial. He 'testified to the arrest of the prisoners *and [their] partial confessions*' (*FP*, 14 October; my emphasis). Cross-examined, 'He said he knew Berry since he was a baby and never knew anything against his character until this ... [H]e gave similar evidence respecting McLaren. He never had Kelly under his charge before this, and he never knew anything against either of their characters ... [H]e did not know much of O'Brien, but he knew that his family were very respectable people' (ibid.).

Lawyer Gibb, on behalf of O'Brien,

appealed to the men [of the jury] to free their minds from all outside influence which might have been brought to bear on them before they entered this court house ... [T]hey should pay no attention to the idle rumors and gossip of the town, which were calculated to deprive the prisoners of the fair play to which they are entitled ... The evidence showed that the prisoners had nothing to do with the inception of the charivari but had merely been attracted there by the noise. There was little evidence whatever concerning client O'Brien ... The stones which were thrown at the house, he said, were not thrown with the intention of hurting anybody; but merely out of a spirit of horseplay. He laid stress upon the fact that no attempt had been made to injure either Mrs Cooper or Mrs Wetherill when they went out. He thought evidence showed that even accounts of the stone throwing had been exaggerated. He complained that the Crown Counsel had put the words into the mouths of witnesses and had violated the rules of court. He said there was not a single word of evidence to show that any of the prisoners were on Emily Street that night at all ... Unless the jury could be satisfied beyond a reasonable doubt that O'Brien was one of the four who were seen on Emily street there was not the slightest ground to convict him of any guilt. He cautioned the jury as to the unsafe character of circumstantial evidence and said that while sometimes valuable, it was often misleading. In the present instance, he considered the circumstantial evidence against the prisoners very slight indeed. He contended that if the jury did find any of the prisoners guilty, they could not find them guilty of the graver offence of murder, but of the lesser one of manslaughter. There was positive proof that Wetherill was excited and if he attacked the person he was running after with his stick and that person in defence had struck a blow which killed him, the act would be perfectly justifiable. He said there was no evidence to show that this was the case but he considered that it was a legitimate inference. There was, however, no evidence to show where Wetherill was killed. In the absence of all evidence to show that O'Brien was on Emily Street at all, or that he was in any way connected with the death of Wetherill, he could not see how the jury could convict him. He concluded by making a strong appeal to the jury to acquit his client. (ibid.)

Lawyer Ward, on behalf of Berry, added,

If his client was guilty of anything, it was of manslaughter and not murder but he contended that Berry was innocent of any crime at all. If Wetherill brought the affair upon himself it would be for the jury to consider whether Berry, if he did anything at all, did not do it in self-defence. If the old man had not been so tenacious of his own rights and had yielded a little by giving the $2, he would not have brought this affair upon himself. But he was too stubborn to do this and, instead of giving the small amount asked, he rushed out of the house armed with a stick, determined to wreak vengeance on the crowd ... [He] suggested that Wetherill might have tripped up in running after the crowd and struck his head against the ground, thus producing the extravasation of the blood which caused death. That would be the first point for the jury to consider, and the second would be whether Berry was there at all or not. He was of opinion that the preponderance of evidence went to show that he was not.

Lawyer Mosgrove, for Kelly and McLaren, added,

Hitherto they had been young men of irreproachable character, against whom up till now there had not been the slightest accusation of crime. He alluded to the unfortunate position of the young men, and asked for them a fair trial. There could be no doubt of Wetherill's death … It was true that he came by his death from the effects of wounds upon his head, but how those wounds were received would remain a mystery to the end of time. Pointing to the mothers of the prisoners, who were in court, he said that it would be a hard thing for the jury to take from these widowed women their only sons. He therefore appealed to them to give to this case all the intelligence with which God had gifted them. It was for the jury to say whether there had been a murder committed at all or not, and he asked them, no matter what language they had heard used, to throw that overboard and come square down to the evidence that they had heard … It was nothing less than a calumny to say that the four prisoners had committed [murder] … He argued at considerable length in favor of the inference that Wetherill had been the aggressor in the matter which resulted in his death. It was a principle of law that every man's house is his castle and a man was justified in taking life in defence of that castle. But in the eye of the law he must remain inside the house while defending it. Referring to the statements made by the prisoners to the police after their arrest, he pointed out that in the eye of the law they were not evidence because no one of the prisoners had said anything which could be used against himself. And what any of them had said concerning the others was not evidence against them because it was not sworn to in the witness box. If for one moment the jury felt it their duty to have any reasonable doubt as to the guilt or innocence of the prisoners, then it was their duty to bring in a verdict of not guilty. He would not ask the jury even to bring in a verdict of manslaughter, for with the evidence before them he would be satisfied with nothing less than acquittal. (ibid.)

The lawyers for the defendants constructed their defences in part from what might be characterized as folk views of the charivari and of law. They include the idea that responsibility for what happens at such an event lies with the original perpetrators – others may be drawn to the event by the noise, but are less culpable. As indicated above, this view was not shared by the legal system; bystanders and noisemakers alike were fined as participants. But to most of the audience, since the four charged with murder were not among those who started the charivari, they were not responsible for what happened. The lawyers also constructed the Wetherill charivari as one involving 'horseplay' rather than malice; they advanced this view by showing that neither of the central women involved was injured, though both left the house at least once. A charivari, then, was a light-hearted celebration rather than an indictment of those against whom it was directed. At best, then, the charivari got out of hand; alternatively, responsibility lay with Wetherill for taking it too seriously, not with those who came to charivari.

The latter concept was supported by the direct argument that Wetherill brought his death upon himself by failing to pay a relatively small sum of money to the charivariers, as tradition dictated. According to this view, he should have given the money; and by implication, if he had, he would have survived the night. (Of course, since some of the first set of charivariers – those who were paid to go away – indeed returned, as Bonnell Jr, Foss, and Murphy had, the argument was shaky at best.) Through this turn of responsibility, Wetherill himself was painted as the villain – presumably not only for being a possibly twice-divorced American widower of sixty-five who was marrying a much younger (though still, by the times, fairly aged) woman, which occasioned the charivari in the first place – but also explicitly for being stubborn and vengeful, unable to accept a light-hearted prank.

R.W. Scott, on behalf of the Crown, tried to counter these ideas:

> That [Wetherill] had come to his death by violent means there could not be the slightest doubt, for he was in good health up to the last time he was seen alive. And there was found on his head wounds which could only have been produced by violence ... [T]he evidence ... proved that the four prisoners were the last of the charivari crowd that were seen in the neighborhood, that after the stone throwing had ceased, four men were seen standing on Emily street, that Wetherill had last been seen alive by his wife going around the corner to Emily street, that a man with a white head had been seen running towards the four men, that after he caught up to them near where his body was found he was seen no more alive, and that the four men were seen running away towards town from where the body was found. He thought he was not asking them to come to a violent conclusion when he asked the jury to come to the conclusion that the four men in question were the four prisoners in the dock. When a prima facie case like this one was

proved to show that the prisoners were present at the scene of the murder, it would be a very easy matter indeed for the prisoners to prove that they were not there, if that was the case. He contended that the statements made by three of the prisoners entirely corroborated the evidence of the other witnesses ... He said that it was quite competent for the jury to bring in a verdict for manslaughter if they thought that the evidence would justify them in doing so. If they thought the prisoners had no intention of killing Wetherill, they might consider that they were guilty of manslaughter. (ibid.).

The *Daily Citizen* also noted Scott's assertion, 'As to the plea which had been raised that Wetherill had brought death on himself by going out of the home, it was only needful to say that he was the only man in the house and obeyed a natural and right instinct in going out to drive off the rowdies who were endangering the lives of helpless women and children' (15 October).

Chief Justice Wilson's charge to the jury in essence concurred with the Crown's position. He

showed the jury that the annoyance given by the charivari parties to the people in Mrs Cooper's house was great, and that custom was no excuse for the rowdy conduct which then took place. He condemned the whole practice in strong terms and said there could be no doubt of the household being in considerable fear. Had Wetherill fired on the crowd and killed someone, he no doubt would have been acquitted. Parties who took part in such proceedings as charivaris, if life was lost in them, they were responsible for that loss of life.[36] His lordship pointed out that the conduct of the whole of the parties about the house of Mrs Cooper on the night in question was most unwarrantable and held that Wetherill did not exceed his rights in going out and giving chase to any of them that he thought he could apprehend. He also held that the evidence pretty clearly showed that violence had been used to him, but that there was nothing to show that he had been guilty of violence to anyone. (Ibid.)

The *Free Press* reported in greater detail Wilson's 'condemnation' of charivaris:

He then proceeded to animadvert simply upon the evils of charivaris. He said that in the case in question, there was but a step between the victim's marriage and his grave. Charivaris seem to be generally considered to be a piece of licensed sport, but this was not the first time that that which had begun in sport had ended in death. The practice was at best a senseless, idle, and vicious one. It was frequently carried on by the use of firearms and other dangerous weapons. Cost what it might, the practice must be put down. It was unbearable that people cannot marry who they please but must consider the wishes of all the wicked and idle among their neighbours and that precious lives should be lost to such a foolish custom ... He knew of no way to put a stop to such practices but a rigid enforcement of the law and it rested with the grand jury to call all who had participated in the affair to a strict account. (14 October).

During the nearly two hours the jury deliberated, 'The probabilities of the verdict were freely discussed quietly among those who remained in the courtroom. There was a general impression that the result would be favourable to the prisoners. It was no surprise when the jury returned and declared their decision "not guilty"' (*DC*, 15 October). A current reader might wonder why the result was not at least a manslaughter conviction, given the compelling evidence that placed the four at the scene, and their implication of each other in the result. Presumably, then, the jury were not persuaded of the fundamental wrong of the charivari as a practice. Like those charivariers tried and convicted of unlawful assembly at the same event, they saw nothing improper about charivaris, and felt that the appropriate reaction to one was not to refuse to give money, but to accede to the crowd's demands. Wetherill, then, was clearly in the wrong, responsible for the crime committed against him.[37]

Allan Greer points out that for the crowd, the charivari involves a 'right to regulate certain specific aspects of the life of the community' (1993, 85). The charivari could coexist with more formal systems of regulation, but as the Wetherill event shows, it can pit the rights of the working-class collectivity against those of individuals. It is unclear why in this case the first payment did not end the charivari. The lack of more detailed information about Wetherill himself – and thus about his connection to the charivariers – stands in the way of a specific understanding.

'Wanton Malice': Editorializing on Charivaris

The reportage discussed above comprises myriad judgments, opinions, and speculations about the event and its participants. Though these articles by no means exemplified the concepts of 'objectivity' in journalism that would become standard in the 1920s and later in North America – 'verification, qualification, attribution, and balance' – (Leff 1997, 29) many papers also took the opportunity to explicitly editorialize on the practice of charivari in general, using the Wetherill charivari as their touchstone. An editorial in the Ottawa *Daily Free Press* the day after the murder spoke of 'public indignation': 'The invasion of [Wetherill's] privacy was an outrage for which there can be no excuse' (12 August). Yet in the absence of excuses, plenty of explanations appeared in the Ontario and Quebec papers in the days and weeks that followed. Some suggested the death was an accident: 'Brutal, reckless, blackguardly as the whole attack was, no one can believe that murder was premeditated and those who were unfortunate enough to be the cause of the taking of the old man's life will be best served by being brought to light. That such a deed should be allowed to go unpunished is an idea not to be tolerated in a civilized country. A ready admission would do much to condone the crime, but every attempt at concealment only serves to harden public sentiment against the offenders when they are discovered, and that they will be none can doubt but skeptics of the deepest dye' (*DC*, 13 August).

Yet the same paper's headlines and report on the previous day showed a much less measured response: 'A BRUTAL MURDER / An Old Man Killed on His Wedding Night / THE CHARIVARI NUISANCE / Its Natural Result – The Loss of Life / NO COUNTY CONSTABLE / Dominion Police on the Track of the Murderers' (*DC*, 12 August). 'A more cowardly and ruffianly attack upon helpless and unoffending persons was never perpetrated in this vicinity. An old man of almost seventy years, two weak women, one of them mother of four young children, who huddled terrified about her, were exposed to the insult and fury of this band of howling scoundrels, who pour volley after volley of heavy stones into the place without heed as to whether helpless infancy or old age might be the victims of their wanton malice' (ibid.).

Though there was almost unanimous condemnation of charivari as a practice, other mitigating factors made their way into the papers' analysis. A familiar explanation in current times, then applied to the charivari, is that such tragedies result from an education system that failed to instil in youth appropriate social and psychological understandings:

We suppose that most of the men who were engaged in this equally cowardly and wicked exploit had gone to school and had received some sort of education at the expense of the public. It is plain that they had acquired neither morals not manners ... Surely if there is any country in the world where it would seem impossible for natives not very far advanced in age to be wantonly brutal, it ought to be Canada where there is such ample provision for the training of children. But this is only one out of several recent incidents, especially of outrages upon women, which show that with all the pains taken for the instruction of our young people, there is abroad among us a spirit of ruffianism which is kept somewhat in check in the cities and towns but is too frequently manifesting itself in rural districts where there are no police. (*Montreal Herald*, qtd in *DC*, 17 August)

This belief in not only the civilizing force of education, but also the necessity of a formal authority to control the populace, shows notions of modernity conflicting with the tradition of the charivari. Further, though today the culprit in these situations is more likely to be illicit drug-taking than drinking – the latter now publicly notorious for its implication in vehicular homicides – this argument about liquor is also a familiar one: 'Some of the crowd were said to be in liquor. Let this be a lesson to stop their drinking habits. Every day the press is reporting murder cases by over indulgence in intoxicating liquors. No doubt sober men sometimes are guilty of crime, but in the majority of cases liquor is the primary cause of the crimes and murders committed throughout the world' (*Brockville Recorder*, qtd in *FP*, 17 August).

As I will show below, temperance arguments were mobilized in full force during this period. But in another concept that will be all too familiar to present-day Canadians, one of the sources of the problem was the community where it took place, and the writer argues for the mobilization of formal legal authorities. The *Free Press* concluded, 'The murderous termination of this charivari is unfortunately but the culmination of a series of such outrages which occurred in or near this city of late. At Rochesterville a few years ago a young man engaged in a charivari was shot and badly wounded, a few nights ago a mob assailed a bridal party on the Richmond Road but was bought off with liquor freely dispensed at a neighboring tavern, and now comes this most disgraceful affair of all ... We are not aware whether there is any law bearing directly on the custom of the charivari, but if there is not, we hope the provincial legislature will next session make a stringent enactment for putting a stop to it' (12 August).[38]

In the same paper, a few days later, in their own defence, 'Mount Sherwood people claim that their suburb is a respectable and quiet one. No liquor is sold there, while its entire criminal record only shows one man having been imprisoned from it, and that was for larceny. Whenever disturbances have been created, as that of Wednesday night last, it has been by outsiders who invaded the place. They desire that the suburb should not be given a name for lawlessness that it does not really deserve' (*FP*, 15 August).

I have been unable to determine why Mount Sherwood and Rochesterville were considered problematic locations. Michael S. Cross notes, 'Until well into the 1840s, Carleton remained a frontier area, on the outward edge of significant settlement. And, like so much of Upper Canada, it was a commercial frontier, as the entrepôt of the lumber trade of the Ottawa Valley' (1967, 105). Ottawa itself once had a bad reputation as an unsafe town (e.g., Cross 1973; McBurney and Byers 1987, 45–61). But those who complained that invading outsiders were responsible were only partially correct. The majority of charivariers identifiable in the 1881 census lived in the same division of Nepean: Mount Sherwood and Rochesterville. However, crucially, the three identifiable accused were not; they were from presumably law-abiding Wellington Ward in the city of Ottawa itself. If the residents of Mount Sherwood were to blame, for some writers it was because they were unwilling to pay for policing: 'Mount Sherwood is a small and comparatively isolated community. Being outside the city limits, it does not come within the jurisdiction of the city police, and owing to the penny-wise-and-pound-foolish policy of the Carleton County Council, it is without a single constable, and there is nothing to prevent the lawless element of the locality doing pretty much as it pleases. In consequence of this people who doubtless do know many of the parties implicated in the charivari are afraid to tell what they know for fear that the persons they expose, or their friends, may take advantage of their unprotected situation to have revenge by injuring either their persons or their property' (*FP*, 13 August).

Alternatively, 'The districts in which police officers are most needed are precisely those which refuse to maintain them. The districts around Ottawa are notorious for their lawlessness. The people of a whole township refuse to pay taxes and great crimes are frequent … Some better system than is in use will have to be contrived for the preservation of peace in such notoriously lawless parts of the country as these (*Montreal Witness*, qtd in *FP*, 17 August).

Yet the *Free Press* also seems to suggest a class-based argument:

The people who reside near the vicinity of the tragedy are for the most part of a class who, for some reason it would be hard to explain, have a horror of courts even though they are only called upon to appear there as witnesses, and they are chary of giving any information to the authorities lest they should be asked to act in that capacity ... There seems to be a great dread of arrest among those residents of Mount Sherwood who live in the vicinity of the place where the charivari and its tragical sequel took place. No sooner is the white helmet of a policeman seen in the vicinity than there is a general locking of doors and pulling down of blinds and the whole place is as still as a churchyard at midnight ... There cannot be the slightest doubt that to make a fearless statement of 'the truth, the whole truth, and nothing but the truth' will be the very best course that can be pursued by all who have any knowledge of the matter. (*FP*, 13 August)

The expectation that the truth will simply lead to justice is clearly more of a bourgeois than a working-class notion. If, as it appears, some of those arrested had not actually attended the charivari, but nevertheless had to face the magistrate in Police Court, and if we presume some kind of community solidarity that sees the charivari as warranted in the circumstances, perhaps the reticence of those in Mount Sherwood was not so incomprehensible after all.

Several articles mention the need for more stringent policing. However, greater and more extensive legal repression of the practice of charivari was perhaps the most common call from the newspapers – or at least the one most often repeated in the *Free Press* and *Citizen*. The *London Free Press* advised the legislature to make charivari a 'specially punishable' crime (qtd in *DC*, 15 August). The *Hamilton Spectator* noted, 'A charivari is in itself an outrage and a breach of the peace ... This brutal custom ought to be punished with the greatest severity, and frowned out of existence' (qtd in ibid.). The *Toronto Evening Telegram* wrote, 'The charivari has had its day and has lived five hundred years, and the sooner it is abolished the better' (qtd in ibid.). According to the *Toronto Evening News*, 'When the outraged bridegroom, driven to desperation by annoyance and by fear of the frenzied mob, has taken down his gun and fired into their ranks, wounding or killing some of them, public opinion has usually held him justified ... The occurrence is a disgrace to our civilization' (qtd in ibid.).

Arguing individual rights against tradition, the *Montreal Evening Post* found, 'It is a pretty state of things when roughs and loafers are in a position to annoy people because, in their opinion, they are too old to contract a matrimonial alliance, and to demand a bribe for ceasing to insult them' (qtd in ibid.). The *Brantford Telegram* commented, 'Many good people look upon charivaria as harmless pieces of fun which need not be condemned if they cannot be encouraged. To our mind they are incentives to rowdyism and should not be tolerated in any community ... The murder of the old man Wetherill should teach all law-abiding places that it is not safe to give a rowdy an inch. The thorough-going ruffian is too apt to take an ell when the strong arm of the law is relaxed in the least' (qtd in *FP*, 16 August). Others concurred:

> Whatever might be said of the charivari – or 'shiveree,' as there is some authority for calling it – in the early days of the country, when means of entertainment were low, and a wedding was the occasion of social jollification, it is now only a display of rowdyism of the worst kind. Like the public address, or the annual presentation of a photograph album to the district school teacher, it has been tolerated, although regarded as a social nuisance. No charivari ever occurred that was not an invasion of private rights, but the occurrence at Ottawa the other evening raises the charivari to a much higher degree of criminality and invites the prompt action of the authorities in mercilessly putting down all such inharmonious and illegal gatherings. To state the case plainly, a man was murdered on his wedding eve because he refused to be blackmailed to the extent of two dollars, in order that a gang of rowdy loafers might fill themselves full of whiskey. The man already paid tribute to one crowd, but this was not sufficient for the drunken gang, and the man lost his life in consequence. This is a poor commentary on our boasted civilization and it will be to our lasting disgrace if another such murder is allowed to occur because this one has been unavenged. (*London Advertiser*, qtd in *DC*, 17 August)

Still others combined the arguments into a seamless defence of modernity and civilization:

> It is evident that the worst class of roughs and scoundrels were engaged ... In many cases, it is to be feared, the perpetrators of this form of social outrage are simply ignorant and thoughtless youths spoiling for some sport. The fun, the sole element of which consists of the annoyance caused to others, is unworthy of a civilized being. The practice of compelling the persecuted parties to hand

over … money is robbery, pure and simple, and should be recognized and punished as such. We do not know what remedy the law provides for the punishment of the horn blowing, the tin pan beating, gun firing, &c., and similar form of annoyance, but they should certainly be made indictable offences liable to severe penalties. (*Toronto Globe*, qtd in *FP*, 17 August)

Finally, one article displays the extent to which the reasons for charivari had become obscure to some:

What the motive was for acts which led to such a terrible end it would not be easy to see unless we assume, as we fear there is too much reason for doing, that the exercise of sheer brutality is a high satisfaction to a certain class of people. There was, so far as we can observe, nothing to bring the newly married couple within the restrictions which self-appointed censors and regulators sometimes choose to impose upon their neighbors. There was no miscegenation which excites such anger in the Southern States; there was no excessive disparity of age between the two spouses; nor was there any affinity or other cause which might excite the horror of the refined and subtle theologists and moralists of 'Bully's Acre.' (*Montreal Herald*, qtd in ibid.)

Divorced, widowed, elderly, and with a disparity in their ages, they multiply instantiated the kinds of characteristics that led a couple to be charivaried. The fact that Wetherill was known as a misanthrope and miser would have exacerbated the situation.

Dead Fathers, Widowed Mothers, and the Evils of Drink: Temperance Arguments

It was only a year after the Wetherill charivari that the Judicial Committee of the Privy Council (then the highest court of appeal for Canadian cases), in *Russell v. the Queen*, ruled that the federal government could prohibit liquor retailing in the interests of the British North America Act's 'peace, order, and good government' (see Heron 2003, 156). Lawyer Ralph Fullarton argued for the federal government: 'Drunkenness affects the whole public; it affects the public health; it affects public morals; it affects public crimes and public order … The totality of those individual cases of persons who take too much becomes a public nuisance and even a public terror' (qtd in Risk 1990, 707). Alcohol played an extensive role in nineteenth-century male socializing (see, e.g., Marks 1996, 81–106), and yet temperance crusades were continual (see, e.g., Noel 1995).[39] Bryan Palmer argues that the tavern and the fraternal lodge 'offered divergent routes away from the isolations and constricting individualism of nineteenth-century society' (2000, 211). However, as may have happened in the Wetherill case, 'at moments of high social tension, alcohol was often a stimulus to acts of riot and rebellion' (ibid., 219–20). Its role as such may be partly explained because 'in North American culture, alcohol acts as a symbol of leisure ... as well as a disinhibitor and dissolver of "hierarchy and structure"' (Warsh 1993, 6).

Reginald Smart and Alan Ogborne argue a combined gender and class link for nineteenth-century alcohol use: 'The male character of frontier life ... contributed to heavy drinking by railwaymen, boatmen, lumbermen, and miners' (1996, 14). However, 'contrary to the sermons of temperance advocates and social reformers, violent physical confrontations were not a phenomenon unique to the drunken underclasses and the impoverished' (Wamsley and Kossuth 2000, 405). Yet drink was one motive force for charivaring; the ostensible purpose of the noise-making performance was to extract money from the couple to buy drinks for the charivariers. To folklorists, such *quête* customs allowed for the redistribution of wealth (clearly James Wetherill was by contemporary standards quite well off), as well as giving young men an opportunity to assert power over those they could not normally control. The middle- and upper-class rejection of the charivari, as seen in the newspaper editorials, could in part be explained by just this kind of inversion of the usual social order. But the charivari's association with drink and public intoxication would also mark it as an inherently socially undesirable activity.

Bryan Palmer links alcohol's 'increasing regulation and governance' to 'a vital social imperative: the new capitalist industrial order demanded a rigid separation of work and life ... Drinking ... had ... to be confined to leisure time, most especially the non-waged night' with the result 'a growing saloon culture' (2000, 220). In contrast, historian Greg Marquis suggests that 'the household was likely the location of most drinking in Europe's North American settlements' (2004, 309). However, the accounts of the four accused give another picture. Their own chronicles of the events, reported in the newspapers, show them eating and drinking outside on the grass near the corner of Bay and Lisgar streets rather than at home or at a tavern, and carrying their bottle of whisky with them (see figure 2.6)[40] Perhaps this behaviour was anomalous, but

2.6   Bay and Lisgar streets, Ottawa (Photo Leah Claire Allen)

it does not seem to have been taken by others as such. Marquis notes a model that certainly describes the four charged: 'Arrests and convictions for public intoxication in urban areas ... established a pattern ... : the bulk of offenders were young, male, and single, either "masterless" or lacking the stability of a family relationship ... Like criminals, they were viewed as weak, lacking self-control, and sinful' (ibid., 310).

Marquis also states that 'treating was an important social custom ... during election campaigns, charivaris, and militia musters' (ibid.). Expectations governed offering and accepting liquor, maintaining sociability among participants. In Worcester, Massachusetts, during the same period, 'treating provided the nineteenth-century [Irish-American] with a crucial means of declaring his solidarity and equality with his kin and neighbours' (Rosenzweig 1983, 59). Julia Roberts described mid-century treating as 'carrying a value exceeding its financial worth. The treat extended an invitation to drink and it invoked the need for a reciprocal return, whether in kind or in a more interpersonal sense' (2001, 100). Two kinds of treats are implicated in the Wetherill charivari. First, as men they knew passed by, Kelly and O'Brien offered a drink, which some accepted. Alcohol was shared among acquaintances. Second, at the charivari itself, the newspapers characterized the demand for money to treat the chari-variers as 'paying tribute,' but it also suggests that the drinking sup-ported by Fowler's dollar paid to the first charivari crowd was spent at a bar, since they refer to 'two treats' and the need for Joseph Arneau, who had taken the money, to pay an additional ten cents to cover the full cost.

'In terms of the family in Western, industrial society, alcohol most often has been portrayed as a problem' (Marquis 2004, 308). Indeed, the example of the four charivariers charged with murder shows the interrelation between family and alcohol. 'The family as both a sym-bol and an objective reality was extremely important to competing arguments on the proper role of alcohol' (ibid., 309) – and vice versa; alcohol became a symbol and objective reality pertinent to the fam-ily. For example, Christopher Berry's father, coming from a 'rather aristocratic family in Ireland,' had died of frozen feet, having gone 'to the dogs on coming to Canada.' Dying of frozen feet and going to the dogs are surely code for involvement with drink; the implication is that the family is both literally and figuratively destroyed by Berry Sr's alcohol use. Similarly, James O'Brien, the one most clearly sus-pected by both papers, had both parents surviving, but not living together, the mother having left 'owing to [the father's] being given to drink.' Again, the family has been destroyed by alcohol. Marquis comments that 'temperance created intergenerational or interspousal tensions within families ... Nineteenth-century temperance was closely linked to another Victorian-era reform, the anticruelty move-ment. Drunken husbands, in this discourse, abused the vulnerable members of families, a moral of the classic temperance play *Ten Nights in a Barroom* ... According to contemporary temperance organizations, charity activists, and public health officials and latter-day social historians, money spent on drink by male breadwinners was a threat to the stability of working-class families' (2004, 312–13).

Ten Nights in a Barroom and What I Saw There was a melodra-matic story written by T.S. Arthur, published in 1854 and subse-quently dramatized by William W. Pratt in 1858. A temperance song by Henry Clay Work, 'Come Home, Father,' which begins, 'Father, dear Father, come home with me now, / The clock in the belfry strikes one,' became part of the play about 1864. This tale of the evils of a saloon – accidental homicide, gambling, murder, and insanity – and its prescription of prohibition as the solution, was very popular at the time (Hart 1986). The story was presented as a slide show at temperance lectures, and several film versions were produced: 'As an object lesson, nothing quite matched the moral havoc portrayed in *Ten Nights in a Barroom*. In that famous cautionary tale ... drink did away with an entire village. Small wonder that the book became a kind of dry bible. *Ten Nights* made fearsome enough reading, but when its searing scenes were projected upon a screen in the darkness of some crowded meeting hall, the cowed spectators might sign a pledge just to get their temperance tormentors out of town' (Clark 1964).

With James Kelly's labourer father dead, Christopher Berry's father dead as a result of alcohol, and James O'Brien's father absent also because of alcohol, only one of the four, Robert McLaren, had both parents living together. The weeping of the mothers of those charged only with attending the charivari was explicitly noted by the newspapers, which also reported lawyer Mosgrove's hyperbolic comment that 'it would be a hard thing for the jury to take from these widowed women their only sons.' Of course not all the mothers were widows, nor was each man charged the only son.

Despite the multitude of explanations, pronouncements, and moralizing that the Wetherill charivari gave rise to, which together suggest its links to contemporary issues of concern for those who encountered it in person or through the newspapers, its relation to the tradition remains clear. The urban/suburban working-class location for this charivari suggests that it wasn't occasioned by notions of community continuation, as in rural areas. Instead, given the apparently significant difference in resources between James Wetherill and those who charivaried him, the demand for a treat was, in essence, for the groom to share some of his wealth. Charivari in 1881 Ottawa, then, was still part of working-class culture.[41] But references to Wetherill as a divorced (sometimes twice-divorced) widower suggest that money may not have been the only consideration. Family and economics were inextricably linked among working-class urban families of the time (see, e.g., Comacchio 1999, 32–9). The need for reciprocity that is underlined in the treat was an expectation within the family also. If there was evidence that Wetherill, despite abandoning his wife/wives, nevertheless expected his daughter to work for him, he was not taking part in the implicit family bargain. These young men may have thought to punish Wetherill for his transgression of familial expectation as well as for not appropriately sharing his wealth.

Violence seems to have been part of the Wetherill charivari almost from its beginning. In the next example, in contrast, few people at the time, and few of those who kept the incident in oral tradition, suggest that the resulting homicide was deliberate. Yet nearly thirty years later, and a province away, death was the result of this next charivari, just as it was of the Ottawa one.

3

'A Man's Home Is His Castle': Death at a Manitoba Charivari, 1909

Though most of the information I drew on for the previous chapter came from various sources, including but not limited to interviews, court proceedings, and local gossip, it was filtered through a single discursive form – the newspaper. The newspaper's stories about charivari related it to criminal or more benign behaviour, sought explanation for what they represented as fundamental human nature (extensively influenced by ideas of class), and interpreted the practice as evidence of an atavistic streak running through the fabric of modernity. To those notions I counterposed other possible contemporary understandings, especially about appropriate relations between individuals and collectivities. However, I am fortunate to be able to add to the repertoire of discursive materials in this chapter not only a more extensive legal record, but also a wealth of oral traditions. As suggested in my introduction, these different forms have different stories to tell, especially when considered from a gender-sensitive perspective. The discourses of newspaper and courtroom absent or silence women; those of oral tradition are more inclusive.

However, most sources agree that on 9 November 1909, eight boys and men gathered outside the home of William McLaughlin Jr, just north of Brookdale, Manitoba, to charivari him and his new bride, the former Ethel Burkell. Four days earlier, on 5 November, the couple had eloped to Rosedale (where their marriage was registered), where they were married by the Methodist minister for Franklin. Though several newspapers noted McLaughlin (born 25 May 1874) as 'a man of good character,' the thirty-five-year old had married the nineteen-year-old Burkell (born 7 May 1890)[1] slightly less than eight months

3.1   Harry and Joseph Bosnell headstone, Neepawa
(Photo: Pauline Greenhill)

3.2 Harry Bosnell, death registration (United Church Archives, The United Church of Canada, Conference of Manitoba and Northwestern Ontario)

after the death of his first wife Ella Ennis in childbirth.[2] Burkell's father did not approve. The situation clearly called for a charivari.

Two days after the event, eighteen-year-old Harry Bosnell, one of the charivariers, died in the hospital, in nearby Neepawa, of peritonitis resulting from a 22-calibre rifle bullet fired from the McLaughlin house, which travelled through his stomach and liver (see figure 3.1). The Neepawa Methodist Church register lists the cause of death as 'gunshot wound,' and adds the remark 'shot at a chirarivi'[3] (see figure 3.2).

A couple of weeks later, McLaughlin was charged with manslaughter. Thus, unlike in the Wetherill charivari, the authorities do not seem to have believed the homicide was intentional. The Grand Jury hearing the case during the Spring Assizes in Portage La Prairie in March 1910 returned a 'no bill' decision.[4] The charivari and its aftermath became not only a local scandal, but also the subject of local, provincial, and even national newspaper coverage as well as legal proceedings.[5] The sources frequently differ on everything from the details of what actually took place to the spellings of the principals' names.

The legal depositions – recent memories at the time for those who testified – give wonderful specifics about what happened at the charivari, though they are by no means disinterested reports (see, e.g., Davis 1987; Sangster 1993). Similarly, then, as now – and in the Wetherill example – accuracy of the newspaper accounts was limited. But the more local news coverage, particularly from the two papers in Neepawa, the nearest large town, can be presumed more generally reliable than the farther-flung ones; indeed, when other generally reliable sources address the same issues they tend to agree with the local paper accounts. Closer social and personal connections to the protagonists would encourage staff of the Neepawa papers to check recollections, word of mouth, and gossip more carefully than would those in Carberry, Portage, Winnipeg, or Toronto. The McLaughlin charivari is still known around Neepawa and Brookdale, and at least one descendant of a local resident took the story with him to Alberta. As discussed in the introduction, though sometimes factually inexact, the oral tradition reflects truths about social relations and cultural interactions of the time, and of the present. All accounts illuminate ideas of appropriate and inappropriate behaviour in strongly gendered terms.

Brookdale Area, 1909

Each [Manitoba] town looks roughly the same, with elevators, loading platforms, and coal and lumber sheds on one side of the tracks, main street and the residential area on the other. The school is several blocks back from the tracks so the trains would neither endanger nor disturb the pupils, and the fairgrounds and stockyards are at the extremities of the little hamlets. Often these towns conform to the square-mile survey system, with eighteen blocks to the mile, the streets sometimes unimaginatively named First, Second, Third going west and, for symmetry, First Street East in the opposite direction. (Whitcomb 1982, 20–1)

The village site of Brookdale was laid out in 1902, to serve a branch line of the Canadian Pacific Railway north to Minnedosa and Neepawa or south to Douglas and Brandon. Among the first businesses were a butcher shop, a blacksmith shop, a store, and a boarding house. Soon were added two grain elevators, a warehouse, a hotel, two general stores, a hardware store, a drug and book store, a harness shop, two farm implement warehouses, a coal shed, a lumber yard, a livery and feed stable, a stockyard, ten dwellings, the CPR station and water tank, a post office, and Bell telephone connection (Swanson 1987, 50–2). It was, very clearly, a service centre for the surrounding agricultural region, the farming countryside in which the McLaughlin charivari took place.

The year 1909 was part of a period of rapid growth and profound change for Manitoba. Its population went from 150,000 in 1891 to 554,000 in 1916, but 'whereas in 1891 over seventy percent of the people lived on farms, by 1916 only fifty-six percent did so' (Jackson 1970, 160–1). Throughout the province, 'lumber and flour mills, coal and fuel yards, farm-machinery dealers, meat-packing houses, printing plants, wholesale grocery and dry-goods establishments ... grew, both in number and in volume ... The main purpose of all this activity revolved about the handling of the grain crop, which was increasing by leaps and bounds' (ibid., 161). Grain production was the mainstay of McLaughlin and those who participated in his charivari.

Historian Gerald Friesen identifies a developing subregion in 1886, 'north of Brandon, in an area that included Neepawa and Minnedosa but stretched as far west as Birtle and Russell' (1984, 202). Brookdale is slightly east of Brandon and south of Neepawa, so it would be close to the southeast corner of the region Friesen identifies. He argues that 'the foundation of every district was the agricultural settler' (ibid., 203), and this region is no exception. All the participants were engaged in farming, and most had arrived in the area before the founding of Brookdale.

The area, even then, was no frontier.[6] 'Within a brief period, certainly by the early years of the twentieth century, the frontier had given way to a settled society' (ibid., 314). The charivari's participants show the close connections between residents. And yet 'the co-operative ethos of the frontier had been succeeded by an individualism that would have done business leaders proud' (ibid., 316). There were gradations of affluence from large, wealthy, English-Canadian background families, who would have had servants, through the average and then poorer farmers (ibid.). The charivari participants were either hired workers (probably William Ernest and Joseph O'Hayes and possibly also Charles Bugg, though he had family in the area) or members of a farming family. The only individual directly involved in the charivari, and enumerated in the 1906 census, with non-family members in his household at that date, was William McLaughlin himself, who had a hired hand. However, since he had no children, where large working families were the norm, having a hired hand may have been simple necessity. For example, Bob

Whelpton was living in his father's household with five members in total; the Wiggins family had eight members; and the Burkell family had ten.

The close links between members of the charivari party and the charivaried couple evidence the 'chain migration' that Friesen notes as central to the European settlement of the area. For example, the parents of charivarier Bob Whelpton had relatives in the area when they moved from Ontario in 1881 (Whelpton and Whelpton 1990). At least three Ennis siblings, in addition to Ella, moved to Manitoba: two brothers and a sister (Buchanan n.d.). Further, the direct familial links in the region are clear. Erstwhile charivarier Bob Wiggins was married to Alma Ophelia, sister of charivarier Bob Whelpton (Whelpton and Whelpton 1990). Charivarier Harold Burkell was the bride's brother. Sarah, sister of charivarier Charles Bugg, was married to groom William McLaughlin's brother George (Watson 1987). Harry Bosnell and his brother Joseph attended the charivari together. Peter Griffith and Bob Whelpton had business together, and Joseph O'Hayes and Bugg were living in the same location. A combination of close family and working links may have enabled the charivariers to feel that they had a right to demand recompense from William McLaughlin.

But as historian Mary Kinnear (1998) argues, women's economic contributions to the daily operations of the agricultural system made them and their work indispensable. Households without women, as explained in my introduction, operated at a disadvantage. Women conducted not only domestic labour; in the early years of settlement, they worked clearing, planting, and harvesting, as well as constructing houses and outbuildings, with their fathers, brothers, and husbands. McLaughlin, a widower with an infant and no grown daughters, would have been seriously motivated to find a wife.

The Legal Record:
Mrs Wiggins's Success vs the Men's Failures

According to the *Neepawa Register*, on Thursday, 18 November, a coroner's jury found that 'Harry Bosnell came to his death from the effects of a wound caused by a 22 calibre rifle bullet, fired on Tuesday night, November 9th, 1909, by some unknown party, from the residence supposed to be occupied by Wm McLaughlin Jr, in the Municipality of Langford, Province of Manitoba' (1). Some distinguished members of the Manitoba Bar and Judiciary were involved with the case. D.A. MacDonald, appointed to the Court of King's

Bench in 1906, who became chief justice in 1927, presided over the bail hearing. H.M. Howell, made chief justice of the Court of Appeal in 1906, heard the Grand Jury case at the Spring Assizes of the Central Judicial District in March 1910. F.G. Taylor, then Crown attorney for the Central Judicial District, appointed to the Court of Queen's Bench in 1933, appeared for the Crown when the witnesses were questioned in Neepawa.[7] Unfortunately, McLaughlin's lawyer is referred to only as 'Mr Robertson' and could not be more precisely identified.

The Grand Jury Depositions were taken in the Police Court at Neepawa on 24 November from the two doctors who had performed the autopsy, as well as from Peter Griffith, Joseph Bosnell, Robert Whelpton, Charles Bugg, Harold Burkell, and William Ernest – six of the eight men who had perpetrated the charivari.[8] These records, which survive in the Archives of Manitoba,[9] give remarkably detailed information about the event. It was a dark night, with no snow on the ground. That visibility was extremely poor may in part explain the accident. At no time in these proceedings did anyone suggest the death was anything but unintentional; the charge of manslaughter itself indicates an inadvertent homicide.

Charles Bugg, aged thirty-three (born 23 December 1875), claims he first heard about the charivari two days before the event, but 'I could not say who organised the charivari party. Joseph Wiggins and several in Brookdale told me that there might be a charivari, but I paid no attention to it till Monday. On Monday I told … O'Hayes [called O'Hara, farmer from Langford, in the *Neepawa Press*][10] that I had heard they were going to have a charivari. I told the Bosnell boys the same.' James O'Hayes was 'stopping' with Bugg, and they met William Ernest on the road two miles from the McLaughlin place.

According to Joseph Bosnell,[11] the brothers left home about 8:00 that evening. They picked up Charlie Bugg and Jimmie O'Hayes and proceeded to the McLaughlin house (see figure 3.3). They also called for fourteen-year-old Harold Burkell (born 8 November 1894), the bride's younger brother, on the way, but he followed later on his own. These four were the first to arrive, at about 10:30. Joe Bosnell had a cowbell; 'the other boys had moleboards [*sic*, mould boards],[12] sleighbells, cowbells, and a shotgun in the hands of William Ernest.'

Labourer William Ernest had been threshing at a local farm, and went to the charivari from Brookdale. He set out with Joe Wiggins (aged forty-one, born November 1868), who had apparently planned to be in the charivari party. They met up with Bugg, O'Hayes, and

3.3   McLaughlin house, 2005 (Photo: Pauline Greenhill)

the Bosnell brothers. According to Ernest, 'Mrs Wiggins [Alma Ophelia, his wife, aged thirty-seven, born 20 March 1872] told Joe Wiggins he wasn't to go. I went home with him from Brookdale and when we got there I unhitched his horses and he went into the house. In my opinion Wiggins was intoxicated.' Ernest took a plough mould board, and O'Hayes brought a 12-gauge breech loader shotgun, but

Ernest took it from him, and claimed that he picked the shot out of the shells.

Peter Griffith (aged twenty-six, born 30 September 1883) had known McLaughlin 'for three or four years but am not well acquainted with him.' He had come west from Ontario with his family in 1897 (Anonymous 1987, 318). He learned about the planned charivari from A.R.L. (Bob) Whelpton (aged twenty-eight, born 28 July 1881), who had also first heard of it from Joe Wiggins. Griffith and Whelpton had met on business that night, and they rode together to the McLaughlin place. It was apparently Griffith's idea to attend the charivari, and he took with him a plough coulter[13] and a bolt with which to beat it. Whelpton brought a pair of bells. When they arrived at the McLaughlin gate, the Bosnell brothers – Billie Ernest, Charlie Bugg, and Jimmie O'Hayes – were already there.

The rest stayed, as Griffith said, 'waiting quiet' on the road, while O'Hayes and Ernest went up to the McLaughlin house. Ernest testified that they 'rapped at the door and got no answer. We spoke up and said "Mr McLaughlin there is a bunch of boys there to charivari him." We yelled out that if he would give us $10 we wouldn't charivari him. Before we asked for the money we went around the north side of the house and shot a blank shell to waken him.' The first shot from inside the house came shortly afterwards. Ernest fired a second time, and his shot was again answered from the house.

Ernest and O'Hayes went back down the road and, after some discussion, the full company proceeded up from the gate, in Griffith's words, 'to carry out the charivari intentions,' making noise with the instruments they had brought. Another shot came from the house.

Once again, O'Hayes and Ernest knocked and Griffith heard O'Hayes call, '"Billie, we have come to charivari," but got no answer. They came back and we circled around to the west and north of the house, everybody making noise with what they had.' He claimed, 'O'Hayes said, "We have come to charivari you," and asked for $5 or $10.' Burkell said, 'They got no answer. They decided to start hammering the instruments they had. They started to make a noise.' The two tried a third time, rapping and asking for ten dollars; they stayed about five minutes at the door. Ernest said he heard another shot from the window, and he also shot again.

Then Whelpton and Ernest both claimed they heard four shots from the window. Ernest said, 'When the first shot was fired I heard something strike the ground near me, and then I struck for the water closet. There were two more shots fired from the window before I got to the closet and when I got there I shot twice.' On the third shot from the house, Whelpton 'saw [Harry] Bosnell coming toward [him] and he said "Bob, I'm shot."'

According to Griffith, two shots were fired from the house after Bosnell was hit. Ernest and Griffith put Harry Bosnell into Whelpton's buggy, and Griffith and Whelpton took him to Neepawa hospital. Apparently unconcerned, Joseph Bosnell went home to bed. The whole process probably took less than half an hour, if the first charivariers arrived at 10:30 as Joseph Bosnell reported, and the shooting took place around 11:00, as the *Neepawa Register* reported (11 November, 2).

Local physician and coroner Israel McInnis testified, 'At first condition did not seem serious. After a time, he vomited and from that time he became worse.' Harry Bosnell died less than two days later, 11 November, around 4 p.m.[14] Death resulted from 'peritonitis caused by a bullet.'

Three days after the death, Constable Charles Rooke went to McLaughlin's house to interview him. 'I asked him if he felt like telling me what had happened on the night of the charivari and he said yes he was quite willing to tell me everything that had happened. He said he and his wife were in the house together alone. I did not warn him before he made any statement as I did not know at that time that I was going to make an arrest. I was merely investigating the case. He said he fired four shots that night with a 22 rifle, one from the east window and three from the north.[15] He said he did not know anybody got hit that night until next morning about eleven o'clock. He said he thought he was firing over the heads of the crowd.'

Two weeks after the event, following an information laid by Constable Rooke and also signed by the attorney general, on 22 November, Rooke arrested McLaughlin and confiscated the rifle. On 25 November, charged that he 'did unlawfully kill and slay one Harry Bosnell,' the accused had 'nothing to say.' The records suggest that on the 27th, he was released on bail of $4,000. However, the *Manitoba Free Press* reported McLaughlin's bail at $8,000 and notes, 'McLaughlin has given security for $4,000 his father for $2,000, and a friend named Hamilton, of Neepawa, the remaining $2,000. McLaughlin returned to Neepawa [from Portage La Prairie, where he was held] last evening' (3 December, 2).[16] At the Spring Assizes of the Court of King's Bench in Portage on 16 March, the Grand Jury heard the manslaughter case against McLaughlin. The following day, it returned with a 'no bill' decision: no trial but also no acquittal.

Why wasn't McLaughlin tried for manslaughter? First, the evidence gathered against him by Constable Rooke would not be admissible because he had not cautioned the witness before questioning him. Under the circumstances, Rooke's failure looked like incompetence, or a reluctance to make McLaughlin legally responsible, or both. Second, McLaughlin's counsel properly advised him not to testify, and legal practice could not require self-incrimination. Third, since they were alone in the house, Ethel McLaughlin was the only other possible witness, and a wife could not be compelled to testify against her husband. The case would have been a difficult one to develop.

But there may also have been more personal feelings among the Grand Jury members that influenced the outcome.[17] For example, the Grand Jury record shows the foreman as 'Ramey,' and the only male adult Manitoban by that name in the 1906 census was thirty-six-year-old James Ramey of Portage La Prairie District.[18] His twenty-three-year old wife Mary had given birth to their daughter Florence on 23 April that year. If this is the same individual, given the similarity in their circumstances – an older husband, a younger wife, and a very young daughter – Ramey may have had considerable sympathy with McLaughlin's situation.

That McLaughlin was the only one of the couple ever even mentioned by witnesses seemed particularly remarkable, given that one of the charivariers was Ethel's brother, Harold Burkell. For charivaris, the wife's identity would be crucial when marked by age, race/ethnicity, or marital status as in some way anomalous, though the practice was directed not at her but at her husband. All the legal records made McLaughlin the subject of the charivari, but I am surprised that there was no explanation of what precipitated the event, as there was for the Wetherill charivari in the last chapter, and as there will be for the Varner saluting in the next. Testimony about the plans spoke only in the most general terms: 'there might be a charivari,' 'there was going to be a charivari,' 'the charivari party.' But at the actual event, all witnesses say that McLaughlin alone was directly addressed, '"Mr McLaughlin there is a bunch of boys there to charivari him" ... if he would give us $10 we wouldn't charivari him,' and '"Billie, we have come to charivari."' Though the wedding occasioned the charivari, the bride herself does not appear. Contrary to her actual importance in engendering the event, she is apparently not germane to the legal case.

Given that the legal record and sequence of events made the most pivotal woman absent and silent, the only woman mentioned stands out. 'Mrs Wiggins told Joe Wiggins he wasn't to go.' The men in the testimony were remarkably ineffectual. All their actions were incomplete, thwarted, or futile. Willett D. Burkell couldn't stop his daughter marrying William McLaughlin; William McLaughlin couldn't make the charivariers go away by ignoring them or by shooting; the charivariers couldn't get McLaughlin to pay ten dollars or even five dollars; McLaughlin didn't intend to kill anyone; the doctors couldn't save Harry Bosnell; the post mortem examiners couldn't even initially find the bullet. Perhaps there was a success in Constable Rooke's getting the story from McLaughlin, but the Crown couldn't use the information, and the Grand Jury's decision was neither a vindication nor an indictment. Remarkably, Alma Ophelia Wiggins was the one individual in the entire testimony who did not seem to be a mere victim of circumstance, unable to assert a will over others, change the course of events, or have any effect on the outcome. Apparently by mere words she prevented her husband attending the charivari he had helped organize, perhaps thus saving his life. But we hear no more from her.

The Press: Innocent Young Victim
vs Man Defending His Home

Perhaps the true beginning of the charivari was the end of McLaughlin's first marriage. The Brookdale column of the *Neepawa Register* of 18 March 1909 reported, 'We are sorry to report the untimely death of Mrs Wm McLaughlin, of Belton, who passed from this life at 2:30 o'clock on Saturday, March 13. The funeral service will take place at home on Tuesday at 8 o'clock, when the body will be taken to Neepawa and thence by train to Ontario for burial at her old home. The deceased leaves an infant child and a sorrowing husband to mourn her loss. Most sincere sympathy is extended to Mr McLaughlin in his deep bereavement' (2).

This notice was sandwiched between the usual community column notes: an announcement for a 'big national concert on Wednesday,' a note that 'a goodly number of people from here went to Brandon to take in the winter fair,' the news that an Oddfellows lodge would be organized, a description of the return of a couple from their honeymoon and a reception for them at the groom's parents' house, word of the local physician's son's successful appendicitis operation in the Brandon hospital, and a report about a wedding at the local Methodist church (ibid.). As I have noted elsewhere, local newspapers' community columns generally announce various kinds of visitations by local people beyond the bounds of the community, as well as those by outsiders who travel to it. The late Mrs McLaughlin's return to Ontario could be so understood. Indeed, charivaris themselves constituted particular kinds of visits that addressed links between individuals, and between them and their communities (see Greenhill 1989a, 1989b).

If the notice of Ella McLaughlin's death was terse, the accounts of its aftermath in the charivari were correspondingly ample. Dated Neepawa, 10 November, a 'special despatch to the [Toronto] *Globe*' (Thursday, 11 November, 4) was headlined 'Charivari near Neepawa, Man., Has Serious Ending: The Usual Case of Crowd of Boys and Young Men Annoying Couple until Man Fires Rifle among Them – Harry Bosnell Badly Wounded.' It reported, 'There was a sad and almost tragic ending to a charivari at W. McLaughlin place, near Glendale, last night, when, enraged by the noisy crowd assembled, following his wedding, McLaughlin fired a rifle among them, and wounded Harry Bosnell, aged eighteen. The bullet passed through his stomach and liver, and although he is still alive and in the hospital here, his life is despaired of. McLaughlin was a widower and had been quietly married a few days ago, hence the celebration.'

The *Carberry News*[19] reported, 'Victim of Charivari Tragedy at Neepawa is in very Serious Condition,' and that 'A gay charivari almost ended in tragedy last night.' Referring to the charivari as a 'party,' the article comments that 'their fun was cut short by the untoward accident' (10 November, 1). The *Neepawa Register*, under the headline 'A Serious Shooting Affair,' reported, 'The Brookdale district was the scene of a tragedy on Tuesday evening about 11 o'clock which is likely to have fatal consequences, involving a serious charge against a resident. It appears that a crowd of about a dozen [*sic*, eight] young men decided to "charivari" Mr Wm McLaughlin who lives 2 miles north of Brookdale and who was married to Miss Ethel Burkell of Brookdale a few days ago. McLaughlin's first wife died last April [*sic*, March]. The usual procedure was under way ... Needless to say there is much sympathy expressed for all concerned in such an unfortunate incident' (11 November, 2).

Also on 11 November, the *Carberry Express*, in 'Boy Shot at Charivari,' reported in an account riddled with factual errors that it had received word 'from the Gordon settlement north of Brookdale of a charivari party which ended disastrously to one of the party. It appears that William McLaughlin was married on Tuesday [*sic*, several days earlier] and the boys that night undertook to make a celebration in honor of the event. They proceeded to the home of Mr McLaughlin and began to make the night hideous with pans, horns, etc. The bride groom became desperate and opening a window fired a shot at random [*sic*, several shots in air]. Harry Bosnell ... received the full charge ... the shot coming out the back, showing that it had been fired at close range [*sic*, from an upstairs window]. Another of the lads received some of the shot [*sic*, rifle not shotgun] in the face [*sic*, no one else was injured]' (1).

The papers from Winnipeg seem to have noted the most personal information about those involved (as well as getting some of the facts wrong). The *Manitoba Free Press* reported, 'McLaughlin, who was the subject of the crowd's noisy demonstrations ... buried his first wife last February [*sic*, March] and a few days ago married the 18-year-old [*sic*, 19] daughter of a neighbour, much against the will of the girl's parents. It is said that the father of the girl instigated the charivari and there is as much censure of him as there is of McLaughlin, who is a man of good character (12 November, 1).

The *Weekly Free Press and Prairie Farmer* reported the identical information on 17 November (5), but the following week, under 'Corrects a Rumor,' announced, 'W.D. Burkell, father of Mrs McLaughlin ... writes to the Free Press to the effect that he had no part whatever in the instigation of the charivari nor was he among those who made up the party. He did not even know that any party had been organized until he was awakened by the noise. Mr Burkell states, however, that he had been opposed to the marriage of his daughter to Mr McLaughlin' (24 November, 5).

The *Neepawa Press*, under 'Charivari Tragedy,' judged that 'nonsense has ended in another tragedy and there is death and grief in South Glendale instead of the joy and felicitations that ordinarily follow a wedding.' It describes the wedding as 'a quiet affair, and when it became generally known in the neighbourhood a charivari was organized.' But the 'fun' of 'a crowd of men and boys ... was of short duration' quickly replaced by 'tragedy,' 'death and grief' (12 November, 4).

The most detailed report of the Coroner's Jury was in 'An Open Verdict,' in the *Neepawa Press*, which described the charivariers as 'marauders' (16 November, 1). The article also stated that McLaughlin and his wife 'were called but on the advice of counsel refused to answer any questions' (ibid.).

After the Coroner's Inquest, Portage La Prairie's *Manitoba Liberal* noted that the 'charivari tragedy ... has been the absorbing topic of discussion throughout the district since news of the event was spread abroad and public opinion is pretty well divided. Some condone while others condemn the shooting, while all regret the tragedy and disapprove the circumstances under which it occurred' (18 November, 2).

The *Neepawa Register* reported 'Death of Harry Bosnell': 'Seldom does just so distressing an occurrence take place as was the death of the youthful Harry Bosnell, which closely followed ... after the shocking and tragic events in which he received the death wound ... The sincere sorrow of the neighbourhood in which he had lived was evident from the numbers who attended the last rites. Townspeople were alike sympathetic .... The deceased was but 19 years of age, the son of H.R. Bosnell [*sic*, Henry I.] of Langford. His people came to Canada from England about 7 or 8 years ago' (18 November, 4).[20]

The *Carberry Express* account of the Coroner's Inquest added some potentially telling information. It reported Bill Ernest as saying 'he did not know' who went to the door with him, 'but thought it was either a Scotsman or an Irishman.' (Evidently, those charivaring together need not be close friends or relatives – mere acquaintance, or being around at the right time was apparently sufficient, as it was in the Wetherill event.) Also, 'on being asked who lived in the house, he said Hume used to, but he understood McLaughlin had gone to live there after getting married' (18 November, 4). From Willett D. Burkell's letter, we know that the McLaughlin house was within shouting distance of his, which suggests that McLaughlin relocated perhaps in part to ensure that his wife had family support nearby.[21]

The *Carberry News*, in reporting on the Coroner's Inquest, called the charivariers 'young fellows' (though at least half their number were twenty-six or older; only teenagers Harold Burkell and Harry Bosnell would have been considered young at the time)[22] and editorialized, 'The whole affair is distressingly sad, all the parties connected with it are highly respectable people, the verdict does not implicate any one, but it is not probable that the matter will be allowed to remain a mystery' (19 November, 8).

Winnipeg's *Weekly Free Press and Prairie Farmer*, in a report dated 25 November but published 1 December, noted, 'The charivari fatality has resulted in information being laid against Wm McLauglin, Jr, around whose home the affair was held' (4). The *Neepawa Press* reported that the arrest of McLaughlin by Detective Charles Rooke of the provincial police force was made at his home 'without any fuss or parleying. The prisoner talked frankly to the detective telling all the circumstances of the tragedy ... Inspection of the windows showed that the north one could be raised only about six inches so that there would be liability of firing too low, though the effort had been to shoot high enough to avoid doing harm.' The paper also reported that Rooke took McLaughlin to the Portage La Prairie jail (26 November, 1).

Reporting the arrest, the *Carberry News* again misrepresented the facts, stating that McLaughlin had been 'very frank in his statement before the magistrate,' though McLaughlin never testified in any of the judicial proceedings. The article, however, went on to editorialize, 'This tragedy should serve as a lesson not soon to be forgotten. There have been too many of these ridiculous demonstrations and several have been settled in the courts. The custom is out of step with modern civilization and should be discouraged' (2 December, 4).

No further press coverage relating to the incident appeared until mid-March of the following year. Portage's *Weekly Manitoba Liberal* reported 'No Bill in the Charivari Case,' 'The surprise of todays [*sic*] assizes occurred when the grand jury filed in shortly after 3 o'clock and reported "no bill" in the case of King vs McLaughlin ... [T]he general impression was that a true bill would be found. The grand jury ... had been considering the case all day, and when Foreman Ramey announced the finding a murmur could be heard all over the court room ... The case created much excitement, especially in and about Neepawa' (17 March 1910, 1). The summary wrongly asserted that 'this case came out of a quarrel at a charivari party' (ibid., 2).

On the next day, the *Neepawa Press* reported, 'That South Glendale charivari tragedy that caused such a commotion and many heart burnings a few months ago ended at the Portage La Prairie assizes on Wednesday, when the grand jury returned "no bill" against McLaughlin, who was indicted for manslaughter for having fired the shot that killed Harry Bosnell. The accused, his bondsmen, and witnesses in the case, who went down on Monday and Tuesday, came home on Thursday and resumed the even tenor of their ways. But the bereaved parents of the dead boy have no consolation. Harry Bosnell was the unoffending victim of an escapade organized and conducted by men who should have known better' (18 March, 1).

The *Neepawa Register* also editorialized,

There should be no objection to the act of setting McLaughlin free. There was never any evidence that he was guilty of any crime.[23] A crowd who as our local contemporary says 'should have known better' gathered at his home on the evening following his marriage and one of the gang added to the usual disgraceful conduct of such charivari occasions the extreme provocation of discharging a shot gun ... We have never heard that anyone even suspected [McLaughlin] of any intention of shooting any one of the crowd. Yet a bullet struck Harry Bosnell and he died from the effects.

But while we agree that McLaughlin should go absolutely free, we would like to have seen the case go before the assize court and a verdict of some kind brought in for the sake of the moral effect. As it is now, all the public know is that the grand jury did not entertain the plea of manslaughter. But if the case had gone to a petty jury and a verdict of 'justifiable homicide' or some such[24] brought in, the public would know that in this country a man's home is in a sense his castle and that citizens take long chances in the attempt to carry out a charivari program.

A sad feature of the present case is that the unfortunate victim was a boy just budding out into manhood, and who in all probability was in no way responsible for the planning of the escapade which resulted so disastrously for himself and his family. (24 March, 1)

The *Carberry News* directly echoed the first sentence from the *Neepawa Press* of 18 March, but added its own commentary: 'This exonerates Mr McLaughlin, but it remains an unfortunate incident in his life that will not soon be forgotten' (24 March, 7).

The newspaper rhetoric around the McLaughlin charivari showed some ambivalence. Descriptions like 'party,' 'fun,' 'gay,' 'celebration,' and even 'escapade' suggested harmlessness, whereas 'affair,' 'ridiculous demonstration,' 'custom out of step with modern civilization,' and 'make the night hideous' were more negative. Yet even the last looked relatively mild in contrast to the grandiloquence that flourished when William Wallace of Purves, Manitoba, shot and wounded charivariers near Snowflake a mere three years earlier, on 8 September 1906. Wallace, a forty-two-year-old widower, married Janet Clarke, a forty-four-year-old widow, instantiating two charivari-worthy characteristics: previous marriage, and marriage involving older people. The wounded charivariers didn't press charges. Yet the case was also widely reported. Page one news of the Toronto *Star* under the headline, 'Three Men Wounded at a Charivari: Noisy Young Fellows Fired Upon by Bridegroom – Thirty Grains in One Body' reported, 'Wm Wallace of Purvis was married on Saturday, and a number of young men paid him a visit last night, forming a charivari party. Mr Wallace, not liking the noise, fired shots from a shotgun, wounding three of the company. Charles Phippa was shot below the knee, and is under the doctor care [*sic*] now. Thirty grains of shot were extracted from his body. Percy Dixon was shot in the thigh and another young man received a few grains in the shoulder. They will all recover. The whole neighbourhood is indignant over the affair' (12 September).

Apparently the term *charivari* wasn't sufficiently familiar to its readers, so the following day the *Star* added, 'A Manitoba bridegroom shot three young men who took part in a charivari, although the charivari is in the nature of a compliment, being the marriage ode of the ancients plus the noise and minus the words' (13 September, 6). Local coverage well reflects the evaluation that community members were 'indignant.' For example, 'Tuesday morning the report reached here that a young man was shot and seriously injured while taking part in a charivari at Purves. If young men will persist in disgracing the age in which they live, by such obsolete and barbaric practices, they may, if disaster overtakes them, expect but little sympathy from peaceable law-abiding citizens. The charivari is as much a thing of the dark ages as the thumb screw and the rack or trial by ordeal.[25] At the same time it is impossible to justify the action of a man who will use a gun, regardless of the consequences, on such an occasion' (*Western Canadian*, 13 September).

Apparently the incident remained newsworthy three weeks later, in 'The Charivari: A Relic of Barbarism':

A Manitoba farmer, who has just taken to himself a wife, found his house surrounded by young men who amused themselves shouting and manufacturing other hideous noises on impromptu instruments. The tone if not the volume of their uproar was changed when the enraged young husband fired on the crowd with a shot gun and struck two of the young men. Fortunately for the young fellow the injuries are not of a serious nature, and he will not have to answer for what might have been the most serious consequence of the anger which blinded him to the recklessness of his conduct.

Though his method of ridding himself of his tormentors was unwise and to be severely censured, one cannot help feeling that not only the two who were hurt, but the rest of the crowd deserved some punishment for their disturbing intrusion on the peace of a home. The charivari is a senseless practice, vulgar and impudent, and without a single good quality to recommend it, and the sooner it dies out in a community the better. It is a worse than childish custom for its motive is the malicious one of deliberately annoying two people who are peaceably trying to mind their own business. The application of nice cold water through a hose would have a discouraging effect upon the disturbers, and do them no lasting injury ...

Mr Wallace was threatened with proceedings, first by the injured man and later by friends of his, who took part in the fracas, but they have been abandoned, the parties evidently realising the sorry figure they would cut in a court of justice. It is hoped that the incident will have the effect of discouraging any further demonstration of a similar nature in that district for all time to come. (*Western Canadian*, 4 October)

Probably because of the relatively benign outcome for the Wallace charivari, the papers showed less restraint in characterizing their disapproval of the custom than in the McLaughlin case. (Indeed, the rhetoric much more closely resembles that surrounding the Wetherill charivari's extreme disapproval, some twenty-five years earlier.) But the death of a young community member who had participated in the charivari may have caused reporters to limit their editorializing rather than by implication accusing Harry Bosnell of being the author of his own demise. Because the deceased was one of the charivariers, not the groom, and because most agreed that the result was accidental, the charivari was represented as a tragedy more than as a disgrace. Yet in the Manitoba cases, the news is about the male participants.

While the significant women weren't entirely absent from the newspaper reports, their identities were invariably given in terms of their relationships to men. A 1909 reader might not have been disturbed, as I was, by the absence from her community column death notice of the first Mrs McLaughlin's name, birth name, age, the place in Ontario where she would be buried, or indeed the child's name, its sex, and many other details.[26] But there was other information to be found about Ella Ennis McLaughlin's life and death. One death registration made by William McLaughlin gives her age as thirty-nine years, seven months, notes her birthplace as Cranbrook, Ontario, and gives the cause of death as 'childbirth.'[27] Another registration by her brother Frank Ennis of Eden gives her age as thirty-six years, eleven months, and fifteen days, and gives the cause of death as peritonitis.[28] This variance of ages is compounded in the 1906 census, which notes Ella as twenty-seven and William as twenty-eight; their marriage registration from 16 October 1901 makes Ella twenty-five and William twenty-seven. As already suggested, William McLaughlin may have wanted to minimize the age difference between himself and his second wife – his stated age upon his second marriage, just over eight years later, was also twenty-seven.[29]

Ella Ennis McLaughlin was a similarly unnamed and shadowy figure in some newspaper charivari accounts. Any that mentioned the bride also noted her predecessor. For example, 'young men decided to "charivari" Mr Wm McLaughlin ... who was married to Miss

Ethel Burkell ... McLaughlin's first wife died last April' (*Neepawa Register*, 11 November, 2), and 'William McLaughlin, whose first wife died last winter, took unto himself a second one last week, the bride being Ethel Burkell, daughter of Mr and Mrs Willett Burkell' (*Neepawa Press*, 12 November, 4).[30] Sometimes the mention was extremely oblique: 'McLaughlin, a widower, was married to a daughter of Willett Burkell' (*Carberry News*, 9 November, 1). The former Ethel Burkell was rarely named in the newspaper accounts; most often she was referred to either in terms of her relationship to McLaughlin or of her relationship to her father or both, such as 'W.D. Burkell, father of Mrs McLaughlin' (*Free Press*).

Ethel McLaughlin's unnamed presence was noted at the inquest: 'William McLaughlin and his wife were called but ... refused to answer any questions' (*Neepawa Press*, 16 November, 1), and 'Mr McLaughlin and his young wife were present, but on advice of counsel, did not give evidence' (*Neepawa Register*, 18 November, 1). At the inquest, however, Ethel McLaughlin's predecessor was rhetorically absent. Yet it was as if both women dropped off the face of the earth once the coroner's inquest was complete; they were apparently then insignificant to any discussion. Two principal characters remained – Harry Bosnell, the shooting victim, and William McLaughlin, who was soon clearly understood to have fired the shot.

Between the two there was something of a discursive struggle; reporters and commentators were unwilling to completely exonerate anyone. Referring to murder, historian Angus McLaren asks 'just how far legitimate force could be pushed' (1984, 159), linking the question to ideas about masculinity. This manslaughter case – as well as other contemporary discussion of charivari – offers some useful insights on the question. Masculine obligation included the defence of one's own property, and while contemporary discourse might not consider wives literally part of a man's chattels, their legal and personal identities were still almost entirely subsumed under their husbands' (or, if they were unmarried, their fathers').[31] Perhaps because the result was a death, only the *Neepawa Register* says in condemnation of the McLaughlin charivari, quite mildly for the time, that 'in this country a man's home is in a sense his castle and that citizens take long chances in the attempt to carry out a charivari program.' McLaughlin's actions were understood in terms of his need to defend his home; Harry Bosnell was excused as being young, and it was presumed (perhaps wrongly) that he was not one of the perpetrators of the charivari, but simply went along.

The Oral Tradition: McLaughlin's Best Friend
vs Rivals for Ethel's Affections?

In contrast to the legal testimony and newspaper accounts, the women clearly figure in most oral traditions.[32] For example, I first learned from McLaughlin relatives that the 'infant' survived, and that her name was Gladys.[33] She is listed in William McLaughlin's obituary (he died 2 November 1956), as 'Mrs Stan (Gladys) Foulton of Flin Flon' (*Neepawa Press*, 15 November 1956). No children were recorded. One of her Neepawa cousins recalls Gladys moving out of the province some time in the 1960s, to British Columbia.[34] She lost contact with her during the 1980s. William and Ethel McLaughlin had no other children. Given that it was not at all unusual for families at the time in the area to have half a dozen offspring or more, the fact that Ella's pregnancy was so late (after eight years of marriage) and that Ethel had no children whatsoever is worth noting. Neither Ethel nor William came from a small family. At the 1906 census, the Burkell family had eight children: Ethel, sixteen; John, fifteen; Harold, eleven; Frank, ten; George, eight; Ellen, six; William, three; and Robert, two. William McLaughlin Sr's wife died in 1880 giving birth to daughter Margaret (Watson 1990, 421; Martin 1983, 634), but William Jr had four brothers and one other sister.

The oral tradition speaks extensively to community dealings, the links between charivariers and charivaried, and the devastating effects of the tragedy. It weaves a complex story about gender relations rather than addressing the local morality and justice that are the subject of journalistic and legal discourse. Indeed, it is not entirely clear that the stories (other than that of an eyewitness) recognize this charivari as a mark of community censure. Oral history may presume that the McLaughlin charivari instead took the custom's more recent form – that of a celebration of an appropriate marriage, not condemnation of a problematic one.

My first indication of an oral tradition concerning this event came during an interview on charivari traditions in Brookdale in 2004. The discussion turned to 'stories about shootings' related to charivaris. Indeed, the tradition is quite extensive. In early summer 2005, I began cold calling McLaughlins in Neepawa, hoping I could locate some relatives. As I was describing to one elderly woman my interest in locating kin of Ethel and William McLaughlin because I was studying charivaris, she asked, 'Wasn't there a shooting?' She didn't know a lot more, only that there had been a charivari, a shooting, and a man killed. Her late husband was a McLaughlin and she thought that William was his uncle.

But before I had time to follow up on this lead, I received an email communication in response to a general query about shivarees sent to newspapers across Canada, from Bill Dunn, now living on 'Mosquito Creek Ranch in the foothills of southern Alberta':

I have a shivaree story to share with you and it's a very sad one. It was related to me by my father many years ago but is still fresh in my memory.

For some background on the event, my father was born in Neepawa, Manitoba, in 1901. He lived on the family farm till 1920 when the family moved to the Springfield district east of Winnipeg. That would date his story to be from a period before they came to the new farm.

He told how a young couple had just got married. One night shortly after the wedding, the groom's friends decided it was time to get the newlyweds off to a good start. Late one night they all gathered at the farm and after the house became dark and quiet it was time to liven things up. They proceeded to march around the house making as much noise as possible beating on tin and shouting at the top of their lungs. Suddenly, a shot rang out from the house and the bullet struck one of the noisemakers. He was killed immediately.

The tragic shooting was even worse when the groom found out the man he had shot in the very dark night was one of his best friends! It was an unfortunate accident and must have made a lasting impression on the community. I don't believe there were any charges laid against the young shooter.

My dad told this story to us as kids more than once. He never gave any names or date of when this happened but it must have been news in the community. It would weigh heavily on the area for quite some time.

I hope you find this account interesting as all pranks don't have a happy ending! (29 July 2005)

It's not surprising that some of the details don't fully match. The couple were not both young; not all those attending were the groom's friends; McLaughlin was charged; Bosnell was not killed immediately. Yet a great deal of the information fits: the noise 'beating on tin,' the charivariers circling the house, the bullet striking the victim, the timing, the very dark night, the accidental nature of the killing, and its effect on the community. Considering that one contemporary newspaper got the number of victims and even the type of weapon wrong, this account is remarkably accurate.

Bill Dunn's father, Perry Powell Dunn, would have been nearly nine years old when the charivari happened, and its impression is clear from his story. Charivariers and charivaried are usually near associates in communities where the tradition is practised (see Greenhill 1989b). Today's charivarier is tomorrow's charivaried, or vice versa. Particularly in its current forms, participants tend to be of the same age group and are usually those who socialize together. Even at approval charivaris, accidents – and deliberate actions – can indeed sunder relationships between close friends, sometimes permanently. And at times what is later described as accidental may in fact have been a deliberate attempt at revenge, or at least at levelling the charivari score. On occasion the repercussions are against grievances between individuals, but very often they are specifically against actions at a previous charivari.[35] Extreme trickery, like removing the mattress from the bed and leaving it out in the rain all night, or letting livestock run through the house, creating disgusting messes and permanent damage to household goods, will be revenged if the perpetrator's identity becomes known.

Bill Dunn commented that his father 'seemed to feel strongly that the one shot and killed was the shooter's best friend' (29 July 2005). It's relatively unlikely, however, that eighteen-year-old Harry Bosnell, who arrived in the area with his family from England in 1903, would have been the best friend of a man twice his age whose family had been homesteading in the area since 1879. But other stories about the charivari suggest an alternative for the best friend's identity. Local archivist and historian Don Murray told me that his uncle had heard about the charivari from Bob Whelpton, and had been shown a hole in Whelpton's coat where a bullet from McLaughlin's rifle had passed through. (An undated note I received from him when I visited 7 September 2005 says, 'Bob Whelpton had a bullet go in the cuff of his coat and out at the elbow.') Eleanor Swanson also heard from 'somebody from Brookdale' (interview, PG2005, 13)[36] that a Whelpton had been shot. If Bob Whelpton was a close friend of McLaughlin's, he might not have volunteered the information that he, too, had been shot at during the charivari, since it might make the shooting of Harry Bosnell appear less inadvertent.

But there was another excellent candidate for McLaughlin's best friend – or, perhaps, his former best friend – among the charivariers. At least one person with whom I spoke thought that McLaughlin had been shooting at, and had injured but not killed, Charles Bugg. Bugg and McLaughlin could have been close. They were nearly the same age, and Bugg was an in-law to McLaughlin – in 1900, Bugg's younger sister Sarah married McLaughlin's elder brother George (Martin 1983, 634; Watson 1990, 422). In 1901 at census time, twenty-five-year-old Charles Bugg was still living with his parents, as was William McLaughlin.

What the 'best friend' story about the McLaughlin charivari tells is not only the social proximity of McLaughlin to his tormenters and the extreme emotions involved, but also the profound sense of regret. What it does not accomplish, that the women's stories about the event do, is make the women involved part of the motivation. The involvement of Charles Bugg not only offers a personal motivation for the charivari, consistent in spirit with Bill Dunn's account, but also makes Ethel McLaughlin central to the event. Elizabeth (Chisholm) Ames, who lived across the road from the McLaughlins and was ten at the time of the charivari, explained that Bugg had been courting Ethel Burkell before William McLaughlin married her: 'He was going with Mrs McLaughlin before she was married to him. So he was angry, you see' (Liz Ames, interview PG2005, 19). As local Brookdale historian Eleanor Swanson, who had the story from her late husband who was eight at the time, put it, 'It was a grudge match. He knew there'd be a shivaree, so he was ready for them, he had the shotgun upstairs. And the fellow that got shot got hung up on the fence getting away … That man was married the second time' (PG2005, 13).

Charles Bugg also figures in a story told to local historian Cecil Pittman from around Brookdale: Bugg himself did the shooting, although William McLaughlin was charged (personal communication, 5 November 2005). Again, there may be symbolic if not literal truth in this account. If Charles Bugg organized the charivari, he was ultimately responsible for what happened (as was the case with the Wetherill charivari, where the four men charged with murder were considered not culpable in part because they were not its originators).

Elizabeth Ames's daughter Donna Walker reported her 106-year-old mother's accounts of the charivari for me,[37] originally at the request of local archivist and historian Don Murray:

> In 1909 at what is now the Hart farm north of Brookdale, a shooting took place with a Bosnell boy 16–17 years being killed. Bill McLaughlin married … Ethel Burkell. The story goes that she had been going with the local vet, Dr Bugg.[38] When the Marcus

Chisholm family who lived across the road[39] heard that Dr Bugg
was organizing a chivaree, the boys in the family were told to stay
away as they feared there might be trouble. When the people were
gathering in the yard, Bill McLaughlin started shooting from an
upstairs window.[40] This is when the Bosnell boy was shot. He was
taken by horse and buggy to Neepawa. My mother remembers
hearing the horse and buggy going very fast and they were whip-
ping the horses to go faster, so they knew something terrible had
happened. (personal communication via Donna Walker, 31 August
2005)

A later communication from Liz Ames via Donna Walker added the
detail that 'she remembers a Burkell coming to their place at supper
time and inviting the boys,[41] but a friend that lived with them telling
the boys to stay away from there as he felt there might be trouble, and
so no-one went' (personal communication via Donna Walker, 21 September 2005). Later, Donna Walker identified the friend as Jim Litt.
'Bill McLaughlin was arrested, but his father paid a lot of money to
keep him out of jail and to keep the records hidden. The story goes
that he nearly lost the farm. Bill McLaughlin was not seen around
much after that' (account from 31 August 2005).

Liz Ames had an astonishing and accurate recall, even of details
concerning the event. She was correct, for example, about the then
staggering amount of money paid by William McLaughlin Sr for his
son's bail, and recalled Samuel Holmes, who put up the other half the
bail money, as a Neepawa resident. The charivari must have been the
subject of a great deal of talk among children, as Perry Powell Dunn's
and Liz Ames's accounts indicate. The discussions would have been
memorable in part because they would have been somewhat illicit. As
Donna Walker said, children at the time would not have been told
very much about such events by their parents. Eleanor Swanson commented, 'It was kind of hushed up, and at that time we kids didn't ask
very many questions. We were told to mind, not to bother [*laughs*]'
(PG2005, 13). Liz Ames knew, however, that William McLaughlin
had been married twice and that his 'first wife died when first child
born' (personal communication via Donna Walker, 21 September
2005).

These women's accounts make the two McLaughlin wives, Ella
Ennis and Ethel Burkell, pivotal to the event. In considering Burkell,
particularly, these stories and recollections lead to questions as to
why she married William McLaughlin, who was much older and had
an infant child. Yet clearly Ethel and Gladys were close in later life.

Community memory does not suggest the same was true for William and Ethel. Liz Ames remembers the infant Gladys being sent to McLaughlin relatives in Riding Mountain to be cared for after her mother's death, returning only just before the wedding: 'She was adopted, just looked after for awhile, and then he just got her back when this all happened. She was looked after by a relative up at Riding Mountain' (PG2005, 19).

What was her motivation for marrying a much older man, especially one with a young child? Perhaps having caring responsibilities for only one child could have been something of a respite for Ethel Burkell. As the eldest daughter of the household, she would be expected to help her mother care for her siblings. At the time of her marriage, four of her siblings would have been pre-teens: two boys, eleven and six; and two girls, nine and one.[42]

Community and Marriage

Even with three different discourses – legal, journalistic, and oral traditional – some questions remain. What purposes could the charivari have served for its participants? Why would a wedding be the community's business? The practice clearly speaks to extensive scrutiny and judgment of community members' lives in socially close if geographically far-flung communities like those around rural Manitoba at the turn of the twentieth century and later.

Indeed, it was not only young rowdies who took licence to charivari, but men as old as forty-one-year-old Joe Wiggins and thirty-three-year-old Charles Bugg. Though the married Wiggins had intended to go but did not, all those identifiable men who actually charivaried McLaughlin were bachelors. We don't know O'Hayes's age and marital status, but by the 1911 census, apparently only Peter Griffith can be clearly identified as married. Among those arguably old enough to wed, both Joe Bosnell and Charles Bugg were still living with their parents. Bob Whelpton was apparently living elsewhere, but William Ernest may have been working as a hired hand in Dauphin Township. Marriage, as Cecilia Danysk argued, was fundamental to the economic and social base of early-twentieth-century Manitoba communities – the family farm – and had sweeping cultural implications (1995, 70). The proportion of men to women was skewed; women were in a minority, and thus there was no social stigma on bachelorhood, but marriage was a matter of considerable and broad community attention, as it is today.[43]

Some might suggest that the payment in cases like McLaughlin's would be in recompense for his taking a young woman out of the system of exchange involving young men. Women were a scarce commodity. Taking a second wife, especially so soon after the death of his first, showed insufficient attention to the concerns and needs of others. But that doesn't explain the Snowflake/Purves charivari, involving a widow and widower. As suggested in chapter 1, at issue is fertility. Even the current charivari could be argued as an encouragement to appropriate fertility; some folks in Ontario told me that a couple could be charivaried any number of times until their first child was manifestly on the way.

In this world, then, McLaughlin could be charivaried not only for taking a young woman out of the pool of eligibles, but also because the couple's fertility could be in question, given McLaughlin's previous marriage, and because any further offspring could cause succession problems. The reason charivari died out first in more heavily settled areas has less to do with the ostensible reason usually given – that the noise and drunkenness disturbed the public peace (though indeed, several ordinances were passed in towns and cities explicitly outlawing the practice)[44] – than it did with the lower level of scrutiny of community continuation through family fertility. As larger, more urbanized communities became less closely knit, the ties among all individual members attenuated, with less responsibility placed on any particular group of individuals to maintain the status quo; charivari was no longer rhetorically useful. Charivari survives in rural areas in large part because it not only addresses community notions of appropriate behaviour (unquestioning hospitality, willingness to deal with the unexpected with aplomb, being a good sport, and taking a joke); it also addresses very real needs. By its 'welcome' – the term participants used most to describe the charivari's purpose – it reminds young marrieds that their responsibility is to stay on the farm, continue to do the work their foremothers and forefathers did, and keep the community going by having children. It confirms their community membership and the responsibilities that go along with it (see Greenhill 1989b).

A final mystery, though, is the survival of the tradition of charivari in the Brookdale area in the face of such a tragedy. Surely, as the newspapers suggested, the death of a community member, especially a young one, might end the practice. And yet charivari continued there, at least to the early 1970s, though its form and intention altered considerably (as it has done across most of English Canada) from a statement of disapproval to one of commendation. The main point of the charivari became to party with and play tricks on the newlyweds, rather than to extract money from them. But crucially, as Kathleen Swanson said, 'I think it was a mark of affection in some ways, because you didn't do it to people you were uneasy with, and whose reactions you couldn't predict fairly well. I think that's also the reason why there was never any real damage beyond labels off the cans and that sort of thing.' As Charlie Simpson explained, 'We had to go back and work together, maybe the next day.'[45]

The McLaughlin charivari and its aftermath show that traditions are remarkably resilient. Yet traditions also change; it's more valuable in contemporary rural Canada to mark marriages – at least heterosexual ones – than to convey disapproval of specific matches. The tradition itself has a new purpose, that of marking the recipients' change in personal status upon marriage. Yet it resists social change on a larger scale by implying disapproval of those who leave the farm or lead a lifestyle the community does not support. While very few Manitobans currently practise charivari, strong memories remain of events in which neighbours, friends, and families 'made the night hideous.'

The previous two chapters have dealt with charivaris that came into the legal system as an epiphenomenon of related action. The ostensible purpose of these actions was to get money from newlyweds so that the charivariers could treat themselves to alcohol. However, in the following example, the purposes of the charivari and the law case intersect. The next charivari I discuss was intended to bring shame, and the law case brought by one of the victims was an attempt to remedy the situation by protesting her own innocence and that of the man with whom she was suspected of adultery.

4

'What You Do in Daylight in Eyes of Public Is No Harm': Person, Place, and Defamation in Nova Scotia, 1917

In the previous two examples, newspaper reporting of the event was extensive. In this Nova Scotia charivari case, it was minimal. As in the Manitoba instance particularly, surviving legal records offer great detail about exactly what happened between community members, but here, as I will discuss in detail, they also crucially offer a perspective on the formal regulation of gendered behaviour. The legal records are the primary source for these charivari data, since there seems to be no community memory of it.

On 23 October 1917, Irene Varner drove from Springfield, Annapolis County, Nova Scotia, to the nearby community of New Germany, Lunenburg County, with her friend and neighbour, Lambert McNayr, to visit her father-in-law. (See figures 4.1 and 4.2.) On their return at about 9:15 in the evening, they were met by six neighbours, firing guns, ringing bells, and shouting. All Springfield would have recognized the event as a 'saluting,' the local term for charivari. The intent and meaning of saluting Varner and McNayr would also have been clear to all. They were being judged and denounced as illicit lovers.

This community assessment would be more problematic for her than for him. As Constance Backhouse asserts, 'Double standards, in law and in social attitudes, viewed the adultery of women as more serious than that of men' (1991, 332). Cross-culturally, women hold the honour and bear the shame of society, in both formal legal systems and community customs.[1] 'A fundamental tenet of feminist political critique throughout the twentieth century has been that the law regulated the sexual activity of men and women in profoundly

4.1 Springfield church with McNayr grave marker (Photo: Pauline Greenhill)

4.2   Grave marker, Lambert McNayr (Photo: Pauline Greenhill)

different ways, with heterosexual women subject to stricter policing and harsher stigmatization for sexual activity outside of marriage' (Sangster 2001, 85). The Canadian Patriotic Fund, from which Varner received an allowance, frequently maintained close surveillance and regulation of its recipients (discussed by Morton 2004, especially 65, 99–103). Even an unsubstantiated suspicion that she was having an affair could have had implications for more than her reputation; it could have affected her livelihood. Thus women facing charges – formal or informal – that they had violated sexual mores sometimes found the courage to resist. So Irene Varner took what was then an extremely unusual step; she charged the six who saluted her with defamation, conspiracy, and personal injury.[2]

This legal case is singular. It is the only one I have located in North America that was actually brought to address the traditional aim of the practice: to express disapproval of community members' actions. Though as already indicated, charivaris sometimes led to law cases, in this example its actual aim – publicity and denunciation of a perceived wrong – was at issue in the formal legal system, as it was in the community. This is not to suggest that the charivari and the legal system had parallel concerns, or worked to control the same alleged wrongs. Indeed, quite the opposite is the case. Charivari's intent is defamatory. It declaims and publicizes a purported wrong, whether an inappropriate marriage or, as in this case, an extramarital sexual relationship. Defamation is against the law. Usually – although apparently not in this case – charivari also claims damages in reparation in the form of money or a treat. But the use of similar methods of amends for a wrong shouldn't suggest that the charivari and the law complement each other. The subject of this saluting went to the law for a remedy, and thus this example shows how the two may directly conflict. The case is also unusual for its time, though by no means unique, in that a young woman won at both trial and appeal against six upstanding men of her community. *Varner v. Morton et al.*, however, is especially compelling for the light it sheds upon the relationship (and sometimes, lack of relationship) between folk/community law and formal law.

As well, the facts surrounding the case show how community and legal discourse alike became inflected with the gendered dynamics of wartime, and with the sociocultural construction of space. The implicated performances of gender involve manipulation of the sociocultural environment, including time and space, as well as of bodies and their accoutrements. The *Varner* case shows how multiple audiences – including multiple community audiences and multiple legal audiences – interpret gendered performances, with resulting understandings that can be congruent and harmonious or divergent and discordant. The discourses that result are constructed by, but also themselves construct, perceived realities. In this particular example, the sexing and gendering of space (Bell and Valentine 1995; McDowell 1999) suggests actions, modes, and locations that mark the gendered performances of participants. Throughout, symbolic capital, especially in terms of prestige and honour (Bourdieu 1991), is risked, won, and lost in the case both in the community and in the formal legal system. The crucial importance of symbolic capital is evident in the fact that Irene Varner pressed her case in the first place, and that Morton et al. appealed when they lost at trial. Such individuals would not frivolously engage the legal system to that extent.

Charivari retains commonalities relevant to understanding this case in Europe and North America, and throughout its history, beginning in medieval times, as explicit attempts to control behaviour. Peter Burke says that in France 'the ritual of charivari seems to have served the function of social control, in the sense that it was the means for a community ... to express its hostility to individuals who stepped out of line and so to discourage other breaches of custom' (1978, 200). Natalie Zemon Davis explains that early modern French charivaris, which she describes as 'noisy, masked demonstration[s] to humiliate some wrongdoer in the community' (1975, 97), had specific objects: 'Widows or widowers remarrying were vulnerable, as were husbands deceived by their wives and husbands who beat their wives during the month of May (a special month for women)' (ibid., 100). Carnival forms like charivari, she concludes, 'can act both to reinforce order and to suggest alternatives to the existing order' (ibid., 123).

E.P. Thompson explains the charivari's motivation in eighteenth-century Britain: 'Publicity was of the essence of punishment. It was intended, for lesser offences, to humiliate the offender before her or his neighbours, and in more serious offences to serve as example' (1993, 480). Thompson directly addresses its controlled violence: 'A rough music was a licensed way of releasing hostilities which might otherwise have burst beyond any bounds of control ... The argument that rough music rituals were a form of *displacement* of violence – its acting out, not upon the person of the victim, but in symbolic form – has some truth ... Rough music did not only give expression to a conflict within a community, it also regulated that conflict within forms which established limits and imposed restraints' (ibid., 486).

But social theorists have long been divided on the function, meaning, and significance of these events. Does such gossip and scandal-mongering maintain social cohesion and order by reinforcing communal norms? Or does it create more conflict by publicizing the presence – often, the florescence – of profound differences in the moral order (see, e.g., Merry 1984)? And what about those occasions when general public opinion is misguided, none of anybody's business, or simply wrong? How can someone who has been victimized by a charivari respond and clear her name? The answer, as this case shows, is that changing the community's evaluation can be done only with great difficulty, if at all. Recourse to the formal legal system – as in this case – may be one tactic to attempt to influence local perceptions.[3]

One of the Springfield charivariers commented, 'If a person is married we usually give them a little salute.'[4] Actually, saluting, like some other forms of charivari, was probably at that time reserved for marriages the community saw as in some way different, or potentially problematic. Like other charivari traditions, where salutings continued in Annapolis and Kings counties later into the twentieth century, they also became a celebration of approved matches rather than their original denunciation.

This case shows that neither the community's assessment nor the legal opinions on the matter at hand were univocal. To an extent they spoke to one another, but at times they diverged on the relevant issues. At the community level, concerns about honour and shame were paramount in determining whose actions – those of the saluted or those of the saluters – were blameworthy. During the jury trial, the community issues met in a public forum that required an absolute and polarized judgment for the plaintiff or for the defendants. At the appeal court level, the legal system's view centred on whether or not the practice of charivari could be a cause of action, and if so what kind of tort (or wrong) it formed. Yet community, trial, and appeal alike showed multivocality and competing visions within their own discourses. These centre upon the actions of a group of key players in the social drama that unfolded.

Springfield 1917

Springfield is located on the southern slope of the South Mountain, in the Annapolis Valley of Nova Scotia, just north of the Lunenburg County line, and with Lake Pleasant, the West River, the LaHave Lakes, Waterloo Lake, Joe Simon Lake and River, Lake Spry, and

Mill Brook forming its boundaries. In 1941, there were 500 residents, engaged in lumbering, farming, dairying, and fruit-growing. Only a small part of the area is under cultivation; most of the village is surrounded by deep woods. 'The numerous lakes and streams in the vicinity of the Dalhousie settlements north of Springfield have furnished water power for saw mills and grist mills, while lumbermen have "driven" logs down stream on many of them' (Kendrick 1941, 5). It was originally settled in 1819 by John Grinton and Boyd McNayr (ibid., 7).

Lumbering was the mainstay of the area. Springfield provided both residence and services for many of those who worked in the region's sawmills and lumber camps. In 1905, the Davison Lumber Company established a large mill as well as the town of Hastings, 'named for the president of the company' (ibid., 87). It remained extremely active until 1920, when it went out of business. Springfield, then, in 1917, would have been an agricultural service centre, but also in part an industrial one. According to local historian and genealogist Lloyd Varner,

> The 1911 census figures for the Springfield District includes 813 names, but this covered a broad area far beyond the community of Springfield. Davison Lumber established Hastings with 30 houses before 1910 and the community continued to grow until it went bankrupt in 1920. At the time of the fire which destroyed most of Hastings in 1928 there were still 55 houses ... In 1917/1918 there may have been around 75 houses in Hastings, and at an average of four persons per house (small for those days), its population may have been around 300. I do not think that Springfield would have been larger, as most of the work force at the mill itself lived in Hastings. A reasonable guess would put the population of Springfield itself in the range of 250 to 350, though with the lumbering operations in the surrounding countryside it would have difficult to define just where Springfield ended and the surrounding settlements began. As the railway centre for the area, Springfield would have served as the hub for communities with a total population of around 1,000 people.
>
> There is not much left in Springfield any more. They still had an elementary school a few years ago, but in spite of the fact that it was remote from any other part of that school district it was threatened with closure. The railway line, post office and stores have all gone, and surrounding settlements use the communities of New Germany, Bridgewater and Middleton as their commercial centres. (Personal communication, 15 May 2007)

Statistics Canada gives the total population of Annapolis Subdivision D, in which Springfield is located, at just under 3,000 in 2001. In 1956 the Springfield population was 70 (Pictou-Antigonish Regional Library n.d.); New Germany in 1967 was 800 (Coastal Communities Network 2005–6). With surrounding areas, Springfield currently has fewer than 200 residents (Rosemary Rafuse, personal communication, 16 May 2007; Lloyd Varner, personal communication, 15 May 2007). The Springfield school closed in 2004. (See figure 4.3.)

Dramatis Personae

Irene Louise Hayden was born 24 August 1896. At the time of the saluting, then, she was twenty-one. She first married at sixteen. Her husband lived for fifteen months afterwards and then died of tuberculosis; they had one son. The widowed Irene Davis moved to Springfield in March 1915, to live with her mother, Edith (Wade) Hayden, who had herself been widowed in 1914. The Haydens were not longtime Springfield residents. In 1901 at census time they were living in Granville Ferry, but at some time before Irene's father George Hayden died in 1914, they moved to nearby Hastings, where he had been a millwright.[5] On 19 January 1916 Irene married Albert (also known as Mike) Varner of New Germany, who enlisted 28 January 1916, nine days after the wedding. While he was away, their first child (Milton) was born, 15 November 1916; Mike's enlistment record notes him as childless. Clearly, Irene Varner had experienced considerable adversity in her life. But her ability to bring the court case suggests she had not only considerable personal strength and family support, but also financial resources.[6]

Lambert McNayr was born 2 November 1864. At the time of the saluting, he was days away from his fifty-third birthday. As the Scott Act constable, McNayr enforced the Canada Temperance Act, introduced between 1915 and 1917 in all Canadian provinces. Temperance seems to have been popular in Springfield. The first known fraternal organization there was a division of the Sons of Temperance (1860); a second was formed in 1887, though it closed in 1899 (Kendrick 1941, 90–1). McNayr was also a blacksmith and farmer. He and his still-living wife, Idella Durling, had eight children. The McNayrs were one of two founding families of Springfield (Calnek 1980, 279).

There were six defendants. Isaac B. (known as Burpee) Saunders, sixty-two,[7] a farmer, lived near Irene Varner, and was a cousin of

4.3   Springfield, Annapolis County, Nova Scotia, from school looking south (Photo: Pauline Greenhill)

Lambert McNayr. William Conrad, forty-three, was son-in-law of I.B. Saunders. Wiley Grimm, thirty-three, was also a Springfield resident, and related to J.C. Grimm, the local councillor. Elwood Mailman (another son-in-law of I.B. Saunders) and Albert Morton also belonged to extended, known, and respected local families. Avard Roop, fifty-four, was an agent and relative of LeRoy Roop, the owner of the local general store, where the six gathered to wait for Varner and McNayr to return from New Germany. These were venerable men, not a bunch of rowdy young boys. Their opinions and views (including the judgment that Irene Varner's virtue was in doubt) would have been taken seriously by the community.

Edith (Hayden) Irvin[8] was Irene's mother. She had eight children, three of whom fought in the First World War. At the beginning of Edith's testimony as a witness for the plaintiff, 'I am wife of John Irvine, K.C.' is crossed out. Born 6 April 1880, she was in her mid-thirties when her first husband, George Hayden, died. Her second husband, John Irvin, was present for the trial – at one point he asked the judge to strike evidence, despite the fact that he was not listed as acting for his stepdaughter. The marriage between Edith Hayden and John Irvin was sufficiently recent that most of the trial witnesses called her Mrs Hayden, and referred to her home as 'Hayden's.'

John Irvin was Irene's stepfather. It is possible that he was visiting the Hayden household when the saluting happened, as a local community column reported on 23 October 1917 (the day of the event), 'Lawyer Irving [*sic*] of Bridgetown has been the guest of Mrs Edith Hayden for the past week.' His comings and goings in Springfield made the paper more than once. On 11 December 1917, 'Lawyer Irving was in town last week.'[9] Irvin and Hayden married five days later, in Springfield. Irene Varner and Lambert McNayr were the witnesses. Irvin's influence must have been pivotal in allowing Irene Varner to pursue the case. An anonymous interviewee commented, 'The fact that she actually took this to the Supreme Court of Nova Scotia had to have had something to do with John Irvin, because that's the way it runs ... here; the politics in Nova Scotia still runs that way. If you've got a connection to a particular political party or to someone like [Irvin], that would be the only way it would go anywhere ... For her to even think about taking that to court she had somebody behind her who felt she could get somewhere, or they had connections. Because an ordinary woman from Springfield would have no chance of taking that to court.'

Finally, Mrs Abbie Conn was crucial because she testified for the defendants that she heard Lambert McNayr describe Irene Varner as his wife. This incident apparently provoked the saluting. Conn lived at Cherryfield, seven miles from Springfield. Born 1 May 1858, this German Lutheran farmer was fifty-nine at the time of the saluting. In the 1901 census, Conn was listed as the head of her household and had four children between fourteen and twenty-one living with her. By 1911, her widowed daughter Bessie Demon(e) was living with her, along with Bessie's three children, all noted as 'adopted.' Bessie's husband Ephraim met a tragic and premature death. According to the *Bridgewater Bulletin*, November 1909, 'A man named Ephriam Demone was accidently killed last evening between cars on a train of the Davison Lumber Company, on the further end of the company's line. He belonged to Cherryfield.' Rosemary Rafuse, who provided the latter information, comments, 'I guess, with a widowed daughter and three grandchildren to raise, Abbie had to bootleg for a living. They had to eat and jobs were not too available in the backwoods of Nova Scotia' (personal communication, 28 April 2008). In any case, Abbie Conn sold liquor, paid a fine, and went to jail for it. She must have been arrested by Lambert McNayr, as was her daughter, whom he also arrested on similar charges. Another interviewee concurs with Rafuse that the Conns may have had few alternatives for feeding the family: 'There weren't a lot of options for widowed women. Unless you were selling yourself, you were selling liquor. I had a great-great-grandmother who found herself in that position at the turn of the [twentieth] century. She still had a houseful of kids at home – five or six ... She actually was charged with bootlegging; I don't think she was ever convicted but she was charged.'

Claims and Counterclaims

The main route to understanding both community and legal issues in this case is via the materials for the jury trial. The documentation, including the witness testimony, suggests a great deal about the individuals' motivations, actions, and ideas – and the range of variation they incorporated. As Natalie Zemon Davis has argued, 'Charivari is a hazardous instrument of social control. When neighbours or villagers disagreed strongly about the conduct of domestic life, or about the rights of folk justice, then the clamorous crowd could shatter the community and leave even violence and death in its wake. Envy or fury could push the social ritual of mockery beyond its usual bounds' (1984, 42). *Varner* shows, as do other charivari cases, 'how seriously the matter of honor and reputation was taken ... and how committed people could be ... to local folk justice as a source of control, or amusement, and of solidarity' (ibid., 43).

The six defendants in the case brought by Irene Varner were also convicted late in 1917 of a Criminal Code, Vagrancy Act violation. Recognizance for Morton reads, 'By discharging firearms and by riotous and disorderly conduct, shouting and making loud noises and swearing in a street or highway leading through Springfield [they] did unlawfully and wrongfully disturb the peace and quiet of the inmates of the dwelling house of Edith M. Hayden of Springfield ... situate near the said street or highway.' Their appeal, filed in December 1917, was apparently unsuccessful. The *Annapolis Royal Spectator* (Thursday, 14 May 1918) announced, 'The County Court Judge Grierson presiding, was in session here on Tuesday when the appeal of the King vs Morton was conducted and judgement reserved.'[10] No further comment appeared.

On 4 July 1918, the six received a summons from Irene Varner for 'damages to the Plaintiffs [*sic*] person and reputation by the Defendant's unlawfully conspiring together on or about the 23rd day of October 1917 and making a demonstration by the firing of guns and

ringing of bells.' A simultaneous personal injury claim failed and will
not be detailed here. Varner's Statement of Claim[11] asserted, among
others, that

4. The Defendants who had previously assembled together at or
   near the residence of I.B. Saunders one of the defendants situate on the aforesaid street or highway next to and within a few
   rods of the Plaintiffs [sic] residence suddenly made their
   appearance and unlawfully began and continued for some time
   a disorderly and riotuous [sic] demonstration by shouting
   making loud noises ringing of bells and discharging and firing
   of guns and rifles loaded with shot and rifle balls

10. It is customary in Springfield ... and other places in Nova Sco-
    tia to celebrate marriage by a demonstration of the friends and
    neighbours on return of newly married couples.

11. The Defendants well knowing the said custom unlawfully and
    maliously [sic] combined and conspired together to insult
    annoy, and bring the Plaintiff into disrepute and injure her
    character as a chaste married woman by falsely pretending that
    there had been a marriage between the Plaintiff and ... Lam-
    bert McNayr and to celebrate such pretended marriage ... with
    the purpose and intent to induce individuals and residents as
    well as the general public to believe that there had been and
    was then existing immoral and improper relations between the
    ... Plaintiff and ... Lambert McNayr.

12. She was injured in her reputation as a married woman in the
    eyes of the public, who were induced to believe by the acts and
    demonstrations complained of and did believe that immoral
    and improper relations existed between the Plaintiff and ...
    Lambert McNayr where the Plaintiff has suffered damages
    and loss in her reputation as a married woman and has been
    prevented from obtaining teams and assistance in driving to
    her friends and relatives and in doing her necessary business
    whereby she has suffered damages. The Plaintiff claims dam-
    ages $400.00. (Varner case)

In answer, the six defendants denied the asserted presence, assembly, and disorderly conduct, but in the alternative they denied

10. ... that they unlawfully or maliciously combined or conspired
    ... to insult annoy or bring the Plaintiff into disrepute ... and to
    injure her character as a chaste married woman ... by falsely

pretending that there had been a marriage between the Plaintiff and ... Lambert McNayr or to celebrate such pretended marriage ... [or] to induce ... the general public to believe that there had been or was then existing immoral or improper relations between the plaintiff and ... Lambert McNayr ...

The defendants ... say that the plaintiff had no character or reputation as a married woman in the eyes of the public and had no character as a chaste married woman in the community where the defendants live and they deny that any members of the public were induced to believe or did believe by any acts demonstrations [sic] complained of that immoral or improper relations existed between the Plaintiff and ... Lambert McNayr ...

12. ... since the departure of the Plaintiffs [sic] husband overseas the plaintiff has been guilty of vile and unchaste conduct both in regard to ... Lambert McNayr and ... others and in that regard her character or reputation has not suffered in the community in which she lives.

13. The Plaintiff in the absence of her ... husband has been infatuated with ... Lambert McNayr and ... [they] have been living in immoral relations ... Lambert McNayr has been driving the Plaintiff around the country and has been in the habit of visiting the Plaintiff and remaining with her until late hours of the night.

14. It was well known in the community that such improper and immoral relations existed between the Plaintiff and ... Lambert McNayr and that they passed off on several occasions as man and wife and had represented themselves as being married. (Ibid.)

Varner, as plaintiff, demanded particulars, and received the following. A better catalogue of community gossip is difficult to imagine:

1. Lambert McNayr on the 28th day of September, 1917, while driving through Cherryfield with the plaintiff said to Abbie Conn 'I have brought my wife with me this time' – thereby representing to ... Abbie Conn in the presence of plaintiff that the plaintiff was the wife of ... Lambert McNayr.

2. The plaintiff some time in 1917 or 1918, the exact date is unknown to the defendants, got drunk with one, Sabeans or Sibbons, and they slept together.

3. During the month of April, 1918, the plaintiff around the station in Springfield was hugging and sitting down on a bench with a man not her husband.

4. The plaintiff in front of LeRoy Roop's store in Springfield ... met a man, not her husband, and hugged and kissed him some time in 1917 or 1918, the exact date of which is unknown to the defendants.

5. Some time during 1917 or 1918, the exact date of which is unknown to the defendants, the plaintiff with some man not her husband came out of a ditch in the evening where they had remained for some time.

6. ... Lambert McNayr during the years 1917 and 1918 and two or three days in every week in said years before the commencement of this action visited the plaintiff at her house and spent hours with her alone in the absence of her husband, who was then overseas.

7. The plaintiff during the years 1917 and 1918 and in every month of said years before the commencement of this action went driving around the country with ... Lambert McNayr. (Ibid.)

In the County Court for Nova Scotia District No. 3 before J.A. Grierson Esq., Varner and witnesses appearing on her behalf answered some of these accusations. In response to the claims that Irene Varner and Lambert McNayr drove around the country together because they were having an affair, McNayr's evidence was, 'I often done jobs for plff's mother around place and assisted them with my team. I considered it was my duty as a neighbour. I thought I owed it to them as they had sent their men to the war. I repaired buildings, cut wood etc. Did some driving for her. I have a pair of horses. Did driving for Mrs Varner. I have driven mother and plff to Hastings singly and together. Have driven Mrs Varner to New Germany several times' (ibid.). His explanation for having Irene Varner with him on other occasions was, 'I am Scott Act Constable. There was a lot of business a year ago. Abbie Conn and Mrs Demon were prosecuted. In driving down took Mrs Varner. I located a distillery. I had Mrs Varner as I did not care to leave my team alone, and I wanted a witness' (ibid.).

Along with other defendants, Elwood Mailman tried to suggest the object of the saluting was Lambert McNayr, not Irene Varner: 'I kind of thought saluting would shame Mr McNayr so he w'd stay home.' Wiley Grimm commented, 'If Mr McNayr was a man I c'd have considered a respectable person I w'd not have thought anything wrong.

I c'd scarcely go into a store or a blacksmith shop in Springfield but that I heard things that were not to Mr McNayr's credit.' The defendant's relative LeRoy Roop asserted, 'He does not move in respectable society in Springfield. I do not claim that he is in society at all.'

Defendant I.B. Saunders said, 'I came home one morning and the boys s'd he has introduced her to old Mrs Conn as his wife in the road. We thought if we gave him a little serenade he w'd take the hint and go home and act like a man. We went there with object of letting McNayr know we were on to him. Did not celebrate for purpose of impugning Plff's character. If I had acted as Mr McNayr acted and people celebrated it, I would say they did right. I would thank them for it and give them a cigar in morning. If a person is married we usually give them a little salute. We did not want the people to think by saluting that Plff and McNayr were doing as newly married people do' (ibid.).

But the majority of testimony referred to Varner, who faced the recitation of extensive, detailed, and damaging gossip against her, already suggested in the request for particulars above. Testimony for the defence from her neighbours damned her in the words of the times: she used profane language, she took the Lord's name in vain, 'She had a bad reputation in Springfield and I think community could get along without her.' Abbie Conn's words suggest that the two were flaunting their relationship: 'He s'd I brought my wife this time so you won't have to wink to her. Mrs Varner was in waggon with McNayr. She was the woman who turned around in waggon and laughed' (ibid.).

Blanche Mailman, wife of Elwood and daughter of I.B. Saunders, said, 'Have known plff for some time. I know Bamford Arkin. Have seen him go around town with plff with arms around her and have seen them go in Barn. Her actions have been very much talked of in that community and fact she went with McNayr.' Bella Morton, wife of Albert, reported, 'Her driving around together with McNayr has been very remarked. I would think they were courting if I didn't know they were married ... She had a bad reputation driving around with men. Also she swore or used profane language. She took Lord's name in vain. She said by God. She said Damn.' Defence witness Jennie Haines asserted, 'I know Archibald Simonds. She told me she had sexual intercourse with him in the dining room of her own home.'[12] Another relative of a defendant testified, 'I saw plff and Harry Roy in street together in front of my store in day time. He put his arms around her.' And later, 'I have an intent in good name of place. It had become a public scandal [McNayr] driving this woman around. If I had known that all McNayr was doing was going to plff's to help I w'd not have thought anything of it. I did not know what he went there for' (ibid.)

Defendant Elwood Mailman testified, 'The plff's reputation as to men is not very good in [Springfield]. I w'd call it bad ... I have helped to celebrate when people got married ... They claimed they were married and so we celebrated. I didn't know that McNayr was not married to Mrs Varner. I did not think anything about it. They told Mrs Conn they were married. This is the only one I heard they told. The only reason we celebrated was they claimed they were married' (ibid.).

I.B. Saunders was also quite explicit about his disapproval of Varner: 'Was it a lady's part to go with McNayr as a witness? I do not think she would be doing right to drive around with him as much as she did. I do not think it w'd be right as I do not approve of it.' Defendant William Conrad testified, 'When I heard that McNayr had introduced Plff as his wife I thought it w'd be a good thing to serenade him ... I do not know who told me. It was rumoured in Springfield.' Another defence witness attested, 'I was Station Master at Springfield. There is a ditch near Station House about 200 yards below station and about 3 or 4 feet below level of road. I frequently saw Plff around station. I saw her go into the ditch one day with a commercial traveller by the name of Purney. I could see Mr Purney greater part of time. They were down 10 or 15 mins'[13] (ibid.).

Defendant Albert Morton showed a similar disapproving scrutiny of Varner's actions, 'I know Mrs Varner. I have seen in her what I considered not being as a chaste married woman. One time I was going around station at Springfield with mail bags. I saw plff sitting there with his arm around her. I don't know the man. I think it was last April. There were not many people there. I saw her coming down road hooked arm to a young man in the evening. This was Seth Langille. They were arm and arm. Know nothing more except her driving around with McNayr and him going there so much ... As far as liquor is concerned McNayr is a respectable man. I think he does things that are not respectable, for instance driving these women around as he does. If I w'd go to a house 2 or 3 times a week when men were not there w'd not think it respectable' (ibid.).

These comments show not only what was deemed appropriate and inappropriate behaviour for a woman at that time and place, but also the strength of the charivariers' convictions. Yet Irene Varner had answers to the accusations. She denied having sex with Simmonds: 'I know a Simmonds but he enlisted in Nov. 1915. We were engaged to be married in July 1915 on July 26th. On the 23rd of July I broke engagement. He was then in Liquor. I have not seen him since. I never slept with Simmonds and never got drunk with him. There never were any improper relations between me and Simmonds.' She also noted that Simmonds 'kept company with' the witness Jennie Haines's sister (ibid.).

Harry Roy was a family friend: 'I went down road and me him and we walked up together ... I went to Station to see if parcel had come ... Went down RR track picking roses. My brother was with me, he c'd have seen me. I heard what Mrs Morton s'd. My mother was there. It was David Allen. He was sitting along side of my mother. I s'd I am going to get jealous and sat down between them. He put his arm around my neck. I don't remember walking down street with Langille boy, but he is younger than I and I would not want to [illegible] him asking. I feel what you do in daylight in eyes of public is no harm' (ibid.).

There were many fewer witnesses for the plaintiff, but her father-in-law Joseph Varner testified on her behalf: 'After I heard of saluting I did not know what to think. Of course she did not stand as good in my opinion. I did not think there was anything between McNayr and daughter-in-law. Do not now. Can't say anything against my daughter-in-law. I thought if plff had stayed at home this would not have occurred. I couldn't swear that I think there is anything wrong but I suspect it' (ibid.).

Another witness for the plaintiff, Fred Silver, also referred to the effect of the saluting on Varner's reputation: 'I have known Mrs Varner for 10 years. I do not know anything against Mrs Varner ... I heard about saluting. It was a topic of conversation in Hastings. I thought it did not sound very good ... I think it injured plffs reputation in Hastings. Did not hear before that about them driving around. I heard a good deal about them driving around after the saluting. After I heard men talk I thought she was bad. Her reputation was bad after that time' (ibid.).

Her mother asserted, 'This is not an action to get money. I am after getting my daughter's character restored in this suit ... Some in Springfield give me cold shoulder. Nobody hinted to me there was anything wrong between McNayr and my daughter. They acted like it that night of serenade' (ibid.).

Irene Varner defended her right to act as she pleased, with a vehemence equal to that of her detractors. But it is clear from the judge's charge to the jury that Grierson was not impressed by Varner or her supporters:

If it were left to me I would not take very long to decide, but I am not going to tell you what my decision would be ... Did the Plaintiff suffer any damage to her character or reputation by reason of the serenade?[14] ... [You should ask] whether the demonstration made the Plaintiff any worse in the eyes of the community than she was before. Did it alter her in any way as to her reputation in the community afterwards? If it did then you should find the Defendants liable for damages.

You have the evidence of a number of witnesses that the Plaintiff, in their estimation, did suffer damages to her reputation by reason of this demonstration. You have also the evidence that the Plaintiff drove out with a man by the name of McNayr, over the country to New Germany and Hastings, and that she was in company with other men and although perhaps she meant no harm, it occurred to me that I would not like a sister of mine to act as she did. Was she as discreet as she should have been? If she were not immoral she should not have placed herself in a position that would lead people to conclude that she was not a chaste woman. She would be judged by her actions and you know people are bound to talk. Did the celebration itself injure her in her reputation? (ibid.)

Grierson evidently expected a negative answer to his question – especially when he couched the saluting as a 'celebration.' However, the jury apparently did not share his scepticism and found in Varner's favour on the defamation and conspiracy charges.[15] Grierson ordered the defendants to pay her $160 'for damage to her reputation' (ibid.).

The defendants asked that the jury decision be set aside – both the finding that she suffered 'damage to her reputation and character by the acts of the defendants in said celebration,'[16] and the damages of '$200 as to her reputation and character.' They wanted a new trial on the grounds that there was no cause of action; that the findings were 'against the weight of evidence' and were 'perverse'; that there was no evidence to support the findings; that since there was no finding of personal injury there could be no damages; that 'the plaintiff had no reputation or character to lose'; that the defendants were wrongly joined as tortfeasors, and 'because the answers of the jury to the questions in favour of the defendant are against the instruction of the learned trial Judge.' Among other responses to these claims, the judge found that 'in reference to the finding that the plaintiff suffered damage to her reputation or character by the acts of the defendants in said celebration, I think there was some evidence that would warrant such a finding. However, if I had been sitting as a Jury I do not think I should have found as the Jury did. That alone is not sufficient reason for me to set aside the finding in this respect, and order a new trial' (ibid.). The defendants then appealed and so the case arrived at the Nova Scotia Supreme Court, with a decision rendered just more than a year and six months after the event, on 2 May 1919.

As the adversarial court system requires, the claims and counter-claims line up in a series of all-or-nothing propositions in both legal and personal contexts: Varner had a cause of action, or she did not; Varner suffered damage to her reputation, or she did not. Similarly, witnesses for the plaintiff assured the jury that Varner was a respectable woman and that it was the saluting itself, not her behaviour, that injured her reputation, while witnesses for the defendants painted her as 'vile and unchaste.' The view in the community would have been somewhat more nuanced, and reading between the lines of the testimony from a community point of view suggests other actions and motivations in play.

The Community's Views

The saluting of Varner and McNayr did not exactly replicate the traditional Annapolis County saluting, in that it was not directed at a married couple. The ostensible purpose, as described by most historians, for denunciatory charivaris was to confirm to those who received it the community's censure of their behaviour. Yet for some this saluting was more an accusation or judgment than a confirmation or affirmation. Rather than simply reasserting a community view of Varner and McNayr's illicit relationship, it manufactured suspicion against them. Clearing one's name from neighbourhood gossip is notoriously difficult; there is no court of appeal in folk law. Yet while gossip lacks legitimacy in formal legal discourses, its reputation as inherently 'informal, almost irrational,' has not always been so negative (Marks 2000, 389). In 1917, in Springfield, the formal charges Varner made against the six men for defamation, conspiracy, and personal injury were undoubtedly the only way she saw to salvage her reputation.[17]

When I contacted the Varner family genealogists and historians and other local history experts about this event, they had never heard of it. This was a considerable surprise to me, particularly because the slightly earlier (1909) charivari in rural Manitoba, the subject of my previous chapter, is still in oral tradition within the family and community and the story has even travelled elsewhere in Canada with a

former resident. I had thought that folks would more likely want to
cover up a manslaughter charge (even though the Grand Jury found
'no bill,' so there was no trial) than to suppress a case like *Varner*,
over matters that to an urban former Ontarian like myself seem much
less weighty.

The family and community helped me to understand that the seriousness of the charges against Irene Varner in the informal court of
public opinion can't be overstated. As family historian and genealogist Lloyd Varner commented, 'Those people really got nasty with
each other and I am not surprised that when it was over nobody was
anxious to talk about it. No one that I have been speaking with had
ever heard it mentioned by anyone' (personal communication, 5 May
2005).[18] Similarly, Rafuse asked her sister-in-law, a great-niece of
William Conrad, 'And she and her sister knew nothing about it, had
never heard it even mentioned. And her grandmother would just have
known everything, and it was never mentioned, that they know of'
(PG2005, 4). When she learned the story, Rafuse evaluated Irene as
'pretty feisty to take them to court ... I admired her. Brave soul'
(ibid.).

I was unable to locate any direct descendants of the couple. In his
extended family, Irene's husband was known but there was some suspicion about Irene herself. Rafuse spoke to a niece, who told her,
'"Uncle Albert used to come to visit, but Irene never came." She was
"different" is the word she used' (ibid.). Another niece, Margaret
McKean, commented, 'I've heard of Mike coming down here and
visiting his brother, but she never came' (PG2005, 6). When I asked
her if she was shocked to learn that such a thing had happened to a
Varner, she corrected me: 'It wasn't a Varner, she was just married to
a Varner ... It wasn't bloodline' (ibid.).

Varner's actions and words show her unconventionality as a rural
Nova Scotia woman. 'Irene's problems with her neighbours were ...
because of her independent nature and unwillingness to conform to
the niceties of the social practices of the time' (Lloyd Varner, personal communication, 5 May 2005).

Varner family genealogist and historian Debbie Vermeulen commented, 'If even a little bit of what they accused her of was true ...
she couldn't have been that innocent, that's all I can say. Not here in
Nova Scotia. She would not have been that innocent ... A lot of the
churches around here ... still do their own moral policing and gossiping and it doesn't take much ... and people start talking! ... Even
in this day and age, that can still happen ... I'm really surprised that
she would win' (PG2005, 1). Lloyd Varner agreed: 'The gossip

spread by Abbie Conn was the spark that caused the saluting incident to occur. The people involved would have been outraged by Irene and this would have been just the excuse they needed to humiliate her. Even her father-in-law, in his testimony on her behalf, said that, while he did not think she had done anything wrong, he thought that she should have been more circumspect' (personal communication, 5 May 2005).

The stakes were high. Eventually, the saluting could have resulted in the end of her marriage. As Thompson asserts, the rough music charivari 'announces disgrace, not as a contingent quarrel with neighbours, but as judgement of the community. What had before been gossip or hostile glances becomes common, overt, stripped of the disguises which, however flimsy and artificial, are part of the currency of everyday intercourse ... The victim must go out into the community the next morning, knowing that in the eyes of every neighbour and of every child he or she is seen as a person disgraced. It is therefore not surprising that rough music, except in its lightest forms, attached to the victim a lasting stigma' (1993, 487–8).

On the return of her husband and brothers from war, and the inevitable breaking of the news of her shame to them, Varner would be expected to prove her innocence. Obtaining damages in a court of law would offer compelling evidence that she was a victim of gossip, not a transgressor against her marriage vows. In Thompson's sense, then, the saluting of Varner was a success, or she would not have taken it sufficiently seriously to commence action against those who perpetrated it: 'Even where no "court" of judgement existed, the essential attribute of rough music appears to be that it only works *if* it works: that is, if (first) the victim is sufficiently "of" the community to be vulnerable to disgrace, to *suffer* from it: and (second) if the music does indeed express the consensus of the community – or at least of a sufficiently large and dominant part of the community ... to cow or to silence those who, while perhaps disapproving of the ritual, shared in some degree the same disapproval of the victim' (ibid., 491–2).

But its success as traditional shaming was unrelated to its legitimacy or validity as a statement about Varner's actions. As Thompson argues, 'Rough music could also be an excuse for a drunken orgy or for blackmail ... It is a property of a society in which justice is not wholly delegated or bureaucratised, but is enacted by and within the community ... And the psychic terrorism which could be brought to bear ... was truly terrifying' (ibid., 530). Damage to a woman's honour by impugning her chastity was by no means a trivial result. As

legal theorist Bradley Wendel argues, 'Although honor is not necessarily a gendered concept, virtually every conception of honor that
has been elaborated throughout history seems fundamentally to
exclude women as people worthy of social prestige. In traditional
honor societies, it is true that both men and women are subject to the
claims of honor, and are potentially liable to lose honor and to be
shamed. The ascription of honor differs between the sexes in what
actions are expected of a man and a woman, and what is necessary to
gain and lose honor. Generally honor for women is associated with
chastity' (2001, 2025–6).

Further, historian Peter T. Cominos argues that at the time in Euro
North America 'the responsibility for purity was entirely feminine,
and women had to bear the brunt of the public censure, the penalty,
and the guilt alone for its loss' (1972, 165). Further, 'women were
classified into polar extremes. They were either sexless ministering
angels or sensuously oversexed temptresses of the devil' (ibid., 167).
Thus, Lambert McNayr's possible contravention of his marriage
vows didn't attract the same level of concern or disapproval as
Varner's. Ultimately, the sexual fidelity of a woman was a greater
issue for her community, and for the legal system; damage to her honour meant damage to her symbolic capital in ways unparalleled for
men.

Yet opinions about the situation and the reasons behind the saluting
were by no means simple. Insofar as the rebuke was aimed at McNayr,
it came from close members of his family and from some of the eld-
ers of the community his ancestors had helped to found. Family and
community alike would have felt quite within their rights to express
their opinions about another member: 'If they were family, that would
make them feel even more justified in doing what they did. Because
families tend to monitor their morals amongst themselves even more
than they would in the community. I mean, they'd talk about them if
they were within the community, but they wouldn't care as much …
It wouldn't take much for a woman to be perceived to have done
something relatively minor to be shunned by her family. So that's why
I can't see that Irene was that naive; she just couldn't have been'
(Debbie Vermeulen, PG2005, 1).

The community members clearly stated their opinions and
defended their right to them – not only in this context but in others.
Irene Varner testified to the following exchange between McNayr
and Saunders: 'Mr Saunders said, you go to hell out of this or I'll
jump the d—— heart out of you. Mr McNayr s'd I will go home
when I get d—d good & ready. Have I not as much right on public

highway as you have. Mr. S—— s'd it makes no difference you got to f—— on home. He said you better be at home with your wife and family than hanging around here.' Lambert McNayr testified, 'Mr Saunders was a neighbour of mine. He s'd Lambert don't you know people are talking about you going to Ruffs. He never advised me in reference to going to Haydens.' LeRoy Roop, who owned the general store where some of the saluters gathered, also clearly disapproved of McNayr, and testified, 'He is not particular friend of mine. I know he has been leaving his family and driving this woman around. I know of a peculiar circumstance that happened when I was a boy about McNayr. I know of nothing I w'd swear to.'[19] The involvement of mature men was unusual because salutings, like the charivaris discussed in the two previous chapters, would usually be perpetrated by much younger boys and men. As I.B. Saunders commented, 'Mrs Hayden [Irvin] s'd to me … what are you doing here this time of night. I should think you sh'd be the last one to be out a gray haired old bugger like you.'

It is possible that McNayr's position as the *Scott Act* constable also influenced community feeling about him. In some locations, these individuals were notoriously unpopular with their neighbours; a friend tells me that some folks from his hometown in Nova Scotia still won't speak to anybody in his family because his grandfather was the *Scott Act* constable there. However, as Debbie Vermeulen said, 'Springfield was a very much a Baptist community, with very strict rules about how society should run … There's no drinking, there's no swearing, there's no smoking … you don't go to church without a hat and gloves … [and] you don't play cards on Sunday. If you do, the devil will get you … Every community was a little bit different, but they all had their little sets of rules, and you didn't violate them' (PG2005, 1).[20] Again, communities are not univocal.

Further, Irene Varner's position in the community – not a long-time resident – may have been relevant: 'She would not be considered community from only having been there as long as she had been. She would be a definite outsider so she would be fair game' (ibid.) – though Lloyd Varner thought her ten or so years in Hastings would be enough to make her somewhat of an insider. But family and community historians have also suggested other possible motivations for feeling against McNayr and Varner. For example, Lloyd Varner pointed out that though the Haydens lived next door to LeRoy Roop's store, they shopped in Hastings. Edith Irvin testified, 'Fruit is kept for sale at Hastings not kept at Springfield. So we go to Hastings.' Apparently petty differences can be the basis for long and deep grudges.

The notion of respectability engaged by these discursive interventions pertains to public behaviour, but apparently presumes private behaviour can be divined from it. Much discourse about Irene Varner from different points of view centred on her actions in what Alan Hunt calls 'heterosocial space.' Noting that '"space" not only has a spatial but also a temporal dimension,' he says that 'by heterosocial space I refer to the shifting and changing sites where ... women and men come into contact and where transactions with potentially sexual dimensions may arise or which others may define in sexualised terms' (Hunt 2002, 2). He argues that contestive uses of heterosocial spaces 'did much to undermine the restrictive regime founded on the ideology of females and males occupying "separate spheres"' (ibid., 27). Hunt's own analysis focuses upon formal and institutionalized regulation of space, but his concept is pertinent to the community interpretations of Irene Varner's actions, and how they affected her position.[21]

Varner and McNayr were never asked during the trial if they were having an affair. Though the defence answer to the statement of claim asserts that they were 'living in immoral relations,' neither plaintiff nor defence directly addressed the issue in the trial. The defence response asserted that she 'had no character or reputation as a married woman in the eyes of the public and had no character as a chaste married woman in the community where the defendants live,' and that she was 'guilty of vile and unchaste conduct both in regard to ... Lambert McNayr and in regard to others' (Varner case). But the sole individual with whom she was directly accused during the trial of having illicit sexual intercourse was Archibald Sim(m)on(d)s, to whom she was briefly engaged – an arrangement that she called off because he was 'in liquor.' Varner categorically stated, 'There never were any improper relations between me and Simmonds' (ibid.). With this one exception, it was not Varner's private acts but her public affection, and her use of public space, that rendered her suspect.

A series of presumptions inflect Varner's and McNayr's actions and locations with sexual meaning. The fact that Varner was physically affectionate in public places with men to whom she was not related lead to the expressed conclusion that she was 'vile and unchaste,' and presumably that she would necessarily go further in private contexts. The fact that McNayr visited the Varner/Hayden home when no adult male relative was present led to an oblique conclusion that his only reason for going there could be to have sexual intercourse with one or both of the women there. The fact that Varner and McNayr drove around frequently together (and presumably Hayden and McNayr did not) led to the conclusion that they were 'living in immoral relations.'

Place combined with gender, and with the unshakeable fundamental belief in heterosexuality and homosociality (that friendly relations can occur only between those of the same sex and that only sexual relations can occur between those of different sexes), to produce only one possible conclusion. Heterosocial friendship being precluded, the only possible relationship between Varner and McNayr was sexual. Though the response to the statement of claim asserted that she was 'living in immoral relations' with McNayr, there was no testimony to that effect. That she must have had sex with him was inferred from the fact that she was physically affectionate with other men in public (note that there was no suggestion that Varner had hugged, put her arm around, walked arm-in-arm with, or gone down the railway line with McNayr). The inexplicit assumption was that all men 'not her husband' were essentially equivalent.[22]

Witness testimony repeatedly argued the propriety and impropriety of the various protagonists' uses of space. In the defence statements, Varner's use of public space was rigorously addressed simultaneously with reminders of her gender: reference to her reputation as a '[chaste] married woman' and such comments as, 'It had become a public scandal [McNayr] driving this woman around.' Reference to Varner's gender was even more pointed in I.B. Saunders's rhetorical question: 'Was it a lady's part to go with McNayr as a witness?'

Further, defence statements referred to physical locations with overdetermined sexual and/or gendered implications, such as the railway station, the store, and the horse and buggy. Irene Varner's accusers contested her actions in highly inflected public places. That she and McNayr went driving together was the most repeated accusation against them. Though not to the extent the automobile later gave, horse-and-buggy rides offered courting couples an opportunity to leave the scrutiny of their community behind. Frequent driving apparently led in this case to a suspicion that courting, not business, was the main intent of the two.[23]

The general store, on the other hand, would be a place where men would be expected to gather (Bauman 1972b). A woman within view (both literal and figurative) of the store would be subjected to the male gaze. As Lloyd Varner commented, 'It would have been normal in those days for men to congregate at the store when not working (the hot stove league), where they would talk about the weather, the war and the neighbours, not necessarily in that order' (personal communication, 27 May 2005). Note that the saluters gathered at the store, and at least two mentioned hearing about the scandal there.

Hunt identifies the railway station as a 'significant site of moral danger ... Railways and railway stations generated both excitement and sexual danger. The bustle and anonymity of the railway station, along with the more prosaic attraction of shelter from the elements, acted as a magnet for many young people. The casual opportunities provided for heterosocial encounters were construed by the moral reformers in more ominous terms. The presence of unattached young women was treated as evidence of the presence of prostitutes and charity girls' (2002, 26).

If we believe Irene Varner, though, she was not 'unattached' at the railway station – she was with her brother – nor was she 'unattached' in the sense of being unmarried. Clearly, any action – no matter how innocent – can become inflected with vile unchastity if the audience wishes to so read it. The station master's accusation conflated persons and place. The highly suspect Irene Varner and the implicitly hyper-sexualized commercial traveller, meeting by chance (or otherwise?) at the railway station and being out of sight part of the time could only speak of a sexual liaison. Irene Varner's obvious sense of freedom to embrace men in public, as well as in her own home, was by her explanations quite innocent, but was rife with innuendo for her accusers.

The defence's only specific accusation that she had sex with a man to whom she was not married was in the context of drunkenness (in the response to the Statement of Claim) and the physical context of her own dining room (in witness testimony). The latter implicitly raised questions not only for her actions but also for their location. Not only is the dining room an inappropriate place for sex, it is also a public/social part of the house compared, for example, with the bedrooms.

Varner answered with an overt defence of her rights in public. In the quotation I use in the title of this chapter, she argued that she should not only be able to use public space as she saw fit, but also to define her public daylight actions as necessarily innocent. Though her assertion was not overtly gendered – she argued generically that what 'you' do publicly during the day is harmless – she was clearly presuming her own right to claim public space, as a person.[24]

The defence's accusations cited McNayr's visits to Varner and to the Hayden place as illicit. Paradoxically, Lambert McNayr was constructed in testimony as belonging at home – that is, in the private, usually female, domain, rather than in the public, usually male, one.[25]

During the saluting, defendant Isaac B. Saunders frequently admonished his cousin to 'go home.' In his own testimony, Saunders argued that his intent was to induce McNayr to 'go home and act like a man.' McNayr was out of place in the Varner/Hayden home; his home place must be with his own family. His very presence at Varner/Hayden's home was questionable in the absence of the women's husbands or other adult male relatives.

Varner won her case at both trial and appeal, but as is too often the situation for women's interactions with the law, the result was more than somewhat mixed. Women's agency in the legal system is strictly controlled, if not actually suppressed, and winning a case does not necessarily mean a victory in the larger sociocultural context. Though she received costs and $200 when the Nova Scotia Supreme Court heard the defendants' appeal from the trial judgment, and though Irene Varner to some extent succeeded in retaining control over the interpretation of her character, the legal system imposed limits as well as considerable personal and emotional cost in pressing it.

Defamation, Slander, and/or Libel

The appeal turned in part on exactly what legal category the charivariers' actions fit. Legal historian S.M. Waddams notes the importance of the distinction between libel, 'defamation by written words,' and slander, 'defamation by spoken words.' Slander was originally not actionable without proof of special damage, with three exceptions: imputing a crime, disparaging professional practice, and imputing a 'loathsome disease.' However, in 1891, another exception was introduced in England by statute 'for slander impugning chastity,' but only for women (2000, 17).[26] The judgment of Chief Justice Harris[27] in *Varner* cites a Nova Scotia Order,[28] which had a similar effect – even if the defamation is slander (spoken), if it refers to 'any woman, imputing to her any unchaste conduct it shall not be necessary in pleading, or to prove at the trial, that any special damage resulted to her from the utterance of such words' (ibid., 8).

Thus it became extremely important in the case to detail the content as well as the intent of the charivari, since Varner's attempt to prove special damage via her personal injury charge was unsuccessful, she did not address special damage for the defamation charge, and charivari is neither a written nor a spoken form of defamation. Harris was 'inclined to the view that the acts of the defendants were equivalent to saying or speaking of the plaintiff that she was unchaste' (ibid., 10). Thus, he decided, no proof of special damage was necessary. However, he was still concerned to identify exactly how to describe the charivari in legal terms. His decision was extremely hedged and equivocal: 'After giving the matter careful consideration I have reached the conclusion, though not without much doubt, that the acts in question are of that intermediate character between slander and libel to which the rules applicable to libel apply' (ibid., 10). Having concluded that the defendants' acts were a form of libel 'or, being slander, the Order XIX rule 29 is applicable and obviates the necessity for proof of special damage' (ibid., 21), Harris dismissed the appeal with costs.

Justice Mellish[29] concurred: 'The plaintiff had a right to the uninterrupted use of the highway. The demonstration complained of was deliberate and malicious and intended to insult the plaintiff and clearly defamatory. I think it was in the nature of a libel. The remarks, however, made by at least one of the defendants, would, I think, in view of the contemporary conduct, amount to slander' (ibid., 53). In noting the 'remarks,' he cemented the case for slander – that there were spoken words that would be slanderous and actionable because they impugned the chastity of a woman. He couched his final judgment, however, in more general terms: 'I think substantial justice will be done by allowing the verdict and judgment to stand' (ibid.). Mellish was the only NSSC justice who did not take an opportunity to upbraid Varner.

Justice Chisholm[30] offered a dissenting opinion. 'So as far as the demonstration of the defendants was criminal in nature they have already answered for they have been prosecuted for their breach of the peace' (ibid., 42). He employed an extremely narrow interpretation of textbook definitions of slander and libel, and thus avoided the conclusion that the charivari was a form of defamation. He quoted Odgers on libel and slander, according to which 'a man's reputation may also be injured by the deed or action of another without his using any words; and for such an injury he has an action' (ibid., 47). He found that charivari could not be included in the non-word libel forms described by Pollock on torts: 'significant gestures (as the finger language of the deaf and dumb) ... [or] drawing, printing and engraving and every other use of permanent written symbols to carry distinct ideas' (ibid., 48). Thus, he concluded that 'in the absence of proof of special damage, I do not think she can recover' (ibid., 51).

Two other justices also had difficulty finding the charivari as defamation. While they concurred that the appeal should be dismissed with costs, they reached their conclusion via another route. Justice Ritchie[31] (with Justice Russell[32] concurring) argued that the charivari should be understood as conspiracy. His description focused on McNayr's actions as reasonable and neighbourly:

> The plaintiff ..., a married woman ... was living at Springfield in the county of Annapolis with her mother. In the summer and autumn of 1917 there was no man about the place, her sons being also overseas; and ... Lambert McNayr helped about the place, planting, cutting wood and performing other neighbourly acts such as it would be natural for a man to for women whose men were fighting the Germans. The plaintiff drove about with this man, McNayr, a good deal, and it no doubt was the cause for remark among the good people of Springfield. The defendants seem to have regarded it as their special duty to take action in regard to the conduct of the plaintiff and McNayr. They saw evil where, so far as the evidence discloses, there was none. (ibid., 24)

The conspiracy case turned extensively on the fact that the action was not directed solely at the plaintiff, but also at McNayr. Ritchie explicitly noted the blamelessness – even praiseworthiness – of McNayr's action. Like Harris, who said Varner – 'had acted most imprudently' (ibid., 3) – Ritchie clearly wished to record some level of disapproval for Varner's actions. The conspiracy argument allowed him to disapprove of Varner while approving of McNayr: 'The conduct of the plaintiff was, I think, indiscreet, and that is all that can be said about her. The mother who, I assume, is a respectable woman, saw nothing wrong in the relations of the plaintiff with McNayr and did not disapprove of her driving with him, and it seems to me that it would have been far better from every point of view if the defendants had minded their own business' (ibid.).

This difference between defamation and conspiracy, then, is crucial to a gendered analysis of the case. The conspiracy issue that Ritchie built was based on the notion that the problem arose less from the impugning of Varner's chastity than from the fact that the defendants gathered to commit an illegal act: 'The conduct of the defendants was absolutely illegal. They assembled together and created a disturbance of the peace of the neighbourhood. They committed a breach of the criminal law. It was an unlawful assembly' (ibid., 25). His comments were much more general about the effects of the charivari on Varner: 'Of course the Springfield people knew that the plaintiff had a husband, and that McNayr had a wife, and I think this action of the defendants imputed misconduct, using the word in the sense which it has acquired in the Divorce Court. An action in this particular form is unusual, but the reason for that is that the circumstances of the case are unusual. If an injury causing damage has been inflicted on the plaintiff it cannot be that the law does not provide a remedy. The scope of an action on the case is wide enough to cover any illegal acts which have caused damage' (ibid., 28).

Crucially, Ritchie found the cause of action to be based on an illegal act that has resulted in damage, rather than on the specific 'damage as to her reputation and character' (ibid., 27) cited in the trial judgment. Hence, he detailed the fit between Halsbury's definition of conspiracy, and the case at hand: 'That there was an agreement between the defendants to meet together and make the demonstration which it is clear was made is shown by the evidence, but apart from evidence such an agreement is to be inferred from the fact that they were all present with the guns, horns, bells and other instruments of torture; such a condition of affairs implies a concerted action. This meeting together of the defendants was an unlawful assembly and a disturbance of the peace of the neighbourhood' (ibid., 35, 36).

In the end Ritchie had to say exactly what the damage was to the plaintiff, and he found 'their action was clearly and obviously wrongful and harmful to the plaintiff, as it imputed improper relations with McNayr' (ibid., 37). But his explanation of the damages was subtly different from that of Harris. Ritchie asserted, 'This case is one for exemplary damages because the defendants acted deliberately, maliciously and wantonly with the intention of grievously insulting the plaintiff' (ibid., 39). Their intentional, deliberate conspiracy, then, called for punitive damages, rather than the unproven damages merited by defamation.

Vile and Unchaste?

The community implication of Varner as 'vile and unchaste' could not only affect her local and family interactions. The end of her marriage, in a context where she was viewed as an adulteress, could result in economic destitution for the rest of her life. That the community took it as their business to conduct this surveillance of Varner's actions can be best understood in the context of wartime.

Some historians have recently argued that the First World War, while a watershed for women's suffrage, nevertheless reinforced gender-polarized views such as that of 'man as the "just warrior" and woman as the moral mother, sacrificing her sons to the cause ... [and the] related theme of men's honourable protection of women and family' (Sangster 2005, 159).[33] Irene Varner's husband was overseas fighting, or she would not have needed Lambert McNayr's wagon and horse to get around. The imposition of the *Scott Act* was a wartime temperance measure, so he would probably not have been out driving so much in the absence of war. Irene Varner's mother, Edith Irvin, had three sons at the front, more than any other family in Springfield. At least one of the men who charivaried Varner and McNayr would have been young enough to have gone to battle. Two, at fifty-three and sixty-two, would have been clearly too old, and another was on the borderline. Evidently they felt it necessary, as men staying behind, to police the morals of a young wife.

The trial foregrounded Edith Irvin as moral mother. Irene Varner was the first to register her three overseas brothers in the testimony and was met with an immediate objection from the defence lawyer. When Edith Irvin noted her sons and son-in-law in her testimony, the defence once more objected. She raised them again during cross-examination. The insistence was sufficiently significant in a jury trial to be disputed. Ultimately, the jury's impressions of the protagonists would strongly influence their decision. Varner's fit with the gendered stereotype of a vile and unchaste woman was overlaid with other, more positive, and ultimately more compelling ones.

The just warriors lurked in the background of the trial testimony; defendant Albert Morton had a son overseas.[34] Apparently no other defendants had close relatives in the war or they surely would have noted them, given the attempts to suppress Varner using her husband and brothers to bolster her symbolic capital. Varner trumped, with three brothers and a husband having served.

A discursive struggle over the position of honourable protector was ultimately won by Lambert McNayr, helping out a widow whose sons are in the war, and a soldier's wife, over the six moral regulators who perpetrated the charivari, policing private morality. Though none of the NSSC justices stated the case as strongly as Varner herself, that what she did was her own affair, Justice Ritchie expressed the modernist notion that people should mind their own business.

The discursive construction of Irene Varner was a centrally contested issue. Was she a woman wronged by the gossip and suspicion of her neighbours, or a repeated transgressor against her wedding vows? Ironically McNayr was in the end more thoroughly vindicated than the actual plaintiff. Varner's boldness in taking the saluters to court in an attempt to redeem her reputation opened her to repeated rebukes from the legal benches of Nova Scotia, as well as a recitation of her shortcomings from the witness stands, and a catalogue of community gossip in the particulars of the charges. Her double victory, at both trial and appeal, was then considerably mitigated. Nevertheless, as Thompson argues,

> Rough music belongs to a mode of life in which some part of the law belongs still to the community and is theirs to enforce … It indicates modes of social self-control and the disciplining of certain kinds of violence and anti-social offence … which in today's cities may be breaking down. But when we consider the societies which have been under our examination, one must add a rider. Because law belongs to people, and is not alienated, or delegated, it is not thereby made more 'nice' and tolerant, more cosy and folksy. It is only as nice and tolerant as the prejudices and norms of the folk allow. Some forms of rough music disappeared from history in shadowy complicity with bigotry, jingoism and worse … For some of its victims, the coming of a distanced (if alienated) Law and a bureaucratised police must have been felt as a liberation from the tyranny of one's 'own.' (1993, 530–1)

Charivari traditions are far from obsolete, though as already indicated, in many parts of Canada their valences have altered. For most English Canadians today, charivaris are intended to welcome a couple to a community, though many such events include tendentious trickery and mess-making (see Greenhill 1989b). Generally, historians and sociologists emphasize charivari's community-making elements over its individual-blaming ones. But internal community discord over a charivari is by no means unusual, as E.P. Thompson's work indicates. *Varner* offers an excellent example of how a woman tried, with some success, to use the formal legal system to defend herself against a community judgment. To the extent that the law saw the charivari as defamation, she succeeded. But note that only one Nova Scotia Supreme Court justice (Harris) was absolutely explicit that a wrong had been committed against Varner because she was female – that she had experienced the special form of gendered defamation. Three justices (including Harris) found that she had acted 'indiscreetly' or 'imprudently.' Only the dissenting judgment and Mellish's make no editorial judgment about the morality of her conduct.

Further, in the trial itself, Varner had to face a recitation of her shortcomings and alleged deviations from the sexual morality of Springfield.[35] At least Varner won her case, with the not insubstantial damages (for the time) of $200. Yet she was subjected to an implicit rebuke by three justices, and indeed won her case despite the fact that three of five justices did not find that she had been defamed.

The denouement of this case is equally telling. When I visited Springfield in summer 2004, I found the graves of four of the six defendants, as well as that of Lambert McNayr, in the Springfield cemetery. They stayed in the village. However problematic McNayr's position may have been, it clearly did not drive him from his home. His gravestone is that of a patriarch, a four-sided column that places his family around him and literally faces all directions to and from Springfield. There were no Conns in the telephone book, and no Irvins.

Irene and Albert Michael ('Mike') Varner stayed in Springfield for a while. The Springfield column of the Middleton *Outlook* on 11 March 1921 reported the death 'on Feb. 20th from scarlet fever of Juanita, the year old daughter of Albert Varner. At the time of writing his small son, Milton, is dangerously ill with the same disease.' The arrival of two more children after Mike returned from war indicates, at the very least, that their sexual relationship wasn't impaired by the saluting. But the Varners eventually moved to Halifax and possibly later to Kingston, Ontario (Varner, Vermeulen, and MacNutt 1993, 47) – though Kingston, Nova Scotia, is more likely. Irene's 1966 obituary is from Shubenacadie; she was survived by Mike and her youngest daughter Eva, but both her sons also predeceased her.[36] In any case, it's clear that for whatever reason, the Varners didn't want to stay in Springfield. The saluting of Irene Varner and Lambert McNayr may have played some role in making it inhospitable for them.

The final charivari example I address has nothing to do with the legal system. It forms a case study primarily because it happens to have been recorded by professional photographers. This event more closely approaches those remembered by most individuals I interviewed or received questionnaires from than the three previous cases. It was a celebration of a marriage, not a denunciation of a couple's relationship.

5

Picturing Community:
Les and Edna Babcock's Shivaree,
Avonlea, Saskatchewan, 1940[1]

The nature and outcomes of the charivaris I've discussed in the previous three chapters might suggest that most such treatments were intended badly, and that in the main they were poorly received and ended in violence, in court, or at best in negative feelings. As I've already suggested, however, a more likely explanation is that the predominance in the literature of charivaris with unhappy results is an artefact of historic written documentation in legal and newspaper records. The authorities and the press were unconcerned with run-of-the-mill charivaris, the vast majority of which were accepted with aplomb. Most recipients demonstrated the tactful qualities of good sports – often under trying circumstances. In the prairie provinces, good sport is a primarily male category: 'At the heart of this designation is a man who will neither shirk nor fear the responsibilities of community life, a man whose character and personality have created, among his neighbours, certain expectations of cooperation and friendliness ..., one who, in the interest of good fellowship, is willing to endure ridicule, humiliation, and even physical pain at the hands of other community members' (Taft 1997, 133–4).

Even the disapproving Susanna Moodie discussed two early-nineteenth-century Ontario charivaris that were received good-naturedly. One involved an older man who married a young widow and eventually paid the charivariers thirty dollars. 'They did not expect that the old man would have been so liberal, and they gave him the "Hip, hip, hip, hurrah!" in fine style and marched off to finish the night and spend the money at the tavern' (1997, 230). Moodie quotes her neighbour as saying '"A charivari would seldom be attended with bad consequences if people would take it as a joke, and join in the spree"'

(ibid., 232–3). The man in the latter example shows good sportsmanship by paying more than anticipated. But women needed to be more
socioculturally resourceful, as the second example from Moodie
shows, in which a widow married a younger man. Though she was
nightly buried in effigy by charivariers, the woman 'wisely let them
have their own way,' commenting that '"as long as she enjoyed her
health ... they were welcome to bury her in effigy as often as they
pleased; she was really glad to be able to afford amusement to so
many people"' (ibid., 233). The charivariers indeed returned night
after night, until the woman invited their leader to dinner. When the
usual disruption began, she commented, '"Here come our friends.
Really, Mr. K——, they amuse us so much of an evening that I
should feel quite dull without them"' (ibid., 234). The charivaring
ended that night.

By 1940, outside Quebec and Acadian Canada, almost all Canadian charivaris had become wedding celebrations rather than denun-
ciations. They indicated the community's acceptance and welcome of
the newlyweds, rather than marking a match that was in some way
problematic. The noise and surprise continued, but the request for
money was replaced by a more subtle *quête* – the expectation of hospitality – and, in many locations, the performance included the enactment of a series of traditional pranks. Yet even as 'welcoming' occasions, many degenerated into contexts for getting even with – or
one-upping – those who had once been charivariers and now were
charivaried. And further, they sometimes led to apparently unmoti-
vated destruction and mayhem. Throughout, men were supposed to
accept them with good humour, and women were supposed to be prepared for them and offer the charivariers the usual farm home hospitality. These kinds of charivaris will be detailed in the last chapter.

But Les and Edna Babcock's shivaree[2] at Avonlea, Saskatchewan,
documented in three remarkable pictures taken by professional photographers Dick and Ada Bird,[3] though it was quite a noisy occasion
and possibly a surprise, obviously wasn't one of these trying ones
requiring male good sportsmanship – though it probably did require
female preparation and hospitality. First, it took place in daytime
(though most in Avonlea remember night shivarees). Second, its participants were all younger than in most such events – from around
eight to the late teens.[4] Finally, there's no indication there was any
trickery involved, though most current residents of Avonlea remember some pranks played against newlyweds at similar events.[5]

The previous three chapters have depended on court records, newspaper articles, and oral tradition. A visual medium as an information

5.1   Avonlea, Saskatchewan (Photo: Pauline Greenhill)

source is new, and the photographs serve as the fulcrum for the present chapter. However, I have been unable to locate any other accounts of this shivaree, and all the general discussions of the practice in the locale are memories from at least twenty and sometimes as long as seventy years ago. Paradoxically, then, though it is the most recent, this example has the least lively and elaborate verbal testimony. It may strike some as incongruous that of all the case studies, this most recent example is the thinnest on details of what actually took place at the shivaree. I couldn't find anyone who remembered being there. And the general recollections offered by folks from around Avonlea and nearby regions of rural Saskatchewan lack the immediacy and specifics of the court cases.

But this lack of detailed testimony is not, after all, so surprising. When the other three charivaris went astray, the authorities and the newspapers alike tried to find out as much as they could about what happened – to develop their cases and/or their stories. The court case and newspaper memories of the first three charivaris are from mere days or weeks after the event. For Les and Edna Babcock's unre-

5.2   Shivareers with dog (Saskatchewan Archives Board)

markable shivaree, I'm asking people to think back sixty-five years or more to an event that was entirely run-of-the-mill. The event, and its accounts, offer a striking contrast to the uproar and strife of the previous examples. The structure of this chapter (and the final one that follows) also differs from the last three. I place this shivaree in its local context, and then detail its similarities and divergences from the tradition, rather than focusing directly upon it.

Michael Taft once called the daily traditions of Saskatchewan people 'dull lore.'[6] Indeed, this case study lacks the excitement and drama of the previous three. There's no interpersonal conflict, no vio-

lence, not even the interruption of sex. It's a pretty tame affair in contrast with the previous three. And yet, the shivaree of Les and Edna
Babcock undoubtedly more closely resembles what would usually
happen, even at the earlier disapproval charivaris, than those that led
to court cases. A bunch of people drop by the newlyweds' house. The
couple greet them and treat them. Then the visitors go away. I would
hate to think, however, that this shivaree's relative lack of mayhem
makes it intrinsically uninteresting. That this event was a great deal
of fun for the participants is obvious from the photographs. And, like
the other three, it also shows a great deal about what life was like for
those people at that time.

In the first photograph in the series, Les and Edna, the honoured
couple, can just be seen peeking out of the house doorway (see figure 5.2). Over thirty shivareers, girls and boys, bang pots and pans
and hit a barrel and a pail with two-by-fours and sticks. A dog, perhaps brought by one of the shivareers or attracted by the noise,
watches the crowd. Most of the girls face the camera, posing in the
traditional smiling mode expected of them – note, for example, the
little girl standing at the right of the photograph with her hands
folded. Only one boy in this picture appears even to notice that a photograph is being taken. In all three shots, most of the boys are gathered to the right and most of the girls to the left.

In the second photograph, Les and Edna, the honoured couple,
have descended from the house and have joined the shivareers at
street level (see figure 5.3). Edna has her hand in a basket on which
she, Les, and several nearby children are focused. They appear to be
oblivious to the noise and mayhem going on in front of them. Are Les
and Edna treating the shivareers, or receiving a gift from them?
Almost all the girls look at the camera, including one in the fore-
ground with her fingers in her ears. Again, only one boy pays attention to the photographers.

In the last photograph, three girls seem to be posed with sticks
above their heads to beat a second barrel, which was obscured by cir-
cles of girls in the other two photographs (see figure 5.4). Les and
Edna converse with one boy. Another figure is visible in the doorway
of the house, watching the antics. A boy directly in front of Edna
appears engrossed with a small object in his hands – perhaps unwrap-
ping candy from the basket.

What do these photographs show about the shivaree and about life
at the time in Avonlea? In order to understand them as the complex
documents they are, it's necessary to look at the general social surround, the community in which the shivaree took place, the partici-

5.3   Shivareers with sticks and barrel (Saskatchewan Archives Board)

pants, and local shivaree practices. Each shivaree is a unique event, but also has qualities in common with others. The photographs give an opportunity for a case study of an event otherwise not likely to be documented, and for drawing on the memories of residents of Avonlea and of contemporary shivareers and shivaree recipients. In comparison with the three previous examples, however, the results may seem somewhat mundane; happy events make for less compelling reading, even though they are clearly more enjoyable for participants!

For those who support them, shivarees are about (re)creating and expressing community. It's a matter of pride for many Canadian rural

5.4   Shivareers with sticks (Saskatchewan Archives Board)

residents that they demonstrate qualities that differentiate them from city folks. For example, as former southeastern Saskatchewan resident Sandra Kochie commented, 'City people, when you talk to them, they look at you as if you've got two heads nine times out of ten. And in a little town you talk to everyone whether you really know them or not. If you say "hello" or "good morning" or something, a lot of times people [in Winnipeg] look at you as if you're really nuts' (PG2006, 2). Gertrude Bircher, who grew up in Craven but was married in Regina, commented that she and her husband had avoided being shivareed when they first married: 'Nobody in Regina did that, to my knowledge, at least in all my circle of family and friends and in-laws. It was more of a country thing, a rural thing … I have never heard of anybody in the city being shivareed. And probably [that would be] because of the noise factor … At a lot of these dos there is liquor served and/or brought and so nobody wants to fight the police's impromptu drop-ins' (PG2006, 35).

The nuisance, noise, and possible police interference are frequently offered as an alibi for the lack of urban shivarees. But I think that the reason goes deeper into social relations. Simultaneously friendly and a test of the recipients' qualities, the shivaree exemplifies a rural–urban distinction, positively drawn by the majority in most smaller communities. However, some locations seem to have tested their members less stringently than others. Further, some individuals managed to escape the more difficult aspects of the shivaree, as Les and Edna Babcock did. In this chapter, I will trace some of the contemporary and more recent shivarees' signal aspects and purposes, but I will also try to indicate how and why Les and Edna's shivaree was both exceptional and typical.

Avonlea

'The rural family forms the foundation of rural life. Agriculture provides the main material base of rural society; the family is its social base … The rural community in this predominantly agricultural province [Saskatchewan] is an institution close to the hearts of rural people. The rural community is a trading or service center, or a combination of these centers, together with the surrounding territory and people which they serve. Farm people identify themselves with the center or centers and thus a community is built. It is an association hard to define but, on an emotional and traditional level, very close to the people involved' (*Royal Commission on Agriculture and Rural Life* 1957, qtd in Smith 1992, 266).

If you draw a line between Regina and Moose Jaw, then form an equilateral triangle directly south, Avonlea (population 449) is at the bottom point. It's a very pretty village, with well-kept houses and parks, in an attractive setting. Unlike some other small prairie places, it is still a very much a going concern. The former railway station has been made into a museum. There's a community hall, a library, a municipal office, a branch of the Bank of Nova Scotia, an insurance office, a John Deere dealership, a Co-op store, and more. Avonlea is primarily a local hub, not a tourist town, though the brick factory in nearby Claybank has been turned into a museum.[7] To the west, the Cactus Hills are visible; just to the northeast is the ranch once owned by Les Babcock, a small section of badlands. To the south, beyond the Dirt Hills, the rolling prairie continues to the U.S. border. And it was in Avonlea that Ada Bovee, sister of Edna Bovee (Babcock) met photographer Dick Bird, and where Edna Bovee and Les Babcock were married.

European settlement began in the 1880s, when several ranchers operated in the vicinity. By the turn of the twentieth century, settlers from Ontario, the Maritimes, and the United States, as well as English and European immigrants, began moving into the area. The Bovee and Babcock families were among the earliest. The founding and naming of the town is narratively marked. Local historian Jean Kincaid notes a story 'about Lucy Maud Montgomery's relatives living in the area and that's why it was named Avonlea' (PG2006, 33).[8] The two daughters of C.T. Babcock and Bertha (Davis) Babcock (parents of Les Babcock) made no mention of this connection when they wrote, 'In 1911, when the railway came as far as Avonlea, we, with quite a few others, were all there to meet the train. Mrs Frost broke a bottle of wine over the engine and named the town Valley Forge, however it was later named Avonlea. As I remember it, one of the engineers said, "What a waste of good wine"' (Lundrigan and McRorie 1983, 256). Another, much more detailed version of the story recounts,

> It was mid-afternoon on August 24th, 1911, when the first Canadian Northern official train whistled long and loud and stopped at the end of the newly laid rails in Sunshine Valley … Two ladies approached the front of the engine; the older one tossed a bottle of champagne across its head. Her companion, a young lady, Margaret Muir, recently from Ayr, Scotland, threw a large bouquet of flowers toward the engineer. 'Why didn't you just give me the bottle, the iron horse doesn't need a drink,' he said. 'I wanted to call the village 'Valley Forge',' Mrs Frost replied. The late Thaddeus Babcock, accompanied by his wife and two children, Vera and Leslie, Mrs James Bovee, John Johnston and son Shirley, elated, stood close by forming a welcoming committee. 'This will be Avonlea,' the engineer said. (*Record of Activities* 1963, 9)

The engineer won over the locals in naming the village, but the locals have won most of the social, economic, and historical battles since; Avonlea has survived where other places have faded into the prairie. By 1963, local historians could report that the Village has a population of over four hundred people and has a large business section and expanding residential area, stretching several blocks on either side of Main Street, to the highway on the East and the C.N.R. on the West. The sports ground separated several homes in the Annex from the rest of the village. In the last few years, the old board walks have been replaced by miles of cement sidewalks, the muddy streets graveled and lighted by mercury vapor lights. There is now a sewage disposal system with a lagoon just outside of town, and in 1961, natural gas was piped to the Village. In the fall of 1962, a modern filtration plant was officially opened and most homes are now enjoying the convenience of running water, quite a contrast to the tank and pail delivery system of the past from the town well on the outskirts. (ibid., 8–9)

Cora Seghers, Les and Edna Babcock's daughter, left Avonlea for Regina when she graduated from high school in the late 1960s, but confirmed that 'there is a lot going on there and always has. You curled, you played hockey, whatever. And of course the park out there has been a huge, huge draw for people and getting even more so' (PG2006, 27). Berenice and Archie Sanderson remembered Avonlea when they were growing up in the 1940s:

> BERENICE: I would have said it was a really close community. There wasn't, I suppose, much to do. I can remember my parents … would play cards at somebody else's house, and we'd go and play with the ones that were our age that were at the same place … There were dances that everybody went to. We would come in [from the farm] with our parents and sit at the back of the hall and watch them dance …
> ARCHIE: … We lived about seven and a half miles from town, and … it wasn't until I was thirteen or fourteen that I came to town on a Saturday night with my brothers. My parents died when I was very young, but my brothers used to come to town on a Saturday night and I came with them. At one time there were movies at the town hall and, of course, if you had a spare nickel or a dime you could get in, and you'd get a bag of popcorn too. That took up an hour and a half or two hours of your evening. But I guess being on the farm there were a lot of young people of my age and I never got to town that often.
> BERENICE: You went to dances out in the schoolhouses on the weekends.

ARCHIE: Yes, and I took my grade 11 and 12 at the local high school here. (PG2006, 37)

For children, recreation might be paramount, but Jean Kincaid also recalls a livery stable, blacksmith, police barracks, a doctor, 'a pool room and a bowling alley. I remember we used to come in to bowl Saturday nights. I thought that was great. A couple of general stores and a hall and a couple of hardware stores. Café, hotel, Chinese restaurant ... a Masonic lodge, and there was an Orange lodge, a butcher shop, a garage, an implement dealer ... We had three churches in town: United, Anglican, and Free Methodists' (PG2006, 33). The Chinese restaurant 'was always a place to stay for salesmen and have meals and for us to go on Saturday night and sit and have pop and pie ... It was always a favourite spot to go because they'd treat you with a piece of candy or something. We figured that was great' (PG2006, 34).[9] Marian New says, 'It's just always been a good town. You know, there's never been too many big troubles or trials. Well, Main Street burned down about '38, I think ... It was all wiped out, the whole street' (PG2006, 31).

Mavis Leakey recollects,

I prefer small towns. I have been in many cities and there wasn't one I would have preferred. I'd like to stay here. It's easier to raise kids in a small town. You know where they are, or can find out if you really want to ... It was very friendly. I remember in the evenings, we always played out under some streetlight, someplace or other, lots of games that kids now don't even know. We entertained ourselves with less. We played kick the can and all sorts of games like that. Where my mother and dad finally moved the house into town and redid it there, it was a good place, on Main Street, with a good streetlight, and that was where we congregated. And I had a town full of relatives, which made it very nice to live in. We had aunts, uncles, cousins; I mean, there was a bunch of us. I really feel bad to see small towns dying out. I hope some of them remain because there are lots of good points about them. In this day and age you're not even an hour from other facilities that we might be lacking.

I've been on council for eighteen years. I'm quitting this year. But we've had a few new businesses, which has been great. I was just reading today, Yorkton or someplace got two canola plants, and I thought, 'Ooh, I wish one of them had come here.' But we have an excellent manor [retirement home] here. It's progressive.

You either go ahead in small towns or you die, is my opinion. How long it will last nobody can predict. But so far we are doing all right. Right now we need a new water plant. It's in the works, but they're getting so many new regulations about the dumps and lagoons and water plants. And I can't say they're bad, all I say is they're very expensive, and it's pretty difficult for small towns ... They do give some grants, but really, compared to what they cost, not enough. But anyhow, we are working on a water plant ... We don't have a choice. They come up with new regulations and then we've got to meet them.

And this year, I just read in the paper the other day, we got twenty-eight new students. If somebody moves to town the first thing you always say is, 'Have you got any kids for the school?' Because I suppose the day could come when our school might close ... Right now it is in pretty good shape because we have taken in a few communities around us, as far as students are concerned ... They can't afford a school in every small town in Saskatchewan any more than they can afford all the hospitals that used to be around here ... I'm a nurse, and it's just financially impossible to maintain them with the facilities they need. And I always tell everybody, they worry about moving to the manor here because there's no doctor in town, and I say, 'I can't remember anybody who's ever died on the way to Regina.' Sometimes you can get somebody into the hospital just as fast from here as some of the outside points in Regina ... Our highway was probably one of the best things that ever happened to us. I mean, it may not be the best, but it was a tremendous thing for the community. (PG2006, 38)

The year 1940 was pivotal, and not just for Les and Edna Babcock. For people in Avonlea, after developing their town and surviving the Depression and drought of the 1930s with its unemployment, decreased incomes, farm debt, and resulting economic and social catastrophe (see Whitcomb 2005, 39–45), the Second World War brought labour shortages. 'Saskatchewan was not saved from Depression by its own government or by the federal government but by the outbreak of World War II in Europe ... Canada itself was not particularly threatened, and at first Canadians volunteered mainly to escape the depression' (ibid., 44). At the same time, 'The war produced a massive demand for Saskatchewan's foodstuffs. Increased demand, the return of normal weather, higher yields, and good prices brought prosperity for the first time since the 1920s' (ibid.). Just a

5.5   Five roads into Avonlea (Photo: Pauline Greenhill)

year after Canada's declaration of war on 10 September 1939, Les and Edna's wedding on 13 September 1940 would have brought welcome relief from the turmoil of the period.[10] That most of the shivaree participants were young – we return in this event to the average age range of the Wetherill charivari, or even younger – probably reflects the town's historic demographic. A wartime marriage would have brought mixed feelings for people in Avonlea. While they might have been happy personally for Les and Edna, a wedding would also be a reminder of husbands and sons serving overseas.

The Individuals

Les Babcock was born 13 March 1900 in Iowa. His niece recalls, 'They called him Leslie Maine Babcock 'cause he was born the day the boat *Maine* sank. They were from the States originally' (Marian New, PG2006, 31).[11] His parents, Charles Thaddeus Babcock and Bertha May Davis, received a homestead patent in the area in 1910. Americans were favoured immigrants at the time: 'The federal government concentrated much of its efforts on Americans because many were of British origin, were English-speaking and democratic, knew how to farm in North America, and had money, machinery and connections to other people who might immigrate ... Americans assimilated almost immediately into the new Canadian environment ... Their influence, however, was profound. That is partly because they reinforced the Anglo-Canadian minority and made its culture dominant' (Whitcomb 2005, 22).

Les Babcock was telephone lineman from 1927 to 1954 (*Record of Activities* 1963, 26), and almost everyone I spoke to in Avonlea remembered him as 'the rural telephone man.'[12] As such, 'if there were lightning strikes, or hail, or wind to blow a pole down or blow the wires down, and if there was trouble on the line or somebody's phone didn't work or came out a loose wire, that's when Les would be called upon to try and fix it ... He had a little shop at the back of their house' (Archie Sanderson, PG2006, 37). Archie Sanderson remembered that 'Les was a tinkerer ... and he was always doing something. After he was married he had a small tractor and a weed sprayer tank and he would contract to spray your field for weeds or one thing or another. And that kept him fairly busy for a lot of his hours in the summertime [and] springtime' (ibid.).

Les's ranch was a family and community gathering place. Jean Kincaid recalls, 'There was a hut there, with a cabin, and the picnic grounds. We used to go out and picnic there quite often after school and weekends' (PG2006, 33). Mavis Leakey commented, 'My uncle was a real naturalist as far as being interested in birds and animals and that type of thing. And he used to go out and live out on his quarter in the summer quite often ... when he had cattle' (PG2006, 38). Dorothy Dunn adds, 'And one of his stories that I remember him telling was this land that he had out there, that's where Jesse James came to. He figured that's where the James brothers hid out. But I'm not sure that wasn't just a story' (PG2006, 39).

One man I met in Avonlea remembers as a child being fascinated with Les's truck and with the tools and implements it held. He recalls Les as being indulgent with the local children, letting them explore the truck's contents while keeping a watchful eye on them. Mavis Leakey also remembers Les's kindness: 'He used to take some of the young boys in town, when he went out on lines, sometimes he would take them if they wanted to go for a ride' (PG2006, 38). Dorothy Dunn concurs: 'Oh, he was the greatest guy with kids ... They followed him like the Pied Piper of Hamelin. And he would play games with them, he'd be walking down the street, and the kids used to play cowboys and Indians, and he'd pause, with his finger up, and "Bang,

I got you!" … And he'd take them on hikes out at the badlands where he had property … He was so kind and … so tolerant of children, I can always remember that' (PG2006, 39).

Les Babcock died in 1960.

Les Babcock married Edna Bovee (born in New Warren, Saskatchewan, on 13 September 1909) on 13 September 1940. They operated the telephone office together. Ada (Bovee) Bird describes Edna's family: 'Our first home was on a homestead SE of Avonlea … In the early 20s we again moved to town … During the years that Aunt Ada had the "Nelson House" [a rooming and boarding house], mother and Edna helped with the cooking and cleaning … There were … over 100 [boarders] with Mother and Edna until the late 60s' (Bird 1983, 272–3).

Archie Sanderson remembered her because 'Edna was my first cousin, so I knew her quite well, all right. She was a quiet person … And actually, I believe that she and Les lived with Aunt Gertie most of their married life. I can remember going over there and she would have cookies made up, and so she was a good cook … But between she and Aunt Gertie, they bandaged a few of my knees too. 'Cause we were on the farm, out two miles north, and so when we came in [to Avonlea] we usually ended up being over at Aunt Gertie's and Edna's' (PG2006, 37).

Dorothy Dunn remembers 'Edna was a little bit shy' (PG2006, 39). Their daughter Cora was born in 1951 (Lundrigan and McRorie 1983, 257). Edna died in 1980.

Dick Bird, the photographer of the shivaree, was born 16 August 1892, in Leamington Spa, Warwickshire, England. He saw his first cinema in 1905, 'an episode in the recent Boer War shown in the Royal Assembly Hall in Leamington,' and 'developed a keen interest in the Cinema at the age of 14 while on family's summer holiday in London watching one of England's first cinematographers engaged in photographing the Sunday afternoon boaters on the Serpentine' (Bird n.d., 1). His family emigrated to the United States in 1907, and his interest in still and cinema photography developed. He worked as an independent film producer from 1910 to the 1960s. In 1919 he 'organized and was elected first President of the Canadian Press Photographers Association [and] organized and became the first President of Local 636 Cinematographers and Motion Picture Craftsmen, I.A.T.S.E.' (Bird n.d., 3).

He moved to Saskatchewan in 1921 and opened the photographic shop Bird Films Ltd in 1928 (Inventory 1992, i).[13] He produced the first known dramatic films in Saskatchewan, the silents *The Seal of*

Prevention (1930) and *This Generation: A Prairie Romance* (1934)
(*What's On* [2002]). He also worked for the National Film Board and
did contract filming for Walt Disney productions (Horne 1997). His
1930s film of 'Fort San,' the provincial tuberculosis sanatorium, is
credited with showing its 'sinister and disconcerting side' (Ring
2002, n.p.). He documented various historical events but 'by the
1930s, Bird had become serious about nature photography' (ibid.).[14]

His first wife died in 1937. He met Ada Bovee of Avonlea when he
was invited to talk to her CGIT group, and they married in 1946.
'Dick and Ada became a successful team, traveling through Canada
and the world producing nature films and conducting lecture tours'
(Inventory 1992, i–ii): 'Throughout his life, Dick Bird received many
honours. He was an Associate of the Royal Photographic Society and
a Fellow of the Zoological Society of London. In 1950 he was the
second Canadian ... to become a Fellow of the Photographic Society
of America. In that year he was also made the first Life Member of
the Saskatchewan Natural History Society. In 1976 Bird received an
honorary Doctorate of Law from the University of Regina' (ibid., ii).

Dick Bird died on 27 September 1986.

Ada Bird – Les's link to Avonlea – was Edna's younger sister, born
in Avonlea in 1917. 'My first recollection of home was the house on
the farm, two miles north of town, with dad doing carpentry work and
barn raising ... Ada attended business college in Regina and was
active in the Sunday School, Mission Band, Young People's groups
and choirs. She was CGIT leader ... when Dick Bird came out to
Avonlea to take the group out to Les's ranch for a nature study. Ada
later went to Regina to work for Bird Films to assist in photographing birds, animals and flowers ... [and retired] after working for Muir
Barber Ltd Hardware at Regina Beach for 13 years' (Bird 1983,
272–3).

Jean Kincaid recalls, 'She went out with him to help him with ...
taking pictures and lots of other things. And a lot, too, were taken out
at Les's ranch because there were different types of birds and flowers
there in the badlands and the Twin Sisters – just a couple of mounds
– just behind Les's ranch ... This was always home and she always
came back. But she was really devoted to Dick and that was her life
job, really, helping him with his filming and running these projectors
at these different schools for lectures. She had a lot to do with his collection of stories' (PG2006, 33).

Marian New also recalls Ada and Dick's meeting: 'He came out
one time [when] I was in CGIT ... to talk about nature and so on to
all the CGIT girls and that's where Ada met him. It wasn't too long

after that she moved in to be his housekeeper. And then when his two girls were grown they were married. And she worked pretty hard because she carried all his big photo equipment and everything, 'cause he was a good age when she married him' (PG2006, 31).

Mavis Leakey says, 'Dick and Ada Bird [would] come out quite often. I remember he used to show slides of their travels at the hall, which were very interesting. We had movies at the hall at one time, but not very often, and so it was a real crowd pleaser' (PG2006, 38). Dorothy Dunn commented, 'Ada had a marvellous singing voice. She had no training but she had a powerful singing voice and she sang right up until her death. She was in the senior choir in Regina and always friendly' (PG2006, 17).

Ada Bird was tragically killed at the age of eighty-five when hit by a car on a pedestrian crosswalk in Regina. Mavis Leakey commented, 'She was very young for her age, very active. Sad really, because there were lots of people her age who would have been sitting in a chair all day doing nothing. And she was far from that' (PG2006, 38).

Shivarees around Southeastern Saskatchewan, ca. 1940

Bertha Farr, who lived in Weyburn, was an outsider to the area when she attended a shivaree, and said, 'At the time I participated, it seemed to me if was only a chance to have a bit of innocent fun with a couple we knew and liked' (Q104 2005). The community ethos surrounding shivarees in southeastern Saskatchewan constructs them as the quintessence of cooperation and sociability, offering a stark contrast to urban life today, as Sandra Kochie again argues:

> We have so many things now. We have TV, we have everything. Nobody really cares about the other guy, or gets together with the other guys, or even knows the neighbours, half the time. But on the farm, the neighbours were like family. If you got sick they'd come put your crop in, and that kind of thing. Everybody knew each other very well. My father and mother even have gone to people's house and they weren't home, and they just went and crawled into their bed, and they waited for them to come home … Nowadays they would frown upon it, they'd think you were kind of nuts. Well, you wouldn't get in the house, it would be locked anyway. Nothing was locked in those years … and if you wanted to go to somebody's house you just went, you didn't have to wait to be invited. Now it's all on invitation only sort of thing. (PG2006, 1)

By far the most common explanation given for holding a shivaree is that it is a 'welcome' to the bride and/or groom. While welcoming might not be the most immediate understanding that a non-participant might have of this kind of activity, locals saw it as 'neighbours getting to know the bride ... So that way everybody got to know the young couple and they got to know their neighbours. And that was important. If you needed help or anything, you needed to know who you could count on ... How else were they ever going to get to know all the neighbours in one fell swoop? And this way they'd have some fun with them, and tell a few jokes, and have a few drinks with them, and have lunch with them ... and after a night of that, you'd know everybody. You'd know who you'd want to really be around, and who you wouldn't want to be around' (ibid.).

From Vantage/Congress, southwest of Moose Jaw, Patricia Thompson remembers her own shivaree pertaining to her outsider status; 'I had lived on the west side of No 2 highway and my new home was "over East." So those neighbours were anxious to know me.' The shivaree was held 'usually after they returned from their honeymoon,' though Thompson remembers tricks happening outside only, along with 'a lot of teasing to the new bride and groom.' The shivareers in this area expected food and drink: 'At our shivaree my mother-in-law made lots of sandwiches (home-made bread and good Ontario cheese) and ladies brought cakes and helped her with coffee' (Q610 2005).

She told a story about a woman who refused to be shivareed:

[My brother-in-law] married a lovely lady (schoolteacher) late December, so in January, my husband and friends decided there must be a shivaree. But the bride had never heard of such a thing, and refused to let anyone in the house despite someone tampering with the chimney. So my husband tried to get in through a bedroom window but the bride saw him and shouted, 'You get to Hell out of here, Doug Thompson,' so he got out, taking the curtains with him! By then the people decided to give up so they went down to the Chinese café and my husband bought pop and coffee, and the ladies brought in their cakes. And they had their party. My poor brother in law was so embarrassed, he said he could never go to another shivaree.

In answer to the query about why shivarees stopped, Thompson replied, 'My 96 year old neighbour who well remembers this, had the answer. People don't get married anymore' (ibid.).[15]

Carolyn Palgrave from near Rouleau remembers her own shivaree in 1971. 'In our case, it was meant to welcome us to our country neighbourhood.' Sociability differed in this location. Rather than the honoured couple providing, the shivareers 'brought all the food/drink and cleaned up before they left.' However, again, the timing was late night: 'They arrived at about 2 a.m. and clanged pots and pans to make loud noise. It was a party mood. Our neighbours stayed about 2 hours – from 2 a.m. until 4 a.m.' There was some minor trickery: 'Some of the women short-sheeted our bed' (Q78 2005).

George Taylor of Bengough said the shivaree was 'to welcome newlyweds into married life,' and the participants were 'friends, neighbours, and relatives from age six to sixty.' Socializing involved 'mostly teasing the groom about incidents in his life concerning his past, present and future.' He also described how 'on one occasion my dad set the horse fiddle[16] against the door and the door flew open. The noise terrorized the house cat who immediately vacated the premises, jumped over Dad's back, and ran to the safety of the barn – screaming all the way. Everyone stopped what they were doing to watch the runaway cat and then went inside to celebrate' (Q794 2005).

Velma Mills from Ogema said she and her husband were shivareed because 'we did not have a wedding dance … I was a new bride to the district, my husband was born on a ranch in the district so he knew everyone and I'm not, so became acquainted with some of the neighbours. I was made welcome, felt part of the community. I have lived almost 50 years in the same area and know everyone.' During her shivaree, the visitors set her alarm clock under the bed and moved furniture. She said, 'The people who came to charivari usually [brought] sandwiches, cakes, cookies, coffee and sometimes some alcoholic drinks, depending on the people who were being charivaried … There was not that many. Most married couples had [a] wedding dance' (Q798 2005).

Participants used different ruses to gain entrance to the house. Apparently, sudden loud noisemaking wasn't used in Disley, as Carl Richter recalled: 'One couple would knock on the door, pretend to be out of gas, then all would walk in.' He also remembered actual music at local shivarees – he played the accordion (Q587 2005).

The late night shivaree was intended to interrupt the newlyweds' sex; it was presumed that newlyweds would be having intercourse on their first night home from the wedding or honeymoon, or within the first few months of their marriage. Though rarely directly disclosed by those who responded to my questionnaire or agreed to be interviewed, this purpose is often alluded to. For example, Sandra Kochie's parents' and grandparents' stories from Tisdale, Yellow Grass, Milestone, and Eldersley noted the shivaree as 'getting newly married people welcomed into the community' but also 'to disturb the couple's wedded bliss ... They brought music, danced, etc., and basically kept the young people up and out of bed. Ha ha' (Q770 2005). When interviewed, she commented that the shivareers would 'make as much racket as they could just to get them out of bed if they were having a peaceful sleep or whatever they were doing.' Success at interrupting coitus wasn't always obvious, but Otto Ulrich remembers a specific shivaree:

> In Moose Jaw, shortly after WWII about 12 people got together to have a shivaree for a couple who had a very small wedding. In this case we told the groom only, but didn't tell him we were having a shivaree with a little surprise, and would later on in the evening all go to a show. We told him (groom) to tell his wife that he was taking her to a show, and while she was getting dressed upstairs, to signal us with drawing the blind in the front room and letting it up again at which time we all went into the house after taking off all our shoes at the front door and going inside without any noise. While we were waiting for her to get dressed there was this sweet voice from upstairs. 'Honey, do you think we have time for a quickie before the show?' What an embarrassment for her when she came downstairs and saw us all there. She eventually got over that. (Q799 2005)

Given these distinctly adult purposes, it's not surprising that most shivarees involved adults, usually the honoured couple's peer group. There were exceptions, though, as Thompson indicated: 'The last [shivaree] I remember was in the war years. This young man was a neighbour; [he] served [in the armed forces] and came home on leave and he brought a Dutch war bride. So, of course we had to have a big shivaree. They lived just about a mile from us up on top the hill, and I remember this man with the bagpipes. He was still going strong so he cleaned up his bagpipes, and I remember him marching up and down the knoll to their place and he had about four or five little boys, [including] my youngest son, who loved the bagpipes' (PG2006, 29).[17]

But Daisy from Cardross in south-central Saskatchewan remembers no tricks and cited the shivareers as folks of 'all ages but not usually children under twelve years of age.' Daisy also described the shivaree as being held 'usually about three weeks after wedding.' From Craven, Gertrude Bircher recalled, 'It was just married couples who would shivaree the new neighbours in the district – a new bride or a new bridegroom ... I don't recall hearing of anybody taking babies or little kids to a shivaree' (PG2006, 35).

Individuals' reactions to their shivaree helped to determine how they would be seen by the community – as good sports or otherwise. More than only an offer of help or a welcome, it would also be a barometer for gauging the couple. A negative response to shivaree tricks would not generally halt the pranking: 'It would just make it worse ... so they better just get over it' (Kochie, PG2006, 2). In extreme cases, almost always involving actions taken outside the house, the tricksters would return for reparation: 'One time we took all the wheels off a guy's car and hung all the tires off his car on the trees and left the truck up on the bales. But that was sort of a bad joke because we had to go back and put it all back together again ... We tried to do things that we don't have to rectify' (ibid.).

Gertrude Bircher commented,

> To me, it's your outlook on life if you consider it lucky or unlucky to be shivareed ... We thought it was a blast to shivaree people, so you bloody well better be willing to take it. That's the way we looked at it. But I think it's the way we were raised, too ... One person phoned her mother the next day crying they put cornflakes in her bed – the most normal boring thing ... I mean it's clean. You wouldn't even have to wash your sheet. All you have to do is shake it out and put it back on the bed ... Her mother told everybody she had phoned. She had been a whiney kid, and she always was a whiner. Her mother told her to grow up ... Everybody thought it was funny that she had phoned her mother crying, and it was funnier that her mother had told her to grow up. (PG2006, 35)

In this part of Canada, the tradition of the *quête* was referenced. Pat Thompson recollects, 'Nobody brought a gift to ours, I don't think ... We often had popcorn and I made lots of candy, but if it's a surprise you are not stocked up with these things' (PG2006, 29). Similarly, one of Thompson's neighbours recalled that directly after weddings 'the kids ran behind with cans and making a noise and then they all went to Western and the husband had to buy the men cigars and the children candy.' William P. Dumur from Kisbey in southeastern Saskatchewan remembers, 'We were all given a 5 cent coin. At one chivaree we were invited in for treats (cookies, etc.)'

(Q583 2005). Evidently, then, treating children at shivarees was known in the area.

Yet the treating at these events went further. Part of the shivaree's purpose was to embarrass the bride in particular, including trying to ensure that she fell down on her gendered duty to always have nearly unlimited amounts and varieties of food available at all times of the day or night for any eventuality. While such an expectation might be patently unreasonable, not to mention potentially expensive and wasteful (and thus contrary to the notion that good farm women would be thrifty and careful consumers), it was common. Gertrude Bircher noted, 'They'd try and catch the bride with no bread in the house. Everybody baked their own bread. But the ultimate disgrace was if you didn't have any cake to feed them. If you didn't have any bread in the house to make sandwiches for them, that was oooohhh! the talk of the district ... Not that they'd want to be fed, it was just that they'd act like they were starving to embarrass you' (PG2006, 35).

Combining with the expectation of a treat in the form of lunch from the bride would be tricks, like the aforementioned cereal in the bed, that involved wasting food – otherwise anathema. For example, Bircher recalls, 'They sprinkled rice in drawers ... Just messy, slow clean-up but not dirty or sticky stuff' (ibid.). Sometimes, indeed, the couple would be able to predict the trickery and circumvent it, or they would be well prepared for the feast. Occasionally, the shivareers could turn the tables on their tormenters. Bircher, who was shivareed in 1976 after her twenty-fifth wedding anniversary, found her bed full of crab apples: 'We just picked up the sheet and dumped them into a tub and threw the sheet in the laundry room and put clean linen on the bed and fell into bed. A day or two later, I washed the crab apples and made crab apple jelly. I canned them all ... Gave the person a jar of crab apple jelly because we knew whose farm the crab apples came from, because they were at the shivaree too ... I told them, "They were damn good crab apples [laughs]. Thanks for bringing them so that I didn't have to go out and pick my own"' (PG2006, 35).

Yet Bircher's shivaree experience was by no means an unmixed pleasure: 'The first ones to leave were sneaking around ... One of them took our car keys off the key board in the back entry, went out and opened up the garage door ... They lifted the trunk lid of the Chrysler up and they filled the box, the cab, and the interior of the half ton truck ... All around the steps was piles of hay and ... our back porch was plunked full of bales' (ibid.). I asked how long it took to clean up, and Bircher answered,

Oh, it didn't take long at all. I suppose with the three of us working, basically my husband and I and my son who was a strong kid, I guess half a day. Whatever. Doesn't seem too long ... The other irritant was because it was harvest time, and my husband and another fellow worked together ... I was on holidays from my job in the city and I had cooked a meat and potatoes meal for dinner and another one for supper, made pies and everything. And so I thought, 'I've got leftover chicken and I've got leftover roast beef and I've got two pies still, I won't have to cook tomorrow.' [But the shivareers] passed around, 'Who wants apple pie, who wants this?' I could have killed them. I thought, 'Oh God, I'm not going to have anything left for tomorrow.' And, well, I did! That was a good gotcha. They couldn't quite finish all the meat and they couldn't quite finish all the pie. (ibid.)

Avonlea Shivarees

In the Avonlea area at the time, 'I wouldn't say everybody got a shivaree, but I would say 75–80 per cent would ... all right!' (Archie Sanderson, PG2006, 37). Shivarees are explained in Avonlea, as elsewhere, in terms of welcome:

> ARCHIE: It was just a fun thing in a sense ... Mostly just a welcoming party, welcoming and congratulating them, and welcoming them to the community and meeting their neighbours. I don't know if there was any real purpose in it other than to say, 'Well, you're married and we're glad you're here.'
>
> BERENICE: It was probably a night out for a lot of them [*laughter*]. They didn't have that much to do otherwise. (PG2006, 37)

Archie Sanderson remembers,

> The word got around that we were going to shivaree so-and-so, and we'd all meet at eight or nine o'clock, and not make any noise, drive up and leave the cars back in the lane someplace and walk up to the residence. Of course, we had pots and pans to bang on, or one thing or another. And then we would bring food – tea or coffee, plus maybe some sandwiches. It wouldn't be a long deal ... [But] it was quite a surprise to the couple that all of a sudden there was all of this noise outside and they wondered what was going on. Most rural homes, in fact even in town here, were very seldom locked ... But I guess for privacy's sake, we just stayed outside

until the young couple got up, they had [*ahem*] time to be dressed and kind of presentable. Maybe twenty-five to thirty people would usually be the count at a shivaree. And of course you didn't advertise it on the telephone because it was rural lines and it wasn't a separate line to each home ... and of course always some people listened to every phone call. (ibid.)

Jean Kincaid recollects only mild shivareeing practices: 'It was all just bring some tricks and some eats and have a party ... Some of them were bound to sneak away and put cornflakes in their bed or fold the sheets up so they couldn't get in, or things like that' (PG2006, 33). The Sandersons recalled no destructive trickery:

> ARCHIE: Sometime later on somebody'd sneak around and put something in their bed ... rolled oats or the cereal of the day.
> BERENICE: I think they also tied the sheets all up and pillowslips and everything.
> ARCHIE: Somebody would distract the young couple, and somebody would sneak around. They wouldn't do any damage of any kind, but just little tricks ...
> BERENICE: I think rice was one thing that was so hard, when they put it in the sheets, to get out again. For the next couple of nights, they'd be lying on a little piece of rice, which would feel like a rock.
> ARCHIE: I don't know if there'd be much else. I think the young couples expected a shivaree, but of course they would never know when it was coming.
> BERENICE: But it was just food they took? They wouldn't take, say, tea towels or something like you do for a shower as well?
> ARCHIE: They might, yes. Maybe a little gift of some kind.
> BERENICE: 'Cause it would be too bad to cause all that trouble and not give them something, a wedding gift of some kind. (PG2006, 37)

Clearly the ethos in Avonlea, as described by this couple, is somewhat less confrontational to newlyweds than in many other locations. Indeed, sometimes the newlyweds received a warning so they could prepare. Archie Sanderson noted, 'It was kept as much a secret as possible. But I think on a few occasions somebody maybe in the conversation blurted out something about a shivaree ... or else somebody purposely maybe made a comment to them that they might get a surprise party' (ibid.).

Marian New's warning attempt, however, was unsuccessful: 'It was my friend who lives on the next street over. And I knew they were planning this shivaree and the girl who was talking about it thought it would be just great to put dead fish under their pillows in their bed and a little chaff in and around. They lived in a trailer out on the farm at that time. So I phoned my friend and I said, "Now this is what they are planning. Lock your trailer and go to your brother-in-law's house." Well, they didn't and I thought, "How dumb could you get that you would let them do that?" I think all they did really was the chaff in the bed, which was enough. I don't think they put the fish in. I didn't go to it ... I don't go for that' (PG2006–31)

The pranking shivaree was clearly part of Avonlea's tradition, as shown by the experience of Dorothy Dunn, who married about two years before Les and Edna:

> My husband and I were married on December the thirteenth, and it was snowy and cold and miserable, and there were snow banks in the yard. I don't know if we were getting ready for bed, but I remember that I heard some noises, like banging on pots and pans. I had not been to a shivaree. I had lived away from home, and I'd only been home a couple of years when I got married. So anyhow, I'm not wanting to be involved in some shenanigans that was going on. I had no idea what it was. And one man climbed through our window, and I was scared to death ... And they came banging on the doors but he also climbed through the window, hoping that we would be in bed. Well, we weren't. And that's what they liked to do, catch you in bed. And kidnap the husband, or something. The men did that. And ... they would bring canned goods and home-cooked food or chickens. They brought gifts, but nobody had any money ... It was winter, but you got things that they had stored away, like potatoes and carrots. And sometimes they would bring chokecherry wine because they had made that in the fall ... I remember my sister – I don't know if she came or if it was just her husband – I know she sent divinity fudge because she made that so well. So, that was what I remember about my own.
>
> But there are many stories about shivarees. One that I remember hearing was of a couple much older than I am. They lived on the farm south of here, and they had a little house ... And there were homemade stairs that went up to this other level which was the bedroom. [And the shivareers] all came into this house, and there was so many that the beam holding up that upper level broke, and

a lot of people fell. I don't remember if anybody was hurt. And in those days you didn't sue anybody for anything like that. (PG2006, 39)

Overall, standard Avonlea shivarees happened at night, mainly involved the honoured couple's peer group, and could include tricks. With a daytime, young peoples', prank-free event, the only common points that Les and Edna's shivaree seem to have are the noisemaking and treat.

Les and Edna's Shivaree

What, then, were the reasons for this anomalous shivaree? Les and Edna both belonged to founding families of Avonlea, and both were upstanding members of the community. Jean Kincaid described Les and Edna as 'really down-to-earth people ... They were both really well liked. And Les ... kept the kids really occupied with his stories' (PG2006, 33). However, they were also considered to have taken their time about marrying and reproducing. As with almost all personal relationships in small towns, Les and Edna's courtship and marriage clearly took place under considerable community scrutiny. Marian New commented, 'Les and Edna went together for eighteen years before they got married and then they were married thirteen years before they had Cora ... Times were hard and Les was nervous about money ... He lived at home with his folks till he got married ... Everybody was pleased that they were getting married' (PG2006, 31).[18] Jean Kincaid noted, 'They had gone together for quite a while' (PG2006, 33). Dorothy Dunn said, 'They weren't young teenagers or anything ... [Les] was different than a lot of guys. He was an older bachelor ... And I don't know how old Edna would be when she got married ... I don't know anything about the romance, I don't know what happened, how long they went together, but it was years' (PG2006, 39, 40).

Les and Edna were married at the United Church in Avonlea. Their daughter Cora Seghers commented, 'They were married on the thirteenth of September, they had thirteen guests at the wedding, there were thirteen leaves on the wedding cake, my dad's birthday was March the thirteenth and my mother's was September thirteenth. And they had thirteen gifts at the wedding. So thirteen isn't unlucky, at least for them' (PG2006, 27). Edna Babcock kept full lists of every shower (she had three) and wedding gift received and the names of the givers, along with all the cards (including the gift cards). The goods they received included housewares: 'covered casserole and custard cups – Pyrex – a set of four goblets, double boiler, tablecloth and cream and sugar bowl, towels, tea cloths, fancy cups and saucers,' and food: 'one dressed chicken, a jar of marmalade, milk, eggs, tomatoes, cinnamon buns, cookies, citron, pumpkin, vegetable marrow, tomatoes, muskmelons, potatoes, one dressed turkey and vegetables' (ibid). Given Edna's archival details here, the lack of a note about a shivaree gift suggests none was offered. Mavis Leakey commented, 'I would be inclined to think that they were handing something out' (PG2006, 38), and the evidence supports her conclusion.

The shivaree took place in front of Edna's mother's house, where the newlyweds lived after they married.[19] Cora Seghers, recalling family stories about her parents' shivaree, characterized it as 'quite calm' (PG2006, 27). Les Babcock isn't described as the kind of person who would put up with pranking at his shivaree. Cora Seghers remembers hearing that her 'father threatened to do somebody serious harm if they bothered to go too hard on them. And he wasn't a violent man, but they just knew that if my dad said, "Get away from me, leave me alone," you did that!' (PG2006, 27).

Though by no means unknown across Canada, daytime shivarees were far less common than those at night.[20] Les and Edna's daytime event may be a function of the young ages of the participants; most pre-teens would be in bed by the time more conventional shivarees started. Mavis Leakey speculated, 'I know [Les] led a boys' group ... So that might account for the young people being there ... The one I was at ... I don't remember any other kids there at all ... It was people more the age of the couple involved that went to them' (PG2006, 38). Archie Sanderson noted that 'the young people would be left back at home to babysit any of the younger ones. The [shivarees] I remember were more of an adult crowd' (PG2006, 37). And yet those shivareeing Les and Edna Babcock are clearly their juniors. The Babcock shivaree was apparently on their actual wedding day; they were wearing the same clothes as in their wedding photographs. A wedding day shivaree would also be unusual. Marian New saw the event as so atypical that she judged, 'I don't think this would be a real shivaree' (PG2006, 31).

Apparently, then, Les and Edna Babcock's shivaree was aberrant for their area, held during the daytime on the actual wedding day, involving no trickery, and apparently organized and conducted by children and teenagers. The context of war, and the absence of younger married couples (with many young men serving in the armed forces), would have made a conventional shivaree difficult, if not impossible. But clearly, even in wartime, some folks in Avonlea saw the need for a special event to mark Les and Edna's wedding.[21] They were popular as individuals, and as a couple. Their marriage was apparently long expected and warmly welcomed. Their young friends, not invited to the small ceremony, probably wanted to celebrate with them nevertheless. The children and youth probably disclosed their plans to Edna's sister Ada Bovee, who had been involved with their CGIT group, and recognized the opportunity for · Dick Bird to document a prairie practice. As she was in the wedding party, it would not have been unusual for her friend and employer to be there, and he would be expected to bring a camera. The three photographs that show Les and Edna's shivaree, then, offer a view of an event that was both common and uncommon, both traditional and anomalous.

The Rural Idyll

Rural communities are by no means the utopias that insiders sometimes paint. Though Les and Edna's shivaree was probably entirely enjoyable for all involved, the tradition itself – even as practised in Avonlea – was not always so. Yet clearly those who stay in such places do so at least in part because they find them preferable to the alternative. But that does not mean that they remain untouched by change. In 1957, Saskatchewan's Royal Commission on Agriculture and Rural Life reported,

> The size of the average farm family has decreased. People are marrying at younger ages than in the past. Greater mobility of farm families, movement of farm families to urban centers, and increased opportunities for recreation and community work outside the home, have encouraged individual rather than family activities ... The clear-cut division of labour responsibilities along age and sex lines is disappearing. The father's dominant role as decision-maker is changing, though he is still looked upon as 'the income earner.' The farm family of the present does not provide help or personal care for older relatives to the same extent as the family of an earlier day. There is still a strong desire to have children continue in farming as a career, and an intention to help children become established in farming, but these aspirations are more apparent among families with better-than-average incomes. (Smith 1992, 266)

As the final chapter will detail, with the above-described extensive changes in the ethos of rural communities, charivari has become a tradition that relates to encouraging and supporting those who stay in the local area and in farming – those who will be producing children to continue the community. However, in areas where rural depopulation is too extensive, the tradition is waning to some extent, though it is maintained in others. In English-speaking New Brunswick, for example, the tradition of charivari continues. But in another twist of its purpose, as for Gertrude Bircher's, it can be used for housewarmings and milestone anniversary celebrations as well as for marriage celebrations. The flexibility of this tradition, then, remains.

6

'Great Fun' / 'A Nuisance':
Seeking Recent Shivaree Discourses

When I first embarked upon a proposal to conduct research on chari-varis[1] in English Canada, I never expected to find anything like the amount and variety of material I did, but at times the data seemed to be throwing themselves at me. One of the external reviewers of my application for funding from the Social Sciences and Humanities Research Council of Canada, however, was even more sceptical than I about my chances for success in this endeavour. She or he was certain that my queries to local newspapers for information on current, recent, and remembered practices would be entirely fruitless. But instead of a paucity of information, I have been grappling with a flood of responses from across the country since I first began field and archival research in 2004. With interviews and questionnaires from nearly a thousand individuals, I have material to keep me writing for years.

I hadn't expected at the outset to find such good historical case studies, either. When I applied for the grant, I had already located the *Varner v. Morton et al* Nova Scotia appeal case from 1919 (the subject of chapter 4), and had begun analysis of the reported and published text. But to find three more examples with excellent data, so nicely ranging in time and moving well across the country, was beyond any hope I had ever dared to entertain. I have often said that this work has been blessed by the best research karma of my entire academic career. Thus, I can't credit anything but luck and coincidence for my finding Sackville, New Brunswick, genealogist and local historian Lloyd Varner, who was so indispensable to my understanding of the Nova Scotia case, by cold-calling Varners in Ontario, because I had been told that Irene Varner and her husband had moved there (though it turns out they probably did not actually do so); contacting (thanks to the kindness and knowledge of local historian Don Murray) Liz Ames, the second-oldest living Manitoba resident at the time I was conducting my investigation, who had lived across the road from the 1909 Brookdale charivari, and remembered it well; locating the Ottawa 1881 charivari by a search of an American news database that the University of Winnipeg library was testing (and did not eventually subscribe to); and telephoning the Saskatchewan Archives in Regina for directions to their premises when photo archivist Tim Novak was on the desk to direct me to the Dick and Ada Bird photographs. Not just the result of diligence, these blessings remain in the realm of chance.

All the model books in my introduction focus on sensational incidents, and all begin their conclusions by recounting what happened afterwards – to the family of Hilda Blake's victim (Kramer and Mitchell 2002), to Ida B. Wells, to Alice Mitchell after she was committed to an insane asylum (Duggan 2000), and to Michael Cleary, who upon his release from prison emigrated to Montreal in 1910 (Bourke 1999). The murders that Duggan, Kramer and Mitchell, and Bourke discuss were very clearly ruptures in the quotidian. Thus, the return to everyday life provides a rhetorical and dramatic resolution for descriptions of the cases and for the books.

But shivarees were – and where they are practised, still are – very much a part of everyday life, not extraordinary events. They were made to fit into the cycles of sociability, house-visiting, and biological, social, and cultural reproduction that community members deal with daily. I have elsewhere argued their continuity with, but also their rupture of, patterns of community house visiting (Greenhill 1989b). And even accidents, errors, and gossip like those that led to the court cases in my first three studies are part of daily life – however much we may wish them not to be.

Some commonalities manifest where the tradition persists. Shivarees currently take place only in locations where marriage remains a subject of absorbing *community* interest. The friend of Patricia Thompson who said that shivaree was dying out because people weren't getting married anymore was not too far from the truth. In places where the perseverance of marriages – in the face of high divorce rates, for example – is a matter of pride, shivarees are being applied to milestone anniversaries. In New Brunswick, most of the recent shivarees I heard about were anniversary, not marriage, celebrations.[2]

Where marriage has become a marker of social prestige and consumerism (see, e.g., Matrix 2006), shivarees are unlikely to take place. But contrary to the usual explanation from participants or former participants, they are not absent because the couple live in a city and would be subject to noise ordinances. Urban folks are perfectly capable of making lots of noise and disturbing the neighbours, with both ritual and individual motivations. But shivarees simply don't relate to the intentions of conventional urban marriage to celebrate romance and capitalism (see Matrix and Greenhill 2006). Sometimes they are entirely irrelevant to or potentially at cross purposes with those aims.

In the shivaree's current and historical manifestations, gendered meanings seem particularly salient. I argued for a gendered community concern in the shivarees I studied in Ontario in the late 1980s – that these events marked the particular semiotic location of brides as welcomed female outsiders, contrasting with the unwelcomed masses of women, men, and children moving into former farmlands in the subdivisions being built across southern Ontario at the time. As one respondent from Schomberg described the social surround, 'I think the way of life has a lot to do with the shivaree not being held now. In my days the community of farmers all *KNEW* each other and welcomed a newcomer. Today in the area where I had lived the neighbours change and move so often that sometimes people a couple of miles apart do not even know each other. Many women work now and everyone is up and off to work. They do not socialize like they used to; it's a changing way of life' (Q11 2005).

The examples I have drawn on here underscore the gendering of shivaree, from the male-to-male violence of the Ontario and Manitoba examples – where, arguably, men literally got away with murder – to the commentaries on appropriate and inappropriate gendered behaviour in Nova Scotia, to the gendered expectations of good sports in Saskatchewan.

I have argued that the Ontario and Manitoba charivari examples were directed primarily at men, and men were the primary participants. These two events offer insight into the construction of masculinity on a variety of levels and in different discourses. In the Nova Scotia saluting, the gendered critique was turned by men against a woman, though there was some implicit – particularly local and familial – negative commentary against the male recipient as well. The Saskatchewan shivaree appears more gender-inclusive. The photographs are of 'Les and Edna's shivaree,' and an approximately equal number of girls and boys attend. Yet this does not mean that the shivaree has become more gender-neutral in its application or in its intentions.

Thus, despite the newspaper and institutional rhetoric of modernity manifest particularly around the Ontario and Manitoba events that makes charivari outdated – even regressive – like all traditions, it retains multiple possibilities. Nevertheless, it remains a practice that is not without its problems. E.P. Thompson's comment on its cognate, rough music, involving humiliation, hostility, stigma, terror, tyranny, and suffering can also apply to historic and current shivarees, despite the perennial explanation from those who participated that it was and is a welcome. My own experience of attending a shivaree in Ontario in 1991 and the evidence from the some 10 per cent of responses to my interview and survey questions that view the practice critically, suggest that now, as well as in the past, it is not always welcomed as an unmixed blessing.

Of those responses that criticize the shivaree or express deep reservations about it, the great majority come from women. As discussed in my first shivaree article (Greenhill 1989b), women are now the primary subjects of this practice. Though ostensibly directed at the couple, the most severe treatment – which is not rectified the next day by participants – is in the woman's domain, and is her job to clean up, buy replacements for damaged goods, and otherwise restore order to the domestic environment. An Ontario couple I interviewed together expressed this idea quite well at the conclusion of our discussion. When I asked them how now they felt about their shivaree, looking back on it, they spoke simultaneously. He said, 'Great fun.' She said, 'A nuisance.'

Gendering Discourses: Song

Each of these charivaris – including the Saskatchewan example in chapter 5, which had no interactions with the law – despite its commonplaceness, in some way merited extraordinary discursive attention. Yet the charivari itself is a form of discourse, a traditional commentary with conventional but variable forms that also reflect its creators, audiences, performance contexts, and sociocultural surrounds. Indeed, the *Varner v. Morton et al* case is actually about whether the charivari can be defined in terms of a recognized form of (il)legal discourse, that of defamation. But the charivari is also, throughout this work, linked with, interacting with, constructing of, and constructed by other discursive forms, including gossip, oral history, family and community narrative, newspaper reporting, legal testimony, and photography.

Consider, for example, 'Sullivan's Shivaree,' with lyrics by Joe Grant and Steve Ritchie of the group Tanglefoot, written in the late 1980s.[3] It exemplifies a conventional male view of current shivaree forms across Canada as 'great fun':

Pete Sullivan he was a shy young man with a big round face like
     a frying pan
And when he smiled it was full of teeth, a little red whisker
     underneath.
Peter found himself one day, plighting his troth to a fair young
     maid.
Met her at the minstrel show; very next day to the church did go.

Now Rosie Jones, that blushing bride, had Peter all puffed up
     with pride.
Sullivan, he the jealous groom, could hardly wait to take her
     home.
Fifteen days of wedded bliss. The neighbours planned an end to
     this.
The time was set, the hour agreed, to shake the house with a
     shivaree.

Chorus: Shout in the dark and roar like thunder,
Bang on the barrel like a drunken drummer,
Fire that gun, scream blue murder; Sullivan's Shivaree.
Shout in the dark and roar like thunder,
Bang on the barrel like a drunken drummer,
Won't be a wink of sleep tonight at Sullivan's Shivaree.

Great Uncle Jim was the head of the gang, says he, 'We'll start
     this off with a bang,
I'll give the signal when the sun goes down. One big blast from
     me old shotgun.'
Billy Banks with an old jawbone, Tommy Riddle with a big
     trombone,
A fiddle and a whistle and a couple of boys with the highland
     pipes to generate noise. (*Chorus*)

Rosie sat up straight in bed, she grabbed Pete's arm and then she
     said,
'There's a ghost or a beast walking 'round outside. Be a man: go
     see what you find.'

Peter being the cowardly sort, he grabs his jug and takes a snort,
Arrives at the door all on the run, lets fly in the dark with his old
    shotgun.
Hearing that noise the company scream out their lungs and Peter,
    he
Thinking his time has surely come, falls to his knees and drops
    his gun. (*Chorus*)

Young and old go streaming by with marble cake and rhubarb pie
Maple syrup and jugs of tea all for Sullivan's Shivaree. (*Chorus*)
    (Tanglefoot 1993)

In this song, shivarees are about 'noise, food, and interrupted sex' (Joe Grant, PG2008, 2). Men are the noisemakers at this event, and they are named, but I surmise that the 'young and old … streaming by with marble cake and rhubarb pie' are female. The only named woman in the entire song is the bride, Rosie. Joe Grant noted that the story came from co-writer Steve Ritchie's family, about a man who had started his own shivaree. Since the usual signal to start such an event was a shotgun blast, the song's point is that Sullivan, by shooting out his door, actually begins his own shivaree. Though Grant was aware of pranks at shivarees, the focus of his song was Pete Sullivan's trick on himself, and on his intention for 'fifteen days of wedded bliss' – implicitly, sexual. It's particularly appropriate that the closing emphasis on communal food (rather than, for example, on the tricks that were played, as those who disapprove of shivaree remember) exemplifies the male view of the shivaree as 'great fun.'

Grant is well aware of the tradition. In a description of his mother's community's tradition of *polterabend* (see Klassen 1998), he noted that 'she said that typically somebody would tie a cowbell under the bed and then they would all be outside the window to see if the cowbell would ring. And the other thing they would do is put baking soda in the pee pot so that when the young lady got up to pee in the middle of the night it would all froth up and she'd think something was wrong with her.' Note the attention to sexual activity – as Grant himself said, 'There was a mildly sexual kind of connotation to many of these things that they used to do' – but also the gendered link specifically to the woman in his description of using the chamber pot. As Grant says, 'I wasn't trying to write a story about a representative shivaree. It was about this particular one where the guy runs to the door, shoots the gun, and they mistake it for the signal.' Those are worthy artistic intentions. I'm not criticizing the song at all, and certainly not because it doesn't fully and adequately represent the shivaree as a tradition. That was not the song's aim, and I'm not suggesting that there should have been another focus for the song. But given the huge range of artistic choices available for someone writing about shivaree, I don't think it's entirely coincidental that the choice emphasizes the 'great fun' aspect. That is most men's view of the tradition, and thus, not surprisingly, it was Grant and Ritchie's.

Gendering Discourses: Pranks

Folklorists have attended to some examples of such nuisance, particularly in the form of practical joking,[4] which is arguably central to current forms of charivari. An early attempt at definition suggested that 'the practical joke is a shape-shifting genre' (Tallman 1974, 259), and talked about it in terms of functions: 'release from suppressed tensions ... and group identity, solidarity and conformity' (ibid., 260). Predictably for its time, this article did not address the ways that practical joking can in fact exacerbate, not release, tensions, and define potential community members not as insiders but instead as outsiders.

A later analysis defined the genre more specifically in communicative terms: 'Practical jokes are built on complex structures of information management, involving dimensions of backstage activity, frame manipulation, fabrication, concealment, and differential access to information about what is going on' (Bauman 1986, 35).[5] Yet Richard Bauman's work similarly understands practical jokes as 'benign fabrications, in which the victim's moral character or other serious interests (e.g., economic) do not suffer any real damage' (ibid., 36). I argue that in charivari the whole point is to flirt with, risk, and even enact damage to test recipients' – particularly women's – sense of community and play.

Practical joking can be related to particular ritual days of the year, like April Fool's Day (see, e.g., McEntire 2002); Halloween (see, e.g., D'Entremont 2008; Kugelmass 1994; McDowell 1985; Santino 1994), and Mardi Gras. The last, particularly, has been analyzed in terms of its extensively gendered quality. Rural Mardi Gras traditions, for example, manifest androgynously costumed women sexually pranking with usually uncostumed men, who respond by beating them with braided whips (see, e.g., Ware 2007). Moira Smith notes that 'practical jokes ... are often customized to fit the idiosyncracies of their targets' (1996, 588); she argues that folk opinion suggests that the target contributes to her or his own victimization though a 'defect of character' (ibid., 589).

At least some of this work implicates the fundamental seriousness of such trickery, as when a woman used an April Fool's 'prank as a way of noting how her potential long-term partner would react to stressful or unpleasant situations' (McEntire 2002, 144). Mardi Gras can also include risky play, such as child abductions (Sawin 2001, 185). Patricia Sawin notes that one observer 'eventually had to hide in the car to escape from advances that increasingly distressed and frightened her. As with most kinds of teasing and hazing, the person who is bothered by it is a much more attractive target than those who respond with equanimity.' She adds, 'Although I feel more a part of communities where I have been picked on by the Mardi Gras, in some cases tourists must go home with an emphatic message that they do not belong here' (ibid., 191). Barry Ancelet argues that the country Mardi Gras (very different from its more familiar carnival counterpart in New Orleans; see Ancelet 1998) play can include 'close calls' (Ancelet 2001, 148) and 'potential danger' and that 'this level of play may actually be cultivated, consciously or subconsciously, by the group or parts of the group, not only to satisfy a desire for greater thrills but to reaffirm the group by creating a need for it to negotiate between cohesion and disintegration or dissolution' (ibid., 149).

Similarly, most charivari tricks are tests, entering into dangerous zones Bauman says are beyond the pale of practical jokes, precisely because only by entering into such areas could the tests be real. The 'nuisance' side of shivaree, usually associated with pranks, is evident, for example, in Monica Morrison's fieldwork in New Brunswick. The intention of celebration and approval did not mean the shivaree lacked the often obnoxious elements of noise, demand for a treat, or trickery:

> As soon as [the newlyweds] got back [from their honeymoon] the word would get around among the neighbours, usually by telephone, that the couple had returned and that there would be a shivaree for them that night. That afternoon the new husband would go out and buy the treat: hard tack candy, peanuts in the shell, and a couple of boxes of cigars ... Whole families would come together, by wagon or automobile, bringing noisemaking equipment: pots, pans, horsebells, harrow discs, horns, shotguns, and almost always the blade of a circular saw with a piece of steel pipe for hitting it. Just as it was beginning to get dark they would gather in the front yard of the bride's parents' house and start to make noise. By this time the bride and groom had 'retired' to the spare room, usually a front room with a window. (1974, 287)

Noisemaking could go on for twenty minutes or more, and but crucially, the denouement involved friendly interactions: 'Then the couple would appear at the front door dressed in their wedding clothes. If the newlyweds were obstinate and would not come out, the noisemakers would burst in through the front door, go right up the stairs with their horns and circular saw and right to the bedroom door. The couple would usually come out then. Then everybody would go up and congratulate them. The treat was set out in washtubs and cigars were passed out to the men' (ibid.).

The event's pranking was explicitly gendered and sexualized, focusing upon the couple's bedroom: 'Its primary purpose is to make the victim uncomfortable and self-conscious and it is likely that this serves to reinforce the married couple's awareness of their new social status' (ibid., 288). Tricks employed the bed and nightclothes: '"breaking" the nightgown by cutting holes at strategic points; preventing entry by sewing up the pyjamas; putting nasty things inside (filling them with honey); or making them noisy by sewing bells to them' (ibid., 289). Friends might subject the groom to 'blackballing, blackening the groom's genitals with shoe polish ... The women (aunts, sisters, cousins, and best friends) tend to do the bedroom and nightclothes tricks; the men (brothers, cousins, and friends) the automobile tricks' (ibid., 290–1). The gendered and sexualized focus on fertility is capped by 'mock congratulations ("I wish you all the joy, And every six months a boy")' (ibid., 288).

Many quotations from Morrison's informants play down the negative aspects: 'There's no harm in it, you know.' 'Just to play a little trick on them. That's all they'd do.' 'They'd do all those things but they'd never do nothing to hurt anybody' (ibid.). I got the identical story when I interviewed and received questionnaire responses from most shivaree participants (and victims) looking back on the events through the rosy glow of twenty or more years. When, after my 1989 article was published, I actually saw a shivaree, I began to understand why it might lead to negative feelings, and even to violence.

The shivaree I attended near Kitchener, Ontario, in the summer of 1991 celebrated the marriage of the sister of one of my Mennonite students at the University of Waterloo who invited me and my partner to attend. We arrived at my student's house – the agreed gathering place – at about nine on a summer Saturday evening. My student told me (and my partner confirmed on the basis of their behaviour) that the men had been drinking since about 10:30 that morning, when the farmers' market closed. The men continued to drink heavily in the back room of the house while the women in the kitchen prepared food and prank paraphernalia, including Saran-wrapped confetti balls.[6] About eleven, we left the house and proceeded to the newlyweds' farm. We were instructed to turn our car lights off only when we reached the farm gate, since the couple lived on a main road. Given the amount of alcohol that many of the drivers had consumed, at my student's suggestion, I cautiously parked as far away as possible. (Although my own car remained unscathed, I witnessed two fender benders in the farmyard during the evening.)

The noise – most audibly from car horns and chainsaws with the blades removed – began shortly after we arrived and continued until the couple came out – in approximately fifteen minutes. (During the noisemaking, several men toilet-papered the entire yard, trees, farm outbuildings, and the couple's car.) The groom came out, joined his friends, and began drinking. The bride sat alone on the steps of her house while approximately twenty women streamed in and began a series of traditional pranks – moving the furniture to different rooms, tying all the socks and underwear together, leaving confetti balls in drawers, hanging bras from the kitchen cupboards, and so on. I learned that the bride had been shivareed the night before, and so had just returned her house to normal when it was being made topsy-turvy again. She did not look happy. She looked tired and angry. Evidently the balm of time might assuage her feelings, but the sense of welcome and celebration felt by those *looking back* on their shivaree seemed to have eluded the bride during the event I witnessed.

The positive shivaree, then, is not always so for everyone. The shivaree seems to set up men with an opportunity to demonstrate their good sport qualities – and indeed I didn't come across any reports in the interviews and questionnaires of men reacting negatively to the more recent shivaree forms – while it sets up women to fail, or at best it tests them much more stringently than it does their husbands. It's easy to be a good sport if your participation in an event involves being woken up on a summer night to go outside and drink beer with your buddies. It's much harder to react well to your friends dirtying, messing, and turning your home upside down, especially when you know you'll have to clean it up alone the next day. Thus the gendering of shivaree tricks orients them particularly toward giving women and men very different experiences of the event.

Further, the treats and sociability essential to the maintenance of any community, rural or urban, are also strongly gendered. The social activities that follow the noisemaking are produced and directed (quite literally) by women. If a confederate inside the house of the couple to be shivareed prepares a treat, it's her mother, mother-in-

law, sister, or female friend. And the expectation that 'ladies provide'[7] makes this aspect of the shivaree female. Note that preparing
food requires much more time and effort than bringing out a chain-
saw or honking on a car horn. Before the event, women must prepare
the treats (and after it is over, usually one woman – the bride herself
– has to clean up). In some locations, however, particularly in New
Brunswick, the treat is less explicitly gendered. Many respondents
there talked about the shivareed bride and groom bringing out washtubs full of candy and of peanuts, which the shivareers would scoop
up by the handful.

As already indicated, the contemporary event, as 'Sullivan's Shivaree' shows, is about sex – or, more specifically, about interrupting
sex. Sexuality and women are referenced in most shivaree tricks. Not
all shivarees involve pranking, but most that currently take place in
Ontario and probably half of those in New Brunswick (the two locations in which shivaree is still fairly widespread) do. In results from
my questionnaires and interviews, pranks demonstrate not only the
sexualized references of the shivaree, but also its direction at the
bride much more than at the groom.

Most shivarees that include tricks direct them at the bedroom, the
kitchen, and the bathroom. These are the most personal and private
parts of the home, but they are also fundamentally associated with
women's productive and reproductive labour. A Tavistock, Ontario,
female respondent said, 'The guys would go off and to do their thing
and the girls do theirs,' and went on to describe how shivareers would
'hang pictures upside down, [put] jello in the toilet, boil ½ their eggs
and leave the rest raw … drink their booze, [and] take out all the
bride's underwear from her luggage she's taking with her on her honeymoon' (Q561 2005). Grant Ketcheson of Madoc, Ontario,
acknowledged that the shivaree could be 'sometimes a rude introduction to rural life for a city gal' (Q539 2005).

Thus, tricks in the bedroom can include noisemakers attached to
the bed, and sometimes its deconstruction so that any movement will
cause it to collapse. Alarm clocks can be set for untimely hours and
placed in difficult-to-locate places in the bedroom or elsewhere (such
as furnace pipes). Bed linens can be short-sheeted and/or filled with
obnoxious substances such as thistles and/or stained with substances
such as Jell-O. Marion Schweitzer of Simcoe, Ontario, specified the
meaning of 'red jello in bed (bride's "cherry")' (Q545 2005) – a permanent stain marks the permanent loss of the woman's virginity in
her supposed initiation into sex. Evelyn Adams of Major,
Saskatchewan, remembered that 'they would fill condoms (French

safes) with water and put them in chairs, bed, wherever they would sit or lay' (Q565 2005). Closets would be rearranged, and cornflakes, confetti, or worse placed in the drawers, and in earlier times, chamber pots filled with water or soda.

Often, as in some of the above examples, the paraphernalia of the bedroom, and/or of sex, would be located outside its normal contexts. Shivareers could 'dampen the couple's underwear with water and put it in the freezer.' The bride's underwear could be publicly displayed inside or even outside the house, on trees or 'on the TV antennae with a spot-light shining on it' (Antonette Lane, Seaforth, Ontario, Q509 2005). Mixing of media and location would also be evident when underwear would be adorned with ketchup and peanut butter or chocolate to reference menstrual blood and excrement. Actual menstrual supplies could be displayed and/or destroyed – tampons strung from the blades of a ceiling fan or menstrual pads also covered with blood- and shit-evoking substances. Alternately, underwear or sleepwear could be hidden. Chester McMackin recalls New Brunswick and Prince Edward Island shivarees where 'door handles to bedroom doors were removed and hidden in not-too-difficult-to-find locations' (Q25 2005).

The house may need an industrial cleaning after domestic animals have been run through it, and golden syrup or shaving cream has been placed under the door handles. 'One friend has a handseeder and used to put rice or oats in it and go throughout the house spreading it' (Cathy Young, Waterloo and Perth Counties, Ontario, Q517 2005). Water buckets could be rigged over the doors. Shredding toilet tissue or Kleenex throughout the house, as well as upside down lampshades would, by contrast, seem relatively easy to deal with.

The assault on the bathroom could be extremely messy and again require considerable cleaning by the bride as the person responsible for the domestic context. Plastic wrap placed over the toilet bowl (or toothpaste or honey smeared on it) and lipstick smudged on mirrors remain perennial favourites. More unusual combinations include 'putting corn flakes and rice in bath tub and filling with water' (Antonette Lane, Seaforth, Q509 2005). Exemplifying the symbolic notion of matter out of place, Marlene Chornie recalls that in Norwood and Burgessville, Ontario, shivareers 'hid silverware in garage, and took curtains down and hid hooks in a crockery jug' (Q26 2005).

The kitchen also received considerable attention. Since women are generally responsible for preparing meals, they would be the ones inconvenienced (or worse, unable to prepare palatable meals) by finding the labels removed from canned goods or switched, cutlery placed inside a water-filled juice container and hidden in the freezer, breakfast cereals mixed together, or sugar and salt switched. David Barrett, in Upham, New Brunswick, experienced shivareers who 'filled our cupboards and pots and pans with balloons and rice' (Q5 2005).

And the persons of the bride and groom are not safe. An anonymous woman from Prince Edward County, Ontario, 'heard they sometimes dragged the groom into the bathroom or put the couple in a tub of cold water and sometimes covered them in shoe polish' (Q23 2005). Manitoulin Island, Ontario, shivarees usually ended with the couple being dumped in the lake (Marilyn Doughty, Q28 2005).

Shivaree tricks outside the house could inconvenience men, such as confetti in their cars, but more extreme pranks could involve 'nailing big boards across front door with a "condemned" sign' and 'wrapping the house and/or trees in toilet paper' (Antonette Lane, Seaforth, Q509 2005), and could potentially affect both husband and wife. Similarly, both could suffer as a result of outhouse doors being nailed shut. When more tendentious pranks are involved, it may be because the potential victims avoided or tried to avoid being tricked at all, as when 'newlyweds "escaped" (in a brother-in-law's car). His car was hoisted up a tree and chained there' (Grant Ketcheson, Madoc, Q539 2005). Karen Johnson from Dresden, Ontario, commented, 'My mom said that a neighbour's home was saran wrapped, the *whole* house very tightly done; must have cost a lot of money for them to do this' (Q2 2005). Some pranks were potentially dangerous, such as 'when leaving, tied doors from outside preventing exit' (William Dumur, Regina, Q553 2005).

Conversely, however, those who were not known shivaree pranksters might escape the worst. 'I did not participate in tricks, so that is why my wife and I may have gotten off more easily than others. We found confetti in every drawer, under chair cushions, behind drapes, under mattresses, and under throw rugs – everywhere' (William McMillan, Uxbridge, Ontario, Q541 2005). Crucially, though, outside trickery was usually redressed the following day by the shivareers themselves, who came to help the groom get his car out of a tree, reassemble farm machinery, find domestic animals that had been released, and so on. No such help came to the bride, who was and is expected to deal with whatever the shivaree brought to her domain without help and without complaint, as the previous chapter indicated.

Some shivareers more democratically addressed the entire property: 'We were chivaried 47 years ago. We didn't hear them until they were in our bedroom. There were about 20 people, friends and neighbours. They dismantled our bed and just stood it up in another room. We had to find it and set it back together before we could go to bed. We had an old windmill at the south side of our house and it was on the roof when they were finished. They brought lunch and made themselves at home. We were in a daze but had expected it sometime, never knowing when' (Wanda Taylor, Dufferin County, Ontario, Q521 2005).

Or, 'We had moved into a newly built house and had cleaned up all the left behind bits and pieces of building material. It was in boxes at the top of the stairs. The boxes and contents were pushed down the stairs. Our precious barrel of rainwater was emptied. The outhouse was moved about two feet back off the hole after dark. Fortunately we didn't step into the hole. Our car had been pushed from where it was parked into a nearby stockyard, completely hidden by the high fence around the stockyard. It took my husband a day and a half to find it' (Norma M. Chisholm, Roseneath, Manitoba, Q526 2005).

'Sullivan's Shivaree' is about a man who started his own shivaree, but the reverse could also happen. I heard several stories about how couples thwarted, at least in part, some of the worst: 'Some of the young newlyweds didn't have a clue about this devious practice, but our daughter had heard about this happening to former newlyweds so she and her husband were both lying awake dressed in sweatclothes, waiting for the "invasion." They were quite surprised by the number of participants (about 28) and the age of the group ... a couple of the older ones were near eighty' (Marilyn Doughty, Manitoulin Island, Q28 2005).

The couple being thus prepared is a common story: 'The chivaree that really stands out in my mind was my husband and myself. At the time we were sharing a phone line with his Mother and there were party lines at that time and I picked up the phone to use it and overheard her talking to someone else about the chivaree for us that night. So I knew all about it and planned a lunch for everyone without anyone knowing that we knew. We went to bed and didn't even get undressed and laid on top of the bed awaiting the crowd to show up. They finally did and I am sure that they knew we knew, as we didn't let the noise go for very long. That took place in October of 1973' (Wanda Allaby, Upham, NB, Q29 2005). Alternatively, 'Always the hydro to the house was cut off, although I recall several clever couples, who awaited a chivaree in the near future, turning the hydro switch off when they went to bed and thus fooling the shivareers who thus just turned the switch on!!' (Elizabeth McKinlay, Grey County, Ontario, Q533 2005). Similarly,

Shortly after we were married in 1970 we had a friend raised in Nebraska come and visit us for the weekend. We lived in a small apartment, so we offered Jean our bed and went across the street and slept on a hide-a-bed at my sister's. Suddenly Jean was awakened by a terrible bang and racket right outside her bedroom window. It must have been terrifying for her. The poor gal didn't know in the dark where to find our light switches, our phone or what phone number to call in an emergency. Being well-read, it slowly dawned on her that this might be a Canadian custom called a shivaree, so she crept to the window and timidly asked, 'Are you looking for Dick and Cheryl?' We loved the outcome. The loud and boastful revellers, intent on surprising, were surprised and somewhat sheepish. The innocent was unnerved and unsettled. The newlyweds, the chosen victims, slept blissfully. No doubt we told this story oftener than the would-be pranksters. We took delight in their mistake and the prank that backfired.' (Cheryl, Rimbey, Alberta, Q4 2005)

In some locations, the couple were expected to fight back. Diane from Listowel, Ontario, recalled, 'One shivaree that I attended the couple threw water out the bedroom window at us as we were approaching the house, making as much noise as possible. The water out the window was a common response in our community when the newly weds heard the people approaching and it was considered good clean fun' (Q30 2005).

However, it's clear that many shivaree recipients were less than thrilled with their experience. As already indicated, most were women. An anonymous female respondent from Tavistock remembered, 'Our shivarees were harmless pranks, but I did hear of a few that turned nasty. For example, pouring honey on expensive wool sweaters, putting ketchup on sanitary napkins and leaving them around, smearing food on walls and windows ... The nasty tricks played disgusted me. It ruined the whole playful experience. It gave shivareeing a bad name. The good ones were fun. We always had a good laugh over them, even now we reminisce' (Q561 2005).

Krista Jacks of Dresden noted that shivaree was 'Ok as long as it was done in fun. I don't agree with the removal of labels, from cans since that is a cost factor' (Q2 2005). At her own 1957 shivaree, Katrina from Florentine, Saskatchewan, feared being tarred and feathered, and said, 'Dad was furious and threatened to shoot them if they didn't leave ... Everyone left immediately' (Q555 2005). Another woman noted that at 'our "second" shivaree, young friends tore labels off all our canned foods in the cupboard, dumped our big box of Tide in our bathtub, and messed up folded things in our drawers while they insisted we make them pancakes. We were short of cash so I had a hard time seeing the humor in their waste. I did not enjoy our chivaree. Their intent seemed to be to aggravate and annoy rather than honor' (Cheryl, Rimbey, Q4 2005).

From Schomberg/Nobleton, Ontario, one woman wrote that at the shivaree she attended in the 1950s, 'younger people went upstairs to the couple's bedroom and threw the mattresses out the window, at the same time damaging the bride's wedding hat. She discovered the trouble while we were there and came raging into the kitchen screaming and crying (it was a bad scene). To this day I do not know who did the bad deed, but it spoiled the evening. It should never have happened. So my feeling on a shivaree is that it is a fun time if no damage is done' (Q11 2005).

William Sweezey of Miramichi, New Brunswick, recalled from the 1930s and 1940s, 'The most dramatic shivaree was the night that live hens were tossed into the hallway. The hens fluttered in all directions and there was a great flurry to rescue the oil lamps and a great deal of pandemonium within the house. When the bride and groom appeared they were visibly shaken and did not appear very happy' (Q16 2005). Lucille Stuckless, from Chesley, Ontario, recalled her reaction to her own 1991 wedding shivaree:

> Not happy at all. We were nude under the sheets and exhausted after the wedding hoopla. The friends/cousins of my husband broke the door down when we wouldn't get up. My husband got out of bed with nothing on to shoo them out the door. I was embarrassed to be seen in my bed with obviously nothing on under the sheet. They kept banging around and demanding to be fed ice cream. My husband and I got up, packed our stuff and left for a four hour drive home. This was three in the morning. We had come back to my in-laws' cottage for a couple of days before going back to work, and then had this bunch to deal with. We felt that it would be nicer to be alone at our home. They thought we were spoil sports. We thought they treated us with no respect as newlyweds. (Q21 2005)

Looking back on the event, many women condemned shivarees (even if they found reasons for their occurrence). Some of the criticism came in the form of stories about negative results of shivarees or of fears related to specific actions. Sandra Densmore of Upper

Musquodoboit, Nova Scotia, said, 'You gathered in a circle and you grabbed the groom and you tossed him as high as you can as often as you can until ... and why nobody was ever hurt, killed, crippled, whatever, I don't know. I have no idea ... It used to be in some communities, they tossed the bride as well' (PG2004, 64–5). From Prince Edward Island, Kathy Wells concurred: '[Tossings] were uncomfortable for the newlyweds and a couple have been dangerous to the groom' (Q846 2005).

Ruby Kewachuk, a British war bride who moved to Nova Scotia, remembered,

> I was so scared. Of course the idea, the joke was that people had gotten into the house while we were getting married in the church and they hung milk buckets and cream cans to the railings under the bed, and somebody had made an apple pie bed. And then when it was dark – I had no idea what was going to happen – there were people there with pots and pans banging them together and a few idiots with rifles firing them into the air, which really scared the devil out of me, coming from England where this is not known. My God, I didn't know if it was somebody attacking us [*laughs*]. Of course there were screams and yells, 'Bring the bride to the window.' I was so petrified and my husband went down, and I thought, 'He's going to let them have it.' But you're supposed to give them cake or cookies or something, and he was passing out beer to them. I don't know what he gave to the women, I didn't care at that point. I was actually horrified by the whole thing ... And after dark of course, having all these noises in the yard ... I found it really horrible. If I had perhaps ... known what they'd been up to ... I don't mind admitting, I was scared. I thought, 'Are we being attacked? Why are they shooting guns, for goodness sakes?' (PG2004, 52–3)

Evelyn Adams of Major commented, 'I thought they were very crass and stupid. But I realize when people live isolated lives, it was a way to catch up on all the news and make the newlyweds welcome ... I learned a lot about people and how some were merely working out their frustrations and some were downright mean and evil ... I think they died out when people got better cars and trucks and better roads so they could get around the country and to the city to concerts and shows to entertain. Like Vegas!' (Q565 2005).

Lucille Stuckless of Chesley remembered, 'If asked to shivaree, I would state my case and not participate and would warn those who

were to be shivareed ahead of time if I could ... I think they are childish pranks and should be done away with. There really is nothing
good about them, in my opinion. I think it is a hick tradition' (Q21
2005).

Diane from near Listowel had two shivarees. The first was fun for
her, but

> the second one was comprised of our unmarried friends and
> acquaintances and they came with one intent and that was to get
> very drunk and do damage. They attempted to crawl in through the
> bedroom window and we heard them, we quickly went to open the
> door but as we went downstairs, the people on the porch roof
> gained entry to the bedroom and they took apart our bed and put it
> on the roof. When we tried to stop the bed from being put on the
> roof, the people downstairs ripped labels off all the canned food
> and threw the food in the refrigerator on the floors and walls. They
> threw wine on the drapes and took our furniture outside in the
> dampness ... At one point my ex-husband and I sat outside on the
> steps and cried. We couldn't be in as many places as the people
> could and so there was nothing we could do but watch. To this day
> I question why we didn't call the police. Perhaps it didn't occur to
> us to hurt our 'friends,' or maybe we thought it was part of the
> shivaree tradition. (Q30 2005)

In the view of a woman from Ontario, 'They got very silly and
good items such as linens, dishes, and furniture got ruined. I
decided this was not a social event I wanted to be part of ... They
are part of my past agricultural life. I have moved on to higher education and successful professional career and they seem silly and
stupid now' (Q31 2005). Marie Jackson of Napanee, Ontario, commented that shivarees were 'fun – when for someone else. Anxious
about it when for us, wondering when, having food on hand, house
clean, night attire, hair, no makeup, etc.' (Q582 2005). An anonymous respondent from St Thomas, Ontario, who participated in
shivarees in the late 1980s, said she 'sometimes felt a bit guilty
because of the *mess*' (Q574 2005). Eunice Dietrich of Herbert,
Saskatchewan, commented, 'Couple should be notified. I do not
believe in surprises' (Q578 2005). From Nova Scotia, Helen Tallman said, 'Cruel may be too harsh a word but it's the first word I
think of. The couple is tired and it is a special day and night for
them. Would it be better to give the newlywed couple time to themselves?' (Q857 2005).

One of the most thoughtful explanations I received came from Diane, who having experienced two shivarees herself, one pleasant and one unpleasant, still participated in them. 'I felt fine because although it was an intrusion to their sleep and their night and it was done as an initiation into the institution of marriage, it had a far deeper meaning. The shivaree was more about a welcoming and to show we cared about them. I pray that the shivarees I participated in the people would feel that my intention was to be a friend in bad times as well as good, that I was a "back door" neighbour and that the house didn't have to be perfect, that I would take time to be with them when they needed me not just when it was convenient for me. I didn't come to this lightly after the destruction of the shivaree at my home but I was blessed to have been shivareed twice so I had two examples to learn from' (Q30 2005).

Evaluating Shivaree/Charivari

Though many respondents indicated that a couple could be shivareed only once, that rule does not always apply. When I asked for reasons why people would receive more than one shivaree, the responses were that different social groupings might organize events separately, or that they could be shivareed any number of times until their first child arrives. The latter explicitly links the shivaree with fertility, and makes it a negative incentive for reproduction. The connections to sex, gender, and sexuality are multiple. The noise that begins the shivaree is arguably male-associated; the best noisemakers are purpose-built by men or appropriated from tools used in male-dominated work. However, the tricks most obviously directed at women are planned and carried out by women. The shivaree is an example of women doing the work of maintaining mores and practices that are not necessarily in their own interests – or those of their female friends and relatives. There can be an element of collective delayed payback: if I had to put up with these pranks, I'll make sure that you have to put up with them also.

But the consequences for women (and couples) who don't fit in can be dire, especially in locations where they must depend on their neighbours and community for assistance. The seriousness of the test echoes the deep play of the Louisiana country Mardi Gras described by Ancelet, Sawin, and Ware. Failing the shivaree test means you are not part of the group. The anonymous Ontario woman above who 'moved on,' however happy she may be with the ultimate outcome of a professional career, may have had little choice. Those who can't take the surveillance, gossip, and conservative mores of most rural communities generally leave them. But those communities – perhaps Avonlea, Saskatchewan, is an example – that appear to welcome outsiders, and whose shivarees are more friendly than they are edgy, survive and sometimes even flourish.

The fact that shivarees are now understood as intending to welcome newlyweds into the community, as I've stated already, does not mean that they never include dangerous and/or illegal actions, or insensitive and/or inappropriate ones. Like many other traditional practices, shivaree is good or bad, and its outcomes positive or negative, based on the specific congeries of individuals and community expectations with luck and good management. Just about any otherwise innocuous social event can turn ugly, and even the most serious political protests can remain decent and safe for all involved.

That being said, I doubt that I would appreciate being shivareed. I suspect I would not be considered a good sport in most rural communities. I value my privacy, I'm not particularly sociable, and I'm offended by the ritual debasement particularly of women in the sexualized pranks of some shivarees. I would find it overwhelming and frustrating that as a woman I would be expected to suffer in silence through an extensive series of pranks intended to test my ability to endure unreasonable provocation without protest. I'd like to think I would appreciate one or two jokes, and that I would understand them as part of tradition. I do think, however, that the women I've quoted above are justifiably upset about their shivarees. As discussed in the first chapter, the debasement of the couple in shivaree pranks may relate to the idea that no individual or couple should be elevated over others, without some ritual action that pulls them down to the common level. But symbolic explanations don't mitigate the individual effects of shivarees, nor do they comfort those who may be on the receiving end of specific practices.

Finally, because a practice helps to maintain a certain status quo doesn't mean that the status quo is actually worth maintaining. The biological offspring of locals aren't the sole route to community continuation. Groups can be reproduced by migration into them, for example. The division of insiders from outsiders that renders incomers a problem is not a reflection of their actual worth as human beings – or as potential community members. But there's nothing fundamental to the symbolic means of shivarees that make them inherently problematic or otherwise.

Arguably, there was no aspect of the 1881 Ottawa charivari that made the murder of James Wetherill inevitable, and nothing in the

1909 Brookdale event that would have led inexorably to the death of Harry Bosnell. Perhaps even the 1917 saluting of Irene Varner could have been taken as a joke, whatever its intention. And there are lots of imaginable circumstances under which even the friendly and fun 1940 shivaree of Les and Edna Babcock could have led to ill feeling and even to death. There are, of course, limits to this kind of speculation. It would be difficult to divine a positive outcome or benign possibilities for racist charivaris. But it's also difficult to imagine that in the absence of that tradition, interracial marriages would have been innocuous and safe. Shivarees as discourse allow certain kinds of statements to be made, but their specific contents can be extremely variable.

Notes

Chapter 1

1 Folklorists understand the *quête* as the gathering of money or a treat in exchange for some kind of performance. Like the noise-making of the charivari, the performance is not usually solicited and can be unwelcome. As one of the anonymous readers pointed out, 'Charivariers are giving something as well as taking – albeit it's a complex and multivalent gift.'

2 Cressida Heyes usefully notes that, for trans phenomena,

> what is at stake … is the relation between established sex, gender, and sexuality labels on the one hand, and these emergent categories on the other. 'Trans-' terms capture various kinds of sex and gender crossing, and various levels of permanence to these transitions: from medical technologies that transform sexed bodies, to cross-dressing, to passing, to a certain kind of 'life-plot,' to being legible as one's birth sex but with a 'contradictory' gender inflection. For some, the adjective 'transsexed' captures the specific project of changing one's sexed body through surgery and hormones, while for others it more broadly describes a distinctive form of narrative. 'Transgendered' might describe any project of gender crossing or blending that eschews medical interventions, or the term might be used as a catch-all that includes anyone who disturbs established understandings of gender dichotomy or its mapping to sexual dimorphism. (2000, 170)

3 In primarily oral cultures particularly, oral histories of great antiquity and accuracy are maintained (see, for example, Vansina 1961).

4 According to Statistics Canada, the entire population of the Rural
   Municipality of North Cypress, in which Brookdale is located, was just
   under 1,900 people in 2001 and that of Neepawa in the same year was
   3,325.
5 The latter was accessed at the Main Library of the Toronto Public
   Libraries.
6 Visual searches of individual newspapers, without some idea of relevant dates, would be time consuming without offering consistent
   results. I was also able to find case file information in archives pertaining to all three actions.
7 In a work that combines feminist and cultural studies perspectives, Janice Radway's (1984) study of romance novels illuminates the actual
   sometimes resistant motivations and experiences of readers, contrary to
   presumptions that they are only silly, bored, duped housewives, buying
   a fairy story purveyed to them by capitalism.
8 The interpreter, Jennifer Bonnell says, 'I defended my choice of cos-
   tume with the argument that, as a "third person" interpreter, I could
   "step outside myself" to interpret the clothes I was wearing as those of
   a nineteenth-century male servant' (2008, 146). Perhaps she did not
   need to perform such intellectual gymnastics. Indeed, in nineteenth-
   century North America, there is no question that some women dressed
   as men. Speculations about their motivations have ranged from giving
   sexual access to other women, to escape from family and community,
   to entrée into male work, to what might now be called transgender or
   transsex – a sense that they were not actually female but in fact male
   (see, for example, Duggan 2000; Greenhill 1995, forthcoming (a).
9 See, for example, Gizelis (1972) and Pendergast (1988), among a host
   of others.
10 For further evidence of satirical storytelling by First Nations, see Basso
   (1979).
11 Charivari is also now spelled in ways that better approximate its English pronunciation; *shivaree* or *chivaree* can often be found in Canadian
   and American dictionaries. Less standard spellings may be attributed to
   the fact that their users rarely if ever encounter the term in written
   forms.
12 Note that in the United States, other terms are also known, including
   belling in Ohio (Halpert 1948) and Nebraska (Meredith 1933), *serenade* in New England (Hanley 1933), and *polterabend* among Mennon-
   ites (Klassen 1998).
13 Junior Farmers of Ontario is an amalgam of locally based community
   agricultural youth groups (see http://www.jfao.on.ca/).
14 I thank the instructor, DeLloyd Guth, for encouraging this work.

15 For Newfoundland mumming violence, see, for example, Story (1969, 177–80); for Canadian charivari violence, see, for example, Greer (1990, 1993) and Palmer (1978).

16 *Varner v. Morton et al.*, [1919] 46 D.L.R. 597, 53 N.S.R. 180 is an appeal case.

17 'Charivari and the Sexual Regulation of Women in Formal and Folk Law,' SSHRC Standard Research Grant, 2004–8.

18 Many social scientists understand the notion of social control as 'a mechanism by which a person or group expresses a grievance' (Black 1984, 7).

19 Michael D. Bristol argues that Shakespeare's *Othello* can be read as a 'rite of unmarrying,' using the 'specific organizing principle ... of charivari' (1990, 3).

20 The idea that comedic ritual would perform such an action is familiar from theorists as diverse as M.M. Bakhtin (1968) and Northrop Frye (2002).

21 While the actual death of an individual from occurrences such as these may be relatively uncommon, Tony Reader of St Stephen, New Brunswick, recalls, 'Beer was consumed but I recall one chap got very sick indeed from sampling furniture polish left carelessly on the top of the piano!!' (Q597 2005) (sequential number in order that questionnaire was received, year). Questionnaires are written responses to questions, gathered during my original research 2004–8.

22 *Patten v. People* 1869 18 Mich. 314; *Choate v. State* 1927 37 Okla.Crim. 314; *State v. Countryman* 1897 57 Kan. 815; *State v. Adams* 1889 78 Iowa 292; *Havens v. Commonwealth* 1904 26 Ky.L.Rptr. 706; *Walker v. Commonwealth* 1930 235 Ky. 471; *State v. Voss* 1921 34 Idaho 164; *Tharp v. State* 1939 65 Okla.Crim. 405.

23 *Bruno v. State* 1917 165 Wis. 377; *Palmer v. Smith* 1911 147 Wis. 70; *Higgins v. Minagham* 1890 76 Wis. 298; *Gilmore v. Fuller* 1901 99 Ill.App. 272 and 1902 198 Ill. 130; *White v. State* 1879 93 Ill. 473; *People v. Warner* 1918 201 Mich. 547; *Ryan v. Becker* 1907 136 Iowa 273; *State v. Parker* 1964 378 S.W.2d. 274.

24 *Kiphart v. State* 1873 42 Ind. 273; *State v. Voshall* 1853 4 Ind. 589; *Cherryvale v. Hawman* 1909 80 Kan. 170; *State v. Brown et al.* 1879 69 Ind. 95; *Bankus v. State* 1853 4 Ind. 114; *St Charles v. Meyer* 1874 58 Mo. 86.

25 *Bruno v. State* 1920 171 Wis. 490; *Lebanon Light, Heat & Power Co. et al. v. Leap* 1894 139 Ind. 443; *Cline v. LeRoy* 1917 204 Ill.App. 558; *Combs v. Ezell et al.* 1930 232 Ky. 602.

26 *Novelty Theater Co. v. Whitcomb* 1909 47 Colo. 110.

27 Morrison sees the disapproval charivari as a French custom: 'The shiv-

aree is an especially strong tradition [in northern New Brunswick], although in character it seems to bear little relation to the custom among the Acadian French to the north and east where it takes on the flavour of overt community disapproval' (1974, 286). My own recent research suggests that charivaris marking second marriages and marriages of older individuals continue in parts of rural Quebec and Acadia.

28 Indicates interviewer [P]auline [G]reenhill date [2005], and sequence [ninth and tentth audiotape sides]. This is one of the oral interviews I conducted during my original research 2004–8.

29 Disguise is not a common element in English-Canadian marriage charivaris over the last 150 years or so. However, the Ottawa *Daily Citizen*, in reporting the Wetherill charivari (the subject of the next chapter), specifically noted that witnesses 'emphatically have declared that none of the gang were disguised either with costumes, blackened faces, or masks' (13 Aug. 1881). Masking and costuming may appear more often in events with political intent, probably because perpetrators do not want their victims or the authorities to be able to identify them (see Greer [1993] on Quebec charivaris of the early nineteenth century, which evidently were usually conducted in disguise).

30 Racialized violence was by no means unknown in Canada (see Backhouse 1999). Miscegenation was considered particularly heinous: 'In 1860 a riot broke out in Chatham when a black preacher named Pinckney dared to marry a white schoolteacher ... When blacks stray from their place by such presumptions as marrying a white ... some unstable whites have reacted with violence. But they could not have reacted at all if society in general had not already defined that place' (Walker 1980, 88–9). Similarly, Wyatt-Brown discusses the use of charivari along with lynching to maintain 'white order' in the United States (1983, 436). 'For lesser offenses, usually ones committed by whites, the charivari was sufficient. Though different in their levels of violence, both were ceremonies of moral purification through the sacrifice of one or more victims, polluted and profaned [in these] ... ecstatic events. The mingling of justice and bacchanalia, centering about the scapegoat, whether a lowly black or an unpopular member of the ruling class, released social tensions in spectacle' (ibid., 437).

31 This poem is structured without stanzas.

32 In stark contrast, see John F. Szwed's (1971) discussion of bachelor Paul E. Hall and the song he wrote to manage his bachelorhood in the Newfoundland outport where he lived. Szwed argues that bachelors were a threat to outport communities. Though they seem not to be so on the prairies, in both locations bachelors were subject to ridicule. Yet

rare comments on charivaris from prairie papers, and the second charivari example I discuss from near Neepawa, Manitoba, in 1909, show
that bachelors were the charivariers – and that they were usually seen
as a nuisance at best, and a problem to be dealt with at worst.

33 One of the social historians who read my work also argued that the
numbers of such events had obviously reduced over time. I'm not sure
that this reduction is indeed so obvious. We have no idea, and we cannot ever know, how frequent charivaris were in the past. And the tradition's alteration to a celebration of appropriate marriages surely meant
that, in those communities where charivari was practised, the numbers
as well as the proportion of charivaris might actually have increased, if
we presume that there were and are more matches the community
approves of than ones they disapprove of.

34 *Horse fiddle* is a common name for an instrument constructed to produce cacophonous noise. Those I have seen in Ontario and Manitoba are
made from a large plank of strong wood (approximately six feet by two
feet by an inch) into which a crank and a toothed gear are fitted. The
teeth of the gear run against a long piece of metal, so that when the
crank turns a tremendously loud vibration results. If the instrument is
propped up against the house, its door, or a beam, the noise and vibration become even louder and more obnoxious. Another form, from the
western United States, was differently constructed, using 'two enormous
bows, made of hoops, heavily stringed and rosined, with a beef-bladder,
fully inflated, pushed between the string and the bow' (Riley 1854, 94).

35 In this, as in many other newspaper reports, details are missing; presumably the events that precipitated them were sufficiently well known
that they did not require elaboration.

36 In a charivari in Kingsbridge, near Goderich, Ontario, that apparently
resulted in a death, 'It appears that there was some ill-feeling on the
part of people around Kingsbridge because they had not been invited to
the Dalton-Moss wedding ... which was quite a large affair' (*Globe*, 30
June 1906, 1). My research shows that charivaris in Saskatchewan
could also be directed against those who did not give a community
party, eloped, or did not hold a wedding dance. Some were instigated
by those not invited to the wedding. Similarly, according to John Carley of Carman, Manitoba, charivaris were 'often for middle aged people getting married, particularly if they didn't have a public wedding
for the neighbours' (Q771 2005).

37 Indeed, nineteenth- to twenty-first-century Canadian laws enforce the
rights of those who have money, and often protect property more dili-
gently than they protect the Charter of Rights and Freedom's 'life, lib-
erty, and security of the person.'

38 This conclusion is based on my SSHRC grant research, which has involved interviews with and questionnaire responses from some thousand individuals across southern Canada, from Prince Edward Island to British Columbia. Only Newfoundland and Labrador and the Northwest Territories, Yukon, and Nunavut appear to lack charivari traditions.

39 An earlier version of chapter 3, however, has been published (Greenhill 2006).

40 A confusing range of spellings of the murdered man's name appear in the record. I have chosen to use the spelling found in most official records.

41 This and all further quotations from the testimony of *Varner v. Morton et al.* are from the Nova Scotia Supreme Court Case file, in file 4495, box 618, RG 39 C HX, Nova Scotia Archives and Records Management (NSARM), and includes the trial testimony. The casebook is missing.

42 Perhaps blaming victims for their own murders was as popular in that time as blaming the victims of sexual assaults for the crimes committed against them is currently, despite feminist attempts to dispel the stereotypes about women and men on which that idea is based.

43 From my interview PG2004, 58–61, Bridgetown, Nova Scotia, 25 July 2004.

Chapter 2

1 The subject of this charivari was called James Wetherill in the *New York Times* (12 Aug. 1881), *The Ottawa Daily Free Press* (Aug. and Oct.), and the *Toronto Globe* (8 Sept.); usually Weatherill in the *Ottawa Daily Citizen* (Aug. and Oct.); and Wetherall, Witherill, and Wetherill in the *Toronto Globe* (12 Aug.). He was Weatherly on the first page of the Information of Witnesses taken at the Coroner's Inquest; various spellings appear throughout, including Margaret's signature as Weatherl. The *Daily Citizen* suggested that some legal documents used Weatheril Everill (18 Aug.), and some of the first newspaper articles reported his name as Earl or Earle. Marriage and baptismal records called him Wetherill; his burial registration was Wetherell, but Margaret's was Wetherill. To avoid confusion, I use Wetherill throughout, even where another spelling was used in the original. Despite multiple creative searches and a visual microfilm scan, I could not find any James Wetherill in the 1881 census who was born in England, approximately the right age and occupation. There are no names close to Wetherill in Carleton County in 1881. I was also unable to securely identify using multiple spellings and visual scan any Margaret

Dougherty, widow, of the right age, Methodist, and born in Ireland, in the 1881 census. In Carleton County, both a Mary Dougherty at fifty-eight and a Margaret Daugherty at seventy-one, both born in Ireland and living together, are probably too old, Roman Catholic, and since no marital status is given for either, they were probably unmarried. However, the Wetherills' marriage registration gives Margaret's birth name as Taylor. The registration of her first marriage in 1872 lists the surname as Daughty, and her husband's death registration in 1878 gives his name as Daughtry. Since the census date was 4 Apr., before Wetherill's death, the absence of these crucial figures remains a mystery to me, but I'm convinced after a visual search of the microfilm census that they are simply not there (see Curtis 2001 on census inaccuracy). The Ottawa City Directories are slightly more enlightening. Mrs M. Daughty, widow, is listed as a grocer on Ann St W. (that part of Emily St was renamed Ann St in 1880, but all references to the charivari still call it Emily) in the 1881 Ottawa City Directory; in 1882 she appears as Mrs M. Weatherell, widow, in Rochesterville. She cannot be identified with certainty in the 1878–80 City Directories. James cannot be located in Ottawa, Mount Sherwood, or Rochesterville in any part of the Directories from 1878 to 1881 (or, of course, in 1882, by the time Margaret is listed as his widow).

2 Henceforth, dates without years are for 1881.

3 The *Toronto Globe* was first issued in 1844 (Wallis 1908, 166), the *Telegram* in 1876 (ibid., 170), and the *Evening News* in 1880 (ibid., 171); the *London Free Press* in 1849, and the *Advertiser* in 1863 (ibid., 175); the *Brockville Recorder* in 1820 (ibid., 172); and the *Hamilton Spectator* in 1846 (ibid., 174). The *Montreal Herald* first appeared in 1811 (Reade 1908, 149) and the *Witness* in 1846 (ibid., 150).

4 Darnton (2000) considers the roles of gossip and poetry/songs in the communication of news in eighteenth-century Paris.

5 Founded in 1869, edited and published by C.W. Mitchell, the *Free Press* was a Radical Liberal paper (Rutherford 1982, 237).

6 Founded in 1874, edited and published by C.H. Mackintosh, the *Citizen* was a Conservative paper (Rutherford 1982, 237).

7 In addition, I was unable to locate several of the charivariers in Carleton County in the 1881 census.

8 As late as the 1840s, gossip was considered a legitimate source of information in the regulation of members of Protestant churches in Upper Canada: 'Among the majority of the population, and indeed within institutions of authority such as the church, an alternative [to written] form of discourse – the spread of information through oral communication or "word of mouth" retained considerable importance,

as well as legitimacy, particularly at the local level' (Marks 2000, 388). Folklorists generally have not appreciated newspapers as sources. Exceptions include Cohen (1973) and Greenhill (1989a, 1989b).

9 Some forty years earlier, Michael S. Cross argues, 'Wealth, *per se*, does not seem to have been a decisive factor ... [in] the criteria for members of the élite' (1967, 108) and notes that an 'aspirant' could be 'otherwise unacceptable – for personal eccentricity, for moral turpitude, for any-one of a variety of reasons considered important by the oligarchs' (ibid., 108–9). He finds that 'the really important characteristics demanded were the correct attitudes on social and political questions, and the indefinable attributes of a gentleman' (ibid., 109). There is a marriage registration for James 'Wetherall' (whose wife's name is wrongly given as 'James' Thornton) in Rothwell, Yorkshire. James 'Wetherhill' and his wife Rachel are in the 1840 British census in Roth-well; James and 'Rachael' 'Wetherill' appear in the 1850 census in Racine, Wisconsin.

10 As Laurel Leff (1997) trenchantly discusses, objectivity has a particular meaning in current media discourse, one that is not necessarily under-stood outside (or sometimes even within) journalism. Further, my own experiences with current media have severely shaken what little faith I may previously have had in their accuracy.

11 See Finnegan (1992), Foley (1988), Greenhill (1989a), Lord (2000), Ong (1982), and Vansina (1961).

12 Where otherwise not attributed, information about birthdates, locations, occupations, and religions come from the transcribed 1881 census, available at www.familysearch.org.

13 This detail is missing from the 'Information of Witnesses.'

14 Emily St was changed to Ann St in 1880 and then to Gladstone. Bay, Lisgar, and Nepean streets remain in Ottawa, but the Lisgar St in Mount Sherwood is now Bell St (Kosonic 1983). Mount Sherwood and Rochesterville were annexed to Ottawa in 1889 (Brault 1946, 28). Two death registrations were made. One, dated 8 Oct. (#2990) notes 'Wetherell''s death date correctly as 11 Aug., and age at death at sixty-five, gives the cause of death as 'murder (sudden)'; another, dated 26 Aug., gives Wetherill's death date as 10 Aug., his age as fifty, and notes that he 'died by violence at the hands of certain parties now supposed to be in the hands of the authorities.'

15 Coleraine, co. Londonderry.

16 At the time of the 1881 census, Catherine Cooper appears to have had no boarders – the only others listed in the residence with her husband George are their four children.

17 This and all further quotations from the Coroner's Inquest are in file:

O'Brien, James et al., 1881, Murder, Cont. 17, RG22-392-0-664, Archives of Ontario. The rest of the case file does not appear to have survived.

18 Another name with variable spelling.

19 Alexander Scott, thirty-three, stonecutter, born in Scotland, Presbyterian, living near the Coopers and Courtmans as well as Charles Blunt, the lone identifiable adult married charivarier.

20 This and all further orthographic and grammatical errors will not be corrected.

21 This report is somewhat surprising, since a large group of those subsequently accused resided in the same census division as the Cooper house, and since Margaret had run a store in the neighbourhood, later taken over by Hugh McMillan.

22 Police officers at the time wore white helmets.

23 For all further named individuals, those with no date and location of birth, occupation, ethnicity, and/or religion were not identifiable in the census.

24 Despite multiple creative searches, no Robert McLaren sufficiently close to most of the information provided by the newspapers could be found in the 1881 census, and none whatsoever in Carleton County.

25 Though there are two James O'Briens in the census for Carleton County, this James O'Brian is reported as living with Ellen O'Brian, who is listed in the census as married but head of her household with no adult male in the residence. The newspapers reported O'Brien's parents as separated. This O'Brian also lived in the same census division as the other two accused who could be located there.

26 There is another Edward Edwards (b. 1861 Ontario, clerk, Irish Church of England), who is from the same census division as the Bonells, McMillan, and McGrath.

27 His pronunciation of his name is probably indicated by the fact that the paper identified him as 'Morphy.'

28 There is an Edward Murphy (b. 1859 Ontario, labourer, Irish Catholic) from the same census location as the three located accused.

29 Living in the same census area is Joseph Arneau (b. 1859, thus twenty-two, French Catholic).

30 There is a James Dunn (b. 1865 Ontario, clerk, Irish Catholic) in the census, living in the same area as the three accused I could locate.

31 The team involved 'a cross-section of Hamilton's working people' (Humber 1995, 23).

32 Similarly, Colin Howell discusses an attempt to establish a ball club at the University of Toronto in 1885. At least one detractor referred to the 'disreputable characters' associated with the game who were 'of the

lowest and most repugnant character. [Baseball] has been degraded by Yankee professionalism' (qtd in Howell 2001, 41–2).

33 Note that there seems to be some confusion about the location, name, and capacity of the Grand. Another perhaps more academically reputable source suggests that the Grand Opera House in Ottawa was built in 1874 on Sparks Street and destroyed by fire in 1913 (Southworth 1992, n.p.).

34 These notions are not dissimilar from Louis Chevalier's description of bourgeois understandings of links between 'laboring' classes and 'dangerous' classes in Paris at the turn of the nineteenth century (1973, 359–72).

35 There is some confusion here, since Kelly is supposed to be the speaker.

36 In the next chapter, this was the outcome nearly thirty years later in Manitoba. A grand jury found 'no bill' in a manslaughter case against a bridegroom who shot and killed a charivarier, so his case never actually went to trial.

37 One cannot help thinking of current disputes about whether rape victims are responsible for the crimes against them, which similarly use concepts of appropriate gendered behaviour to attempt to explain perpetrators' actions or even to exonerate them (see, for example, Yamawaki 2007). While the actual characteristics and expectations hold different content, as one would expect, given their basis in gendered binaries, the processes are alike. An individual who fails to uphold gendered expectations can be blamed for the alleged consequences of that failure.

38 There was some discussion of 'a charivari on a piece of land a few yards outside the limits of the city of Ottawa' in the Ontario legislature (Ontario 1884, 22).

39 Glenn J. Lockwood makes a fascinating argument that the early development and flowering of the temperance movement in Ontario was related to conflicts between the former American residents and incomers from the British Isles in the 1820s and 1830s, a fight for 'moral legitimacy' between Irish Tories and American Reformers (1990).

40 Some information on hostelries in Ottawa during the nineteenth century can be found in Guillet (1956, 143–74).

41 Charivari was also part of working-class culture in Montreal, as asserted by DeLottinville (1981–2, 10).

Chapter 3

1 Birthdates, where they could be found and are not otherwise attributed, are from the 1901 Census. At the 1901 Census, then twenty-six-year-

old McLaughlin was still unmarried and living with his father – the senior McLaughlin was a widower whose wife had died in childbirth some twenty years earlier (Martin n.d.; Watson 1990) – and three younger siblings. Manitoba marriage registration records indicate that he married Ella Ennis in Neepawa on 16 October 1901. Ellady Jane Ennis was born 28 March 1870 at Cranbrook, Ontario, died 13 March 1909 at Neepawa, Manitoba. 'As I recall from my Dad, Ellady did not like her name ... so went by "Ella"' (Buchanan n.d., n.p.).

2 The infant, named Gladys, survived. Their marriage certificate wrongly lists McLaughlin's age as twenty-seven, along with at least one other error, giving Ethel Burkell's father's name as William (it was Willett). The latter's birth and death dates are given as 1868–1917 in the transcription from the Rosedale cemetery in Manitoba, http://www.west-manitoba.com/cemetery/rosedale.htm.

3 The spelling suggests that the register-maker – probably the minister – was unaware of the term, and possibly also of the practice. The Neepawa Methodist Church register is held at the United Church Archives, housed at the University of Winnipeg.

4 'No bill' means that after the evidence was presented by the Crown, the Grand Jury did not indict McLaughlin. Manitoba had grand juries until 1923. Historian of law Alvin Esau said, 'We abolished Grand Juries here because they were viewed as a waste of time given that for most serious cases, the accused was entitled to a preliminary hearing before a provincial court judge whose job was precisely to determine if there was sufficient evidence for an indictment' (personal communication, 27 Sept. 2004).

5 I first located this event during a word search for *charivari* in the database of the *Globe and Mail*, which turned up a 'special despatch to the *Globe*,' dated Neepawa, 10 Nov., and printed on 11 Nov. 1909, 4.

6 Violence in early western Canada is described by Louis A. Knafla (1995).

7 Further information about these individuals can be found in Bumstead (1999), Gibson and Gibson (1972), and *Pioneers* (1925).

8 I have been unable to learn why no deposition was taken from James O'Hayes (sometimes referred to as O'Hara), the other charivarier.

9 Noted in the Criminal Register for Portage (GR 7188), the Portage case file (M1348) was subsequently transferred with some others to Winnipeg (Criminal Register GR3636), where it currently can be found (M1476), in the Archives of Manitoba. All subsequent quotations that have no newspaper or other sources indicated in the text are from this case file.

10 The *Neepawa Press* (which is still in operation) was established in

1896, announcing, 'It is believed there is room in Neepawa for two live, local papers, and it is proposed to make The Press a clean and creditable journal, trusting to success in this respect to establish a profitable and permanent business' (qtd in Pratt 1967, 50).

11   Joseph Bosnell was eighteen at the time of the 1906 census. He died on 2 Aug. 1914 and is buried with his brother Harry in the Neepawa Cemetery.

12   I have chosen in this chapter to draw attention to mis-hearings and misspellings. The mould board is the front facing portion of a plough that turns over the furrow (Shaw 2002). Sizeable, and made of metal, it would make considerable noise when beaten.

13   The coulter is the vertical section of a plough that runs through the soil (Weller n.d.), also large and metallic.

14   Testimony from John S. Poole (physician and provincial coroner) gave the time of death as 4 p.m; it is stated as 4:30 p.m. in the *Neepawa Press* (12 Nov. 1909, 4).

15   Note that this number of shots is far fewer than reported by the charivariers.

16   The legal record indicates that the other bail guarantor was Samuel Holmes.

17   James Ramey was also the only adult male in Manitoba in 1911 by that name. I'm grateful to Brandon University Archivist Tom Mitchell for pressing me to go further in examining this verdict to see who was on the Grand Jury; unfortunately, only Ramey could be identified.

18   As transcribed on http://automatedgenealogy.com/index.html (to July 2007).

19   The *Carberry News* was established in 1889, and the *Carberry Express* in 1892. They merged into the *Carberry News-Express* in 1910 (Pratt 1967, 167), still in publication.

20   The date of their arrival given in the 1906 census is 1903.

21   Liz (Chisholm) Ames, who was ten at the time, and lived across the road from the charivari location, mentioned that the Burkells were neighbours of her family.

22   Angus McLaren (1984, 174) suggests that youth could be attributed on a class basis, with a twenty-year-old working-class male considered a man and his middle-class counterpart a youth. This result seems unlikely in the less overtly socially differentiated rural culture of Manitoba, and it is highly improbable that men well into their twenties and thirties would be considered youth in any case.

23   Manslaughter, though unintentional homicide, is of course a crime.

24   Justifiable homicide would not be a possible verdict for a manslaughter

charge (unintentional death); the former relates only to intentional acts, that is, a murder charge.

25 Note the use of historical comparisons from the legal context.

26 That the child was not named made me suspect, as it turned out, quite correctly, that she was a girl.

27 Schedule C, held in a private collection.

28 Form 11, obtained from Vital Statistics, Manitoba. Frank Ennis was born in 1865 at Cranbrook, Ontario, and died 15 Nov. 1919 at Eden, Manitoba (Buchanan n.d.).

29 These age differences are something of a mystery. Bruce Curtis's (2001) fascinating work on nineteenth-century Canadian censuses indicates that the census cannot simply be presumed accurate, given that its information was dependent on the sources, the gatherers, and the census structure generally. See also Ingrid Botting's useful feminist critique of the census (2000). Yet the 1901 census and his first marriage certificate agree on McLaughlin's age, as do the local newspapers; I don't know why the 1906 census makes him younger by approximately five years, but social disapproval would provide motivation for McLaughlin to minimize the age difference between himself and Ethel, whose age remains nearly constant in the documentation: ten in 1901, sixteen in 1906, and nineteen on her marriage certificate in 1909. The information on Ella Ennis McLaughlin remains unclear. If she was twenty-five in 1901, she could be neither thirty-six nor thirty-nine upon her death in 1909. The great specificity of the ages at death is equally if not more puzzling. Perhaps she was older than McLaughlin, and that would offer the same motivation – social disapproval – for an inexact marriage registration.

30 The latter was the only indication that Ethel McLaughlin had any female relatives.

31 Women's legal position and its implications in rural contexts are detailed by Kinnear (1998).

32 Similarly, differential gendered understandings manifest in narratives about murdered women in newspapers and ballads (see Cohen 1973).

33 The 1911 census had not been released when I began this work.

34 Temperate BC is a favourite retirement location for winter-weary Manitobans.

35 For example, the first woman I interviewed during this research asked that her name not be used in its communication, because she did not want her best friend to find out that she was the perpetrator of tricks at the friend's wedding some thirty years ago. About 10 per cent of responses to my survey of charivari across Canada describe lasting ill will between individuals as a direct result of actions at charivaris, almost all of which were of the positive, approval type.

36 This identification system for my field recordings notes the interviewer
    P[auline] G[reenhill], the year in which the recording was made, and
    the sequence in which it was gathered.
37 Imagine my joy in discovering that an eyewitness to the events sur-
    vived and was able to tell me about it. I'm profoundly grateful to Don
    Murray, who made the connection to Donna Walker, who not only
    cooperated in helping to get answers to my questions from her mother,
    and helped to arrange a short interview between myself and Liz Ames,
    but also provided invaluable background information (see Nicholson
    2005).
38 There was a Dr Bugg practising in the area around the same time (Gra-
    ham 1983); Charles Bugg is listed as a farmer in the 1901 census.
39 Liz Ames was born a Chisholm, and Marcus Chisholm was her father.
40 One story from Brookdale, reported by Cecil Pittman, was that
    McLaughlin was shooting from his roof (personal communication, 5
    Nov. 2005).
41 Possibly Harold Burkell, who attended the charivari.
42 The Burkell children's names confusingly vary between the 1906 and
    1911 censuses.
43 Anyone who feels that such attention to the identity of married couples
    is anachronistic would do well to compare the current controversies
    over same-sex marriage; exactly whom someone chooses to marry is
    by no means beyond public scrutiny, even today.
44 The *Revised Charter of the City of Winnipeg*, 1918, 198, includes,
    under 'public safety and comfort,' 'For preventing or regulating the fir-
    ing of guns or other firearms, and the firing or setting off of fire-balls,
    squibs, crackers or fireworks; and for preventing charivaries [sic], and
    other like disturbances of the peace' (W.C., s. 703 133).
45 From my interview at the Simpson home near Brookdale, Manitoba, 2
    Sept. 2004 (my record number PG2004, 104).

Chapter 4

1 Countless articles address this issue; for example, see Baron (2006) and
   Dale (2003).
2 *Varner v. Morton et al.,* [1919] 46 D.L.R. 597, 53 N.S.R. 180 is the
   appeal; the Nova Scotia Supreme Court Case file is in file 4495, box
   618, RG39 C HX, NSARM, and includes the trial testimony. The casebook is missing.
3 Michel de Certeau (1984) distinguishes between strategies – related to
   institutions and positions of power – and tactics – ad hoc interventions.
   The law as an institution is fundamentally strategic, but Varner uses it

tactically, mobilizing it as a petitioner – and probably also through her personal connections – to deal with a specific situation, rather than to control the system itself.

4 This and all future quotations from the trial testimony are from Nova Scotia Supreme Court Case file, file 4495, box 618, RG39 C HX, NSARM.

5 In the 1911 census, George Hayden is listed as a 'millman' but his family seems to have been missed.

6 Davis characterizes the targets of the French charivaris she discusses as 'independent and strong personalities, unwilling to allow themselves to be shamed' (1984, 50).

7 I know the ages of these men from their gravestones in the Springfield cemetery.

8 I use this spelling since it was the one noted on the Hayden/Irvin Marriage Register (Province of Nova Scotia 001412).

9 From clippings provided to me by Rosemary Rafuse. Irvin's records have inconsistent spelling and ages, but given his profession and location in the smaller community of Bridgetown, they are undoubtedly the same individual. His name is spelled 'Irvine' in the court records and 'Irving' in the community column. A John Ervin, barrister, aged fifty-one, was listed as practising in Bridgetown during the 1901 census, living with his wife Maggie and two daughters. A John Irvin, barrister, aged sixty-eight, lived in Bridgetown during the 1911 census. John Irvin, barrister (called to the Bar 31 Dec. 1870, crown prosecutor for Annapolis, 1906, and stipendiary magistrate for Bridgetown) is listed in *Prominent People of the Maritime Provinces* (Canadian Publicity Co. 1922, 91), but his wife is still given as Maggie E. Fletcher.

10 John Arthur Grierson was born in Kentville in 1864, and was appointed County Court judge in 1916. He died in 1934 (see Haliburton 2004, 393).

11 Documents other than the trial testimony are found in box 11, AP, C, RG 38, NSARM.

12 According to Lloyd Varner,

There were obviously hard feelings between Jennie Haines and Irene, caused by something that Irene had said to her (the 'slur' mentioned in Jennie's testimony). She did not say what it was, but she clearly took it very seriously. Jennie's father was a younger brother to Joe Varner, Irene's father-in-law, making Jennie and Albert first cousins. Their homes were only a stone's throw apart in New Germany, and Jennie was only two years older than Albert. These were two very large families, both living on parts of the original family grant, so the relationship would have been quite close. Jennie says that she earlier used to go to Irene's house two or three times a day, so we can assume that this was a serious family spat. (Personal communication, 27 May 2006)

13 In the plethora of jokes about them, travelling salesmen were notoriously sexually active.

14 His use of this term suggests he is unaware of *saluting* as the local term and substitutes one that is more familiar to him, or that he chooses to present the saluting in a more benign light as a mere serenade.

15 In seduction trials of the early nineteenth century, 'physical attractiveness and feminine demeanor' led juries to 'measure their awards according to their impressions of the wronged woman' (Backhouse 1991).

16 They take up the judge's minimizing language.

17 Historian S.D. Amussen suggests that 'many defamation suits were attempts to stop a rumour before it became part of the victim's "common fame" and reputation. Observation and gossip not only shaped reputation, but also shamed people and defined particular behaviours as deviant' (1985, 214).

18 I am indeed fortunate that they were nevertheless excited about my work on the case, and most helpful with my research.

19 LeRoy Roop testified that he also shot off a gun at the saluting. I have no idea why he was not also charged.

20 The Springfield Baptist Church celebrated its hundredth anniversary in 1935 (Kendrick 1941, 94).

21 Further discussion of the sexualization of space can be found in Best (1995); McDowell (1999), and Schmidt (1998).

22 Such rationalizations bring to mind the historic discourse around rape, which suggested that unless a woman was a virgin or had never had sex with anyone to whom she was not married, she could be presumed to be 'asking for it.' This notion is understood as so pervasive and ingrained that many jurisdictions have made a sexual assault victim's prior sexual history inadmissible (see, for example, Gotell 2005).

23 When automobiles entered the cultural scene, they became even more associated with heterosexual couples and courting (see Hunt 2002; Scharff 1991). I thank my colleague Tamara Myers for this suggestion.

24 Although women were not deemed persons legally in Canada until 1929, when the British Privy Council declared them so in a famous decision.

25 The saluters themselves belonged at home (that is, they should have been in their own private spaces, not the public space) with respect to the criminal charges against them. The act of vagrancy pertains to

being out of place in public space; it was the men's improper use of the public highway, as well as disturbing the Hayden/Varner household's peace, that was at issue. Vagrancy was frequently deployed against women, particularly those suspected of sex work. But in this case the folks out of place were upstanding men, who felt they were upholding rather than deviating from community morality.

26 *Slander of Women Act,* 54 & 55 Vic. c. 51. In any of these cases, truth would be a defence.

27 Robert E. Harris was appointed judge of the Supreme Court of Nova Scotia in 27 June 1915, and chief justice of Nova Scotia in February 1918 (Canadian Publicity Co. 1922, 79–80). The fourteenth chief justice, he served as such until his death in 1931. He was born at Annapolis Royal on 18 Aug. 1860 (Nova Scotia Barristers' Society 1978, 32). Discussion of the ideological positions of Harris and some of his cohort on the bench can be found in Girard (2004) and in Brown and Jones (2004); see also his colleague Benjamin Russell (1932, 256–8) on Harris's appointment as chief justice. Russell also credits him with adding a new wing to the courthouse, and 'the decoration of the walls with the portraits of the judges who have served their day in the course of the years that are passed. These portraits are all that can be depended upon to keep the bulk of our departed justices in the memory of posterity' as well as devoting 'a goodly share of his wealth to the construction of King's College in practical co-operation with Dalhousie' (ibid. 258) (see also Haliburton 2004, 71, 481; Inglis 1977, 112–19).

28 Nova Scotia Order XIX, Rule 29.

29 Humphrey Mellish, Puisne judge, was born in Prince Edward Island in 1862, was appointed to the Supreme Court in 1918, and served until his death on 19 June 1937 (Nova Scotia Barristers' Society 1978, 77). A barrister remembered him as 'highly regarded in the thirties by the Bar and ... quick with wit and reply ... He ruled over his court as would an Emperor. He loved every moment on the Bench,' and noted his 'piping voice' and 'pontificating' (Kanigsberg 1977, 36; see also Haliburton 2004, 217).

30 Joseph Andrew Chisholm was born at St Andrew's on 9 January 1863, appointed Puisne judge on 8 February 1916, and chief justice in 1931, serving till his death in 1950 (Nova Scotia Barristers' Society 1978, 34). A barrister recalled him as 'a kindly soul; always willing and eager to lend a helping hand to the young practitioner. His silver mane – his gentle voice and his reasoned application of the law won him the love and respect, not only of the Bar, but of the entire Halifax community' (Kanigsberg 1977, 35). He also conducted historical research on the Nova Scotia judiciary (Chisholm 1921, 1949; see also Haliburton 2004, 73, 481).

31 James Johnston Ritchie, born Halifax 27 July 1856, was appointed to
    the Supreme Court 16 Feb. 1912 and served until his death in Bermuda
    in 1925 (Nova Scotia Barristers' Society 1978, 74; see also Haliburton
    2004, 215).

32 Benjamin Russell, born at Dartmouth on 10 Jan. 1849, was appointed
    to the Supreme Court on 3 Oct. 1904. He resigned 3 Oct. 1924 and
    died in 1935 (Nova Scotia Barristers' Society 1978, 70; see also Hal-
    iburton 2004, 207). Russell clearly had a sense of humour, being co-
    author of *Crustula Juris, Being a Collection of Leading Cases on Con-
    tract Done in Verse* (Fletcher and Russell, n.d.). He also wrote memoirs
    (Russell 1926, 1932).

33 Sangster's work focuses more upon the institutionalized regulation of
    women during wartime, but her insights about the treatment of work-
    ing-class women resonate tellingly with the experience of Irene Varner
    in rural Nova Scotia.

34 There is no Morton in the Springfield history among those who served
    in the First World War; there are three Haydens, two McNayrs, one
    Mailman, and four Saunders listed among the twenty-four individuals
    (Kendrick 1941, 59).

35 The testimony also recalls for me the comments of women who press
    sexual assault charges, that the trial is another violation.

36 From a clipping in the collection of Rosemary Rafuse.

Chapter 5

1 Dick and Ada Bird Collection (Credit: Regina R-A27572-1, 2, & 3,
   Saskatchewan Archives Board).

2 *Shivaree* is the term used by participants and locals, so I follow their
   lead.

3 The shivaree took place six years before Dick and Ada married, however, so at the time she would have been Ada Bovee.

4 Edna Bovee (Babcock) was involved in a CGIT (Canadian Girls in
   Training, United Church teen women's) group (Bird 1983, 273), and
   the oldest shivareers there appear to be approximately the age of members – fifteen or sixteen.

5 Pranks did not occur only at shivarees. Halloween and gate night (usually the night after Halloween) brought on relocated and tipped out-
   houses, piles of burning material in the middle of the road, opened
   gates, egging, and a variety of other outdoor (usually negatively
   received) actions. But other events also occasioned pranking: Returning
   to Rouleau from watching election night celebrations in Regina in
   1932, Stirling King and friends were pelted with rotten tomatoes from

Fred Argue's car. King's group stopped at Craig's store to get rotten fruit and rotten eggs, blocked the road entrances into the town, and rotten-egged Argue's. 'In the end, every store front downtown and each of many of the nearby houses received its share of ripe fruit and rotten eggs. So did Fred Argue's gang. And so did all of us' (King 1995, 167).

6 The evidence he musters in *Discovering Saskatchewan Folklore* (1983), however, belies that judgment, showing that what is common need not be boring.

7 The tourist attraction of the area is Rouleau, where the sitcom *Corner Gas* was filmed.

8 The first of Montgomery's Anne books, set in the fictional village of Avonlea, Prince Edward Island, was published in 1908. The author's father relocated from PEI to Prince Albert, Saskatchewan (where he died in 1900) after her mother died. Montgomery herself lived briefly with him there, but returned to PEI in 1891 (Devereux 2007). The Avonlea community website also asserts, 'The community is named after the novel "Anne of Avonlea", written by the famous Canadian author, Lucy Maud Montgomery' (Avonlea 2008).

9 For information on restaurants as cultural centres in prairie towns, see Marshall (2009).

10 Wright's (1955) history of Saskatchewan details these events and their effects upon the people of the province.

11 Actually, the *Maine* was sunk on 15 February 1898, but that does not cast doubt on Babcock's being named after the event.

12 As Les Babcock's sisters noted in the local history book, the telephone system was first envisioned even before the village was named: 'While dad [C.T. Babcock] and two of his bachelor neighbours were in Rouleau one winter day in 1910, a raging blizzard came up and as there were no land marks such as fences, poles or even trails, they decided to stay there overnight ... The men arrived home about three PM and brought three telephones, the first in the community. Rouleau was our first central office. That was the real beginning of the Avonlea Telephone system' (Lundrigan and McRorie 1983, 256).

'The first meeting of the proposed Avonlea Rural Telephone Co. was held June 27, 1913 ... C.T. Babcock was elected chairman' (Watson 1983, 37). The first line was built in Sept. 1913, and in 1915 a switchboard with thirty lines was operated from a local residence (ibid.). The Department of Railways, Telegraphs, and Telephones, Report of Mr Francis Dagger, 1908 stated that 'the development of [rural or farm telephones] is of supreme importance to this province and [I] have no hesitation in stating that, next to railways and good roads, there is an urgent need for telephone communication between the farming communities and the towns in all parts of the province' (qtd in Smith 1992, 176).

13 Still in business, it is run by his great-granddaughter Lori Desjardins, and her husband Marshall (Bird Films n.d.).

14 Bird appeared in *The Canadian Who's Who* (1970–1972), 12:92.

15 Q610 is an arbitrary number, assigned as received to a questionnaire. Composed in 2004, these questionnaires were sent out between 2004 and 2007 to those who answered newspaper and radio notices that I was seeking individuals with information about charivaris.

16 As previously indicated, a horse fiddle is made from a large plank of strong wood (approximately six feet by two feet by an inch) fitted with a crank and toothed gear. The teeth of the gear run against a long piece of metal, so that when the crank turns a tremendously loud vibration results.

17 Charivari parading by young people was part of some Nova Scotia practices. Children marched to the accompaniment of their own discordant pots and pans to the homes of newlyweds, where they would be treated with candy or money to go to the local store and buy candy.

18 Cora was born eleven years after they married, so perhaps the length of the courtship is also a bit overstated.

19 'The house that was in these pictures was a 13 room house. There were five bedrooms, two living rooms, a dining room, a kitchen, a front porch and a back porch, and a garage' (Cora Seghers PG2006, 28). The house was torn down in the early 1980s.

20 For example, the wife of the attending minister at a wedding in O'Leary, Prince Edward Island, noted, in a letter dated 4 May 1949, 'The wedding was very small, just the parents, grandparents and witnesses and a couple of friends ... But following the ceremony and the eating ... a chivaree was held in broad daylight, in the middle of the afternoon. Truckloads of people came in weird costumes, all masked, and they just took over the party' (Colborne 2003, 68–9). Masking was clearly not part of the Avonlea shivaree.

21 Traditions associated with young men are often maintained during wartime by other groups or individuals.

Chapter 6

1 From this point onward I will use the term *shivaree* to refer to current practices, as it is currently the most common spelling, except when another has been used by a correspondent or writer. *Charivari* remains as the historic and generic form.

2 Indeed, I just missed two such shivarees in Sussex, New Brunswick, by a couple of weeks when I visited there in July and August 2006. In discussion with a storekeeper, I learned that she and her husband had been shivareed on their farm outside town to celebrate their twenty-fifth wedding anniversary. An additional shivaree had taken place right in Sussex (the perpetrators had warned both the neighbours and the RCMP in advance), again celebrating a milestone anniversary.

3 Used by kind permission of Joe Grant and Steve Ritchie. Another song about a 1932 Ontario event, 'Murphy's Shivaree,' written about her grandparents by local songmaker Arthur McCormick, was kindly sent to me by Verna Stephenson. It details a considerably more edgy event, in which the bride and groom are torn only partially clothed from their bedroom and required to serve supper to the shivareers. I very much doubt that these are the only songs written about such occasions.

4 The term is interchangeable with *prank* (Smith 1996, 587).

5 Bauman elaborates: 'Engineered fabrications, crafted deceits, practical jokes involve by their very nature a differential access to and distribution of information about what is going on, with the trickster having a more "real" sense of the situation, while the victim has a "false" one. There may also be bystanders to the situation whose information states will vary depending on the extent to which they have been let in on the joke by the trickster and the extent of their knowledge of the features of the victim's informational environment that are being manipulated by the trickster' (Bauman 1986, 37).

6 My student explained that confetti balls were a 'nice' shivaree trick compared to simply strewing the confetti everywhere, as they would not make a mess.

7 'Ladies please provide' is a coded accompaniment to an invitation to a local event in rural Ontario – a community shower or anniversary party, for example – that will be catered by those attending – a pot luck.

References

Alford, Violet. 1959. Rough music or charivari. *Folklore* 70:505–18.

Allen, Barbara. 1979. The personal point of view in orally communicated history. *Western Folklore* 38 (2): 110–18.

Amussen, S.D. 1985. Gender, family and the social order, 1560–1725. In *Order and disorder in early modern England*, ed. Anthony Fletcher and John Stevenson, 196–218. Cambridge: Cambridge University Press.

Ancelet, Barry Jean. 1998. *'Capitaine, voyage ton flag': The traditional Cajun country Mardi Gras.* Lafayette: Center for Louisiana Studies.

– 2001. Falling apart to stay together: Deep play in the Grand Marais Mardi Gras. *Journal of American Folklore* 114:144–53.

Anonymous. 1987. Griffith. In *Quest in Roots*, 318–319. Brookdale, MB: Brookdale Historical Society.

Armstrong, Denis. 2005. Our grand old operas. *Ottawa Sun,* 22 September.

Atwood, E. Bagby. 1964. Shivarees and charivaris: Variations on a theme. In *A good tale and a bonnie tune,* ed. Mody C. Boatright, Wilson M. Hudson, and Allen Maxwell, 64–71. Dallas: Southern Methodist University Press.

Avonlea. 2008. Avonlea, SK, Canada. http://www.avonlea.biz/.

Backhouse, Constance. 1991. *Petticoats and prejudice: Women and law in nineteenth-century Canada.* Toronto: Women's Press.

– 1999. *Colour-coded: A legal history of racism in Canada 1900–1950.* Toronto: University of Toronto Press.

Baker, J.H. 2002. *An introduction to English legal history.* 4th ed. London: Reed Elsevier.

Bakhtin, M.M. 1968. *Rabelais and his world.* Trans. Helene Iswolsky. Cambridge, MA: MIT Press.

Barney, Robert Knight. 1993. Whose national pastime? Baseball in Canadian popular culture. In *The Beaver bites back? American popular culture in Canada,* ed. David H. Flaherty and Frank E. Manning, 152–62. Montreal and Kingston: McGill-Queen's University Press.

Baron, Beth. 2006. Women, honour, and the state: Evidence from Egypt. *Middle Eastern Studies* 42:1–20.

Basso, Keith. 1979. *Portraits of 'the whiteman:' Linguistic play and cultural symbols among the western Apache.* Cambridge: Cambridge University Press.

Bauman, Richard. 1972a. Belsnickling in a Nova Scotia island community. *Western Folklore* 31:229–43.

– 1972b. The La Have Island General Store: Sociability and verbal art in a Nova Scotia community. *Journal of American Folklore* 85 (338): 330–43.

– 1986. *Story, performance, event: Contextual studies of oral narrative.* Cambridge, UK: Cambridge University Press.

Bell, David, and Gill Valentine. 1995. Introduction: Orientations. In *Mapping desire: Geographies of sexualities,* ed. David Bell and Gill Valentine, 1–27. London: Routledge.

Best, Sue. 1995. Sexualizing space. In *Sexy bodies: The strange carnalities of feminism,* ed. Elizabeth Grosz and Elspeth Probyn, 181–94. Routledge: London.

Bird, Ada. 1983. Bovee family. In *Arrowheads to wheatfields: Avonlea, Hearne & districts,* ed. Avonlea Historical Committee, 272–3. Avonlea, SK: Avonlea Historical Committee.

Bird, Dick. n.d. Biographical data. Manuscript in file IV.8.6, R-17, Dick and Ada Bird fonds, Saskatchewan Archives, Regina.

Bird Films. About us. http://www.birdfilms.ca/about.shtml.

Black, Donald. 1984. Social control as a dependent variable. In *Toward a general theory of social control,* ed. Donald Black, 1:1–36. Toronto: Academic Press.

Bonnell, Jennifer. 2008. A comforting past: Skirting conflict and complexity at Montgomery's Inn. *Journal of Canadian Studies* 42 (1): 127–53.

Botting, Ingrid. 2000. Understanding domestic service though oral history and the census: The Case of Grand Falls, Newfoundland. *Resources for Feminist Research* 28 (1–2): 99–120.

Bouchier, Nancy B. 2003. *For the love of the game: Amateur sport in small-town Ontario, 1838–1895.* Montreal and Kingston: McGill-Queen's University Press.

Bouchier, Nancy B., and Robert Knight Barney. 1988. A critical examination of a source on early Ontario baseball: The reminiscence of Adam E. Ford. *Journal of Sport History* 15 (1): 75–90.

Bourdieu, Pierre. 1991. *Language and symbolic power.* Cambridge, MA: Harvard University Press.

Bourke, Angela. 1999. *The burning of Bridget Cleary: A true story.* Harmondsworth: Penguin Books.

Brault, Lucien. 1946. *Ottawa old & new.* Ottawa: Ottawa Historical Information Institute.

Bristol, Michael D. 1990. Charivari and the comedy of abjection in 'Othello.' *Renaissance Drama* n.s., 21:3–21.

Brown, R. Blake, and Susan Jones. 2004. A collective biography of the Supreme Court judiciary of Nova Scotia, 1900–2000. In *The Supreme Court of Nova Scotia 1754–2004: From imperial bastion to provincial oracle,* ed. Philip Girard, Jim Phillips, and Barry Cahill, 204–42. Toronto: University of Toronto Press.

Buchanan, Watson, and related Canadian families. http://bill_buchanan.tripod.com/buchanan/.

Bumstead, J.M. 1999. *Dictionary of Manitoba biography.* Winnipeg: University of Manitoba Press.

Burke, Peter. 1978. *Popular culture in early modern Europe.* New York: Harper and Row.

Butler, Judith. 1993. *Bodies that matter: On the discursive limits of 'sex.'* New York: Routledge.

– 1999. *Gender trouble: Feminism and the subversion of identity.* 2nd ed. New York: Routledge.

Calnek, W.A. 1980. *History of the County of Annapolis.* Belleville: Mika.

Canadian Publicity Co. 1922. *Prominent people of the Maritime provinces.* St John: McMillan.

The Canadian Who's Who. 1970–2. Toronto: Who's Who Canada Publications.

Certeau, Michel de. 1984. *The practice of everyday life,* trans. Steven Rendall. Berkeley: University of California Press.

Chevalier, Louis. 1973. *Labouring classes and dangerous classes in Paris during the first half of the nineteenth century.* London: Routledge, Kegan Paul.

Chisholm, J. 1921. Our first common law court. *Dalhousie Review* 1921: 17–24.

Chisholm, Joseph. 1949. Three chief justices of Nova Scotia. *Collections of the Royal Nova Scotia Historical Society* 28:148–58.

Clark, William M. 1964. Ten nights in a bar room. *American Heritage* 15 (4). http://www.americanheritage.com/articles/magazine/ah/1964/4/1964_4_1 4.shtml.

Clifford, James. 1988. *The predicament of culture: Twentieth-century ethnography, literature, and art.* Cambridge, MA: Harvard University Press.

Coastal Communities Network. 2005–6.
http://www.coastalcommunities.ns.ca/magazine/comm_profile.php.

Cohen, Anne B. 1973. *Poor Pearl, poor girl! The murdered girl stereotype in ballad and newspaper.* Austin: University of Texas Press.

Colborne, Joan Archibald. 2003. *Letters from the manse.* Charlottetown: Island Studies Press.

Collins, Patricia Hill. 2000. *Black feminist thought: Knowledge, consciousness, and the politics of empowerment.* 2nd ed. New York: Routledge.

Comacchio, Cynthia R. 1999. *The infinite bonds of family: Domesticity in Canada, 1850–1940.* Toronto: University of Toronto Press.

Cominos, Peter T. 1972. Innocent Femina sensualis in unconscious conflict. In *Suffer and be still: Women in the Victorian age*, ed. Martha Vicinus, 157–172. Bloomington: Indiana University Press.

Coutts, Robert. 1982. Gold Rush theatre and the Palace Grand. *Beaver: Magazine of the North* 312 (4): 40–6.

Cross, Michael S. 1967. The age of gentility: The formation of an aristocracy in the Ottawa Valley. *Historical Papers* 2 (1): 105–17.

– 1973. The Shiners' War: Social violence in the Ottawa Valley in the 1830s. *Canadian Historical Review* 54 (1): 1–25.

Curtis, Bruce. 2001. *The politics of population: State formation, statistics, and the Census of Canada, 1840–1875.* Toronto: University of Toronto Press.

Dale, Elizabeth. 2003. A different sort of justice: The informal courts of public opinion in antebellum South Carolina. *South Carolina Law Review* 54:627–46.

Danysk, Cecilia. 1995. *Hired hands: Labour and the development of prairie agriculture, 1880–1930.* Toronto: McClelland and Stewart.

Darnton, Robert. 2000. An early information society: News and the media in eighteenth-century Paris. *American Historical Review* 105 (1): 1–35.

Davis, Alan, and Raven I. McDavid, Jr. 1949. 'Shivaree': An example of cultural diffusion. *American Speech* 24 (4): 249–55.

Davis, Natalie Zemon. 1975. *Society and culture in early modern France.* Stanford: Stanford University Press.

– 1984. Charivari, honor, and community in seventeenth-century Lyon and Geneva. In *Rite, drama, festival, spectacle: Rehearsals toward a theory of cultural performance*, ed. John J. MacAloon, 42–57. Philadelphia: ISHI.

– 1987. *Fiction in the archives: Pardon tales and their tellers in sixteenth-century France.* Stanford: Stanford University Press.

DeLottinville, Peter. 1981–2. Joe Beef of Montreal: Working-class culture and the tavern, 1869–1889. *Labour / Le Travailleur* 8–9:9–40.

D'Entremont, Carmen. 2008. Le Vol des soupes aux choux: Une tradition Acadienne de Pombcoup? *Rabaska: Revue d'ethnologie de l'amérique française* 6:69–78.

Desplat, Christian. 1982. *Charivaris en Gascogne: 'La morale des peoples,' du XVIe au XXe siècle.* Paris: Bibliotheque Berger-Levrault.

Devereux, Cecily. 2007. Montgomery, Lucy Maud. Canadian Encyclopedia. http://www.canadianencyclopedia.ca/index.cfm?PgNm=TCE&Params=A 1ARTA0005 395.

DeVoto, Bernard. 1947. *Across the wide Missouri.* Cambridge, MA: Riverside.

Dobash, Russell P., and R. Emerson Dobash. 1981. Community response to violence against wives: Charivari, abstract justice and patriarchy. *Social Problems* 28:563–81.

– 1992. *Women, violence and social change.* London: Routledge.

Dubinsky, Karen. 1993. *Improper advances: Rape and heterosexual conflict in Ontario, 1880–1929.* Chicago: University of Chicago Press.

Dufresne, Martin. 2000. La Police, le droit pénal et 'le crime' dans la première moitié du XIXe siècle: l'exemple de la ville de Québec. *Revue juridique Thémis* 34:409–34.

Duggan, Lisa. 2000. *Sapphic slashers: Sex, violence, and American modernity.* Durham: Duke University Press.

Dunaway, David K., and Willa K. Baum, eds. 1984 *Oral history: An interdisciplinary anthology.* Nashville: American Association for State and Local History.

Dupont, Jean-Claude. 1977. *Heritage d'Acadie.* Montreal: Lemeac.

Edwards, Murray D. 1968. *A stage in our past: English-language theatre in Eastern Canada from the 1790s to 1914.* Toronto: University of Toronto Press.

Ellis, Bill. 1989. Death by folklore: Ostention, contemporary legend, and murder. *Western Folklore* 48:201–20.

Finnegan, Ruth. 1992. *Oral poetry: Its nature, significance, and social context.* Bloomington: Indiana University Press.

– 1994. The poetic and the everyday: Their pursuit in an African village and an English town. *Folklore* 105:3–11.

Flanagan, John T. 1940. A note on 'Shivaree.' *American Speech* 15:109–10.

Fletcher, Mary, and B.W. Russell. n.d. *Crustula Juris, being a collection of leading cases on contract done in verse.* Toronto: Carswell.

Foley, John Miles. 1988. *The theory of oral composition: History and methodology.* Bloomington: Indiana University Press.

Friesen, Gerald. 1984. *The Canadian Prairies: A history.* Toronto: University of Toronto Press.

Frye, Northrop. 2002. The argument of comedy. In *The Reader's Ency-clopaedia of World Drama*, rev. ed., ed. John Gassner and Edward Quinn, 1024–7. Mineola, NY: Dover Publications.

Geertz, Clifford. 1980. Blurred genres: The refiguration of social thought. *American Scholar* 49:165–79.

Gibson, Dale, and Lee Gibson. 1972. *Substantial justice: Law and lawyers in Manitoba 1670–1970*. Winnipeg: Peguis Publishers.

Gilje, Paul. 1996. *Rioting in America*. Bloomington: Indiana University Press.

Girard, Philip. 2004. The Supreme Court: Confederation to the twenty-first century. In *The Supreme Court of Nova Scotia 1754–2004: From impe-rial bastion to provincial oracle*, ed. Philip Girard, Jim Phillips, and Barry Cahill, 140–203. Toronto: University of Toronto Press.

Gizelis, Gregory. 1972. Historical event into song: The use of cultural per-ceptual style. *Folklore* 83:302–20.

Goodwin, Joseph P. 1975. 'We're all a-goin' a-dry-settin' tonight': Christmas mumming and related customs in Alabama. Unpublished.

Gordon, Edith. 1971. A review of the life of a homesteader of fifty years ago. In *A record of activities and reminiscences of Rouleau and district.* n.p.: Saskatchewan Homecoming '71.

Gotell, Lise. 2005. When privacy is not enough: Sexual assault com-plainants, sexual history evidence and the disclosure of personal records. *Alberta Law Review* 43:743–78.

Graham, Jessie. 1983. Dr Edwin Edward Bugg. In *Heritage: A history of the town of Neepawa and district as told and recorded by its people, 1883–1983*, ed. History Book Committee at Neepawa, Manitoba, 408–9. Winnipeg: Inter-collegiate Press.

Greenhill, Pauline. 1989a. *True poetry: Traditional and popular verse in Ontario*. Montreal and Kingston: McGill-Queen's University Press.

– 1989b. Welcome and unwelcome visitors: Shivarees and the political economy of rural–urban interactions in Southern Ontario. *Journal of Rit-ual Studies* 3 (1): 45–67.

– 1994. *Ethnicity in the mainstream: Three studies of English Canadian culture*. Montreal and Kingston: McGill-Queen's University Press.

– 1995. 'Neither a man nor a maid': Sexualities and gendered meanings in cross-dressing ballads. *Journal of American Folklore* 108:156–77.

– 2006. 'Make the night hideous': Death at a Manitoba charivari, 1909. *Manitoba History* 52:3–17.

– forthcoming(a). 'If I was a woman as I am a man:' Transgender imagina-tion in Newfoundland ballads. In *Changing places: Feminist essays in empathy and relocation*, eds. Valerie Burton and Jean Guthrie.

- forthcoming(b). Coincidences and a Thornfield, Missouri charivari, 1962. *Missouri Folklore Society Journal* 26.

Greer, Allan. 1990. From folklore to revolution: Charivaris and the Lower Canadian Rebellion of 1837. *Social History* 15 (1): 25–43.

- 1993. *The patriots and the people: The Rebellion of 1837 in rural Lower Canada.* Toronto: University of Toronto Press.

Guillet, Edwin C. 1956. *Pioneer inns and taverns.* Vol. 2. Toronto: Ontario Publishing Company.

Haliburton, Charles E. 2004. *A biographical history of the judges of Nova Scotia, 1754–2004.* Kentville, NS: Judges of Nova Scotia.

Hall, Frederick A. 1974. Musical life in Windsor: 1875–1901. *University of Windsor Review* 9 (2): 76–92.

Halpert, Florence. 1948. Belling: An Ohio custom. *Journal of American Folklore* 61:211–12.

Halpert, Herbert, and George M. Story, eds. 1969. *Christmas mumming in Newfoundland: Essays in anthropology, folklore and history.* Toronto: University of Toronto Press.

Hanley, Miles. 1933. 'Serenade' in New England. *American Speech* 8:24–26.

Hart, James D. 1986. Ten nights in a barroom and what I saw there. In *The Concise Oxford Companion to American Literature.* Oxford: Oxford University Press. http://www.oxfordreference.com/views/ENTRY.html? subview=Main&entry=t53.e1944.

Haywood, Charles. 1957. Charivari. *Journal of American Folklore* 70:279.

Heron, Craig. 2003. *Booze: A distilled history.* Toronto: Between the Lines.

Heyes, Cressida J. 2000. Reading transgender, rethinking women's studies. *NWSA Journal* 12 (2): 170–80.

Holden, Madronna. 1976. 'Making all the crooked ways straight': The satirical portrait of whites in Coast Salish folklore. *Journal of American Folklore* 89:271–93.

Horne, Gerald S. 1997. Interpreting prairie cinema. *Prairie Forum* 22 (2): 135–51. http://members.shaw.ca/horne/prairiecinema.html.

Howell, Colin D. 2001. *Blood, sweat, and cheers: Sport and the making of modern Canada.* Toronto: University of Toronto Press.

Humber, William. 1995. *Diamonds of the North: A concise history of baseball in Canada.* Toronto: Oxford University Press.

- 2005. Baseball and Canadian identity. *College Quarterly* 8 (3). http://www.senecac.on.ca/quarterly/2005-vol08-num03-summer/humber.html.

Hunt, Alan. 2002. Regulating heterosocial space: Sexual politics in the early twentieth century. *Journal of Historical Sociology* 15:1–34.

Inglis, R.E. 1977. Sketches of two chief justices in Nova Scotia. *Collections of the Nova Scotia Historical Society* 39:107–19.

Ingram, Martin. 1984. Ridings, rough music and the 'reform of popular culture' in early modern England. *Past and Present* 105:79–113.

– 1985. Ridings, rough music and mocking rhymes in early modern England. In *Popular culture in seventeenth-century England*, ed. Barry Reay, 166–97. London: Croom Helm.

An inventory of photographs in the Dick and Ada Bird Collection. 1992. Unpublished manuscript, Saskatchewan Archives Board, Regina.

Jackson, James A. 1970. *The centennial history of Manitoba.* Winnipeg: Manitoba Historical Society.

Jones, Deborah. 1990. Gossip: Notes on women's oral culture. In *The feminist critique of language*, ed. Deborah Cameron, 242–50. London: Routledge.

Kanigsberg, R.A. 1977. *Trials and tribulations of a Bluenose barrister.* Halifax: Petheric.

Kendrick, Mary F. 1941. *Down the road to yesterday: A history of Springfield, Annapolis County, Nova Scotia.* Bridgewater, NS: MacPherson.

Kent, Joan R. 1983. 'Folk justice' and royal justice in early seventeenth-century England: A 'charivari' in the Midlands.' *Midland History* 8:70–85.

Kesterton, W.H. 1967. *A history of journalism in Canada.* Toronto: McClelland and Stewart.

King, Stirling. 1995. Rotten-egged. In *The buckle of the grain belt: Rouleau and District history, 1894–1994.* Rouleau, SK: Rouleau and District History Book Committee.

Kinnear, Mary. 1998. *A female economy: Women's work in a Prairie province, 1870–1970.* Montreal and Kingston: McGill-Queen's University Press.

Klassen, Pamela. 1998. Practicing conflict: Weddings as sites of contest and compromise. *Mennonite Quarterly Review* 72: 225–41.

Klymasz, Robert B. 1985. 'Malanka': Ukrainian mummery on the prairies. *Canadian Journal for Traditional Music* 13:32–6.

Knafla, Louis C. 1995. Violence on the western Canadian frontier: A historical perspective. In *Violence in Canada: Sociological perspectives*, ed. Jeffrey Ian Ross, 10–39. Don Mills, ON: Oxford University Press.

Kosonic, D.M. 1983 Street name changes. Document prepared for the City of Ottawa Archives.

Kramer, Reinhold, and Tom Mitchell. 2002. *Walk towards the gallows: The tragedy of Hilda Blake, hanged 1899.* Don Mills: Oxford University Press.

Kugelmass, Jack. 1994. *Masked culture: The Greenwich Village Halloween parade.* New York: Columbia University Press.

Leff, Laurel. 1997. The making of a 'quota queen': News media and the bias of objectivity. In *Feminism, media, and the law*, ed. Martha A. Fineman and Martha T. McCluskey, 27–40. New York: Oxford University Press.

Léger, Lauraine. 1979. Le charivari en Acadie. *Les cahiers de la société historique acadienne* 10 (4): 164–9.

– 1980. *Les sanctions populaires en Acadie: Région du comté de Kent.* Ottawa: Éditions Leméac.

– 2000. Le charivari en Acadie. *Les cahiers de la société historique de la vallée de Memramcook* 11 (2): 72–4.

Le Goff, Jacques, and Jean-Claude Schmitt, eds. 1981. *Le Charivari.* Paris: École des hautes études en sciences sociales.

Lockwood, Glenn J. 1990. The secret agenda of the Upper Canadian Temperance Movement. In *Consuming passions: Eating and drinking traditions in Ontario*, ed. Dorothy Duncan and Glenn J. Lockwood, 157–83. Willowdale, ON: Ontario Historical Society.

Lord, Albert Bates. 2000. *The singer of tales.* Cambridge, MA: Harvard University Press.

Lundrigan, Lois, and Vera McRorie. 1983. The C.T. Babcock family. In Avonlea Historical Committee 1983, 256–7.

Marks, Lynne. 1996. *Revivals and roller rinks: Religion, leisure, and identity in late-nineteenth-century small-town Ontario.* Toronto: University of Toronto Press.

– 2000. Railing, tattling, and general rumour: Gossip, gender, and church regulation in Upper Canada. *Canadian Historical Review* 81 (3): 380–402.

Marquis, Greg. 2004. Alcohol and the family in Canada. *Journal of Family History* 29 (3): 308–27.

Marshall, Alison. 2009. Everyday religion and identity in a western Manitoban community: Christianity, the KMT Foodways, and related events. *Journal of the American Academy of Religion* 77 (3): 1–36.

Martin, Irene. 1983. William McLaughlin family. In *Heritage: A history of the town of Neepawa and district as told and recorded by its people*, ed. Louise Rey and Myrtle McKenzie, 634–5. Neepawa: History Book Committee at Neepawa.

Marx, Karl. 1852. The Eighteenth Brumaire of Louis Bonaparte. http://www.marxists.org/archive/marx/works/1852/18th-brumaire/ch01.htm.

Massicotte, Edouard-Zotique. 1926. Le Charivari au Canada. *Bulletin des recherches historiques* 32:712–25.

Matrix, Sidney. 2006. 'I do' feminism courtesy of *Martha Stewart weddings* and HBC's *Vow to Wow Club*: Inventing modern matrimonial tradition with glue sticks and Cuisinart. *Ethnologies* 28 (2): 53–80.

Matrix, Sidney, and Pauline Greenhill, eds. 2006. Wedding realities / Les Noces en vrai. *Ethnologies* 28 (2): 5–222.

McBurney, Margaret, and Mary Byers. 1987. *Tavern in the town: Early inns and taverns of Ontario.* Toronto: University of Toronto Press.

McDowell, John H. 1985. Halloween costuming among young adults in Bloomington, Indiana: A local exotic. *Indiana Folklore and Oral History* 14 (1): 1–18.

McDowell, Linda. 1999. *Gender, identity and place.* Minneapolis: University of Minnesota Press.

McEntire, Nancy Cassel. 2002. Purposeful deceptions of the April fool. *Western Folklore* 61 (2): 133–51.

McLaren, Angus. 1984. Males, migrants, and murder in British Columbia. In *On the case: Explorations in social history*, ed. Franca Iacovetta and Wendy Mitchinson. Toronto: University of Toronto Press.

Meredith, Mamie. 1933. Belling the bridal couple in pioneer days. *American Speech* 8:22–4.

Merry, Sally Engle. 1984. Rethinking gossip and scandal. In *Toward a general theory of social control.* Vol. 1, *Fundamentals*, ed. Donald Black, 271–302. Toronto: Academic.

Moodie, Susanna. 1997. *Roughing it in the bush; or, life in Canada.* Critical ed., ed. Elizabeth Thompson. Ottawa: Tecumseh.

Morrison, Monica. 1974. Wedding night pranks in western New Brunswick. *Southern Folklore Quarterly* 38 (4): 285–97.

Morton, Desmond. 2004. *Fight or pay: Soldiers' families in the Great War.* Vancouver: University of British Columbia Press.

Nicholson, Marcy. 2005. 107-year-old city woman second oldest in Manitoba. *Brandon Sun*, 18 August.

Noël, Françoise. 2003. *Family life and sociability in Upper and Lower Canada, 1780–1870: A view from diaries and family correspondence.* Montreal and Kingston: McGill-Queen's University Press.

Noel, Jan. 1995. *Canada dry: Temperance crusades before Confederation.* Toronto: University of Toronto Press.

Nord, David Paul. 2001. *Communities of journalism: A history of American newspapers and their readers.* Urbana: University of Illinois Press.

Nova Scotia Barristers' Society. 1978. *The Supreme Court of Nova Scotia and its judges, 1754–1978.* n.p.: n.p.

Ong, Walter J. 1982. *Orality and literacy: The technologizing of the word.* London: Methuen.

Ontario. Legislative Assembly, *Sessional Papers* (1884), vol. 8,

http://books.google.ca/books?id=r3ROAAAAMAAJ&q=charivari
+Ottawa+land+limits&dq=charivari+Ottawa+land+limits&pgis=1.

Palmer, Bryan. 1978. Discordant music: Charivaris and whitecapping in nineteenth-century North America. *Labour / Le travailleur* 3:5–62.

– 1979. *A culture in conflict: Skilled workers and industrial capitalism in Hamilton, Ontario, 1860–1914.* Montreal and Kingston: McGill-Queen's University Press.

– 2000. *Cultures of darkness: Night travels in the histories of transgression.* New York: Monthly Review.

Pendergast, David M. 1988. The historical content of oral tradition: A case from Belize. *Journal of American Folklore* 101:321–4.

Pettitt, Tom. 1999. Protesting inversions: Charivary as folk pageantry and folk-law. *Medieval English Theatre* 21:21–51.

Pictou-Antigonish Regional Library. Antigonish County placenames. http://www.parl.ns.ca/placenames/antigonishs.html.

Pioneers and prominent people of Manitoba. 1925. Winnipeg: Canadian Publicity.

Pratt, A.M. [1967]. *The story of Manitoba's weekly newspapers.* Steinbach, MB: Derksen Printers/Manitoba Weekly Newspapers Association.

Radway, Janice. 1984. *Reading the romance: Women, patriarchy, and popular literature.* Chapel Hill: University of North Carolina Press.

Reade, John. 1908. In the Province of Quebec. In *A history of Canadian journalism ... 1859–1908*, 146–59. Toronto: n.p.

Reaney, James. 1978. *The shivaree: Opera in two acts.* n.p.: n.p.

Record of activities in connection with the settlement of the Avonlea District: Pioneer reunion, A. [1963]. n.p.: n.p.

Revised Charter of the City of Winnipeg. 1918. n.p.: n.p.

Rey-Flaud, Henri. 1985. *Le Charivari : les rituels fondamentaux de la sexualité.* Paris: Payot.

Riddell, William Renwick. 1931. The 'shivaree' and the original. *Ontario Historical Society* 27:522–24.

Rieti, Barbara. 2008. *Making witches: Newfoundland traditions of spells and counterspells.* Montreal and Kingston: McGill-Queen's University Press.

Riley, Henry Hiram. 1854. *Puddleford and its people.* New York: Hueston.

Ring, Dan. 2002. Qu'Appelle: Tales of two valleys. Mendel Art Gallery. http://quappelle.mendel.ca/en/tales/whoscalling/quappelle/index.html.

Risk, R.C.B. 1990. Canadian courts under the influence. *University of Toronto Law Journal* 40:687–733.

Roberts, Julia. 2001. The taverns and tavern-going in Upper Canada, 1849. In *Canada 1849*, ed. Derek Pollard and Ged Martin, 93–107. Edinburgh: University of Edinburgh Press.

– 2002. 'A mixed assemblage of persons': Race and tavern space in Upper Canada. *Canadian Historical Review* 83 (1): 1–28.

– 2003. Harry Jones and his cronies in the taverns of Kingston, Canada West. *Ontario History* 95 (1): 1–21.

– 2004. Taverns. In *The Oxford Companion to Canadian History*, ed. Gerald Hallowell, 607–8. Don Mills, ON: Oxford University Press.

Rosenzweig, Roy. 1983. *Eight hours for what we will: Workers and leisure in an industrial city, 1879–1920.* Cambridge, UK: Cambridge University Press.

Russell, B. 1926. Reminiscences of the Nova Scotia judiciary. *Dalhousie Review* 5:499–512.

Russell, Benjamin. 1932. *Autobiography.* Halifax: Royal Print & Litho.

Rutherford, Paul. 1982. *A Victorian authority: The daily press in late nineteenth-century Canada.* Toronto: University of Toronto Press.

Sangster, Joan. 1993. 'Pardon tales' from Magistrate's Court: Women, crime and court in Peterborough County, 1920–50. *Canadian Historical Review* 72 (2): 161–97.

– 2001. *Regulating girls and women: Sexuality, family, and the law in Ontario, 1920–1960.* Don Mills, ON: Oxford University Press.

– 2005. Mobilizing women for war. In *Canada and the First World War: Essays in honour of Robert Craig Brown*, ed. David McKenzie, 157–93. Toronto: University of Toronto Press.

Santino, Jack, ed. 1994. *Halloween and other festivals of death and life.* Knoxville: University of Tennessee Press.

Sawin, Patricia E. 2001. Transparent masks: The ideology and practice of disguise in contemporary Cajun Mardi Gras. *Journal of American Folklore* 114:175–203.

Scharff, Virginia. 1991. *Taking the wheel: Women and the coming of the motor age.* New York: Free Press.

Schely-Newman, Esther. 1993. The woman who was shot: A communal tale. *Journal of American Folklore* 106:285–303.

Schmidt, Sarah. 1998. 'Private' acts in 'public' spaces: Parks in turn-of-the-century Montreal. In *Power, place, and identity*, ed. Tamara Myers, Kate Boyer, Mary Anne Poutanen, and Steven Watt,129–49. Montreal: History Group.

Shaw, Christine, dir. 2002. Butser ancient farm. http://www.butser.org.uk/iafplo_hcc.html.

Sibbald, Barbara. 2004. Ottawa's literary environment: Part 4. *National capital letters: Ottawa's literary environment.* Ottawa Literary Heritage Society http://capletters.ncf.ca/capletters/5/ottawaliterary.html (accessed 2 May 2007).

Sider, Gerald M. 1986. *Culture and class in anthropology and history: A Newfoundland illustration.* Cambridge, UK: Cambridge University Press.

Smart, Reginald G., and Alan C. Ogborne. 1996. *Northern spirits: A social history of alcohol in Canada.* Toronto: Addiction Research Foundation.

Smith, David E., ed. 1992. *Building a province: A history of Saskatchewan in documents.* Saskatoon: Fifth House Publishers.

Smith, Moira. 1996. Pranks. In *American folklore: An encyclopedia,* 587–9. New York: Garland Publishing.

Smith-Rosenberg, Carroll. 1975. The female world of love and ritual: Relations between women in nineteenth-century America. *Signs* 1 (1): 1–29.

Southworth, Jean. 1992. Ottawa, Ont. In *Encyclopaedia of music in Canada,* ed. Helmut Kallman and Gilles Potvin. http://www.thecanadian encyclopedia.com/index.cfm?PgNm=TCE&Params=U1ARTU 0002678.

Story, George M. 1969. Mummers in Newfoundland history. In Halpert and Story, 167–85.

Swanson, Eleanor. 1987. Brookdale. In *Quest in roots,* 50–6. Brookdale, MB: Brookdale Historical Society.

Szwed, John F. 1966. Gossip, drinking and social control: Consensus and communication in a Newfoundland parish. *Ethnology* 5:434–41.

– 1971. Paul E. Hall: A Newfoundland song-maker and community of son. In *Folksongs and their makers,* ed. Henry Glassie, Edward D. Ives, and John F. Szwed, 147–69. Bowling Green, OH: Bowling Green Popular Press.

Taft, Michael. 1983. *Discovering Saskatchewan folklore: Three case studies.* Edmonton: NeWest.

– 1997. Men in women's clothing: Theatrical transvestites on the Canadian prairie. In *Undisciplined women: Tradition and culture in Canada,* ed. Pauline Greenhill and Diane Tye, 131–8. Montreal and Kingston: McGill-Queen's University Press.

Tallman, Richard S. 1974. A generic approach to the practical joke. *Southern Folklore Quarterly* 38 (4): 259–74.

Tanglefoot. 1993. *A grain of salt.* Ooze River Music, ORM11-1192CD.

Thompson, E.P. 1992. Rough music reconsidered. *Folklore* 103:3–26.

– 1993. *Customs in common.* New York: New Press.

Underdown, D.E. 1985. The taming of the scold: The enforcement of patriarchal authority in early modern England. In *Order and disorder in early modern England,* ed. Anthony Fletcher and John Stevenson, 116–36. Cambridge, UK: Cambridge University Press.

Underdown, David. 1987. *Revel, riot & rebellion: Popular politics and culture in England, 1603–1660.* Oxford: Oxford University Press.

Vansina, Jan. 1961. *Oral tradition: A study in historical methodology,* trans. H.M. Wright. Chicago: Aldine.

Varner, Lloyd, Deborah Vermeulen, and Tracey MacNutt. 1993. *The Varners of Nova Scotia.* Privately printed.

Waddams, S.M. 2000. *Sexual slander in nineteenth-century England: Defamation in the ecclesiastical courts, 1815–1855.* Toronto: University of Toronto Press.

Walker, James W. St G. 1980. *A history of Blacks in Canada: A study guide for teachers and students.* Hull: Minister of Supply and Services Canada.

Wallis, Arthur. 1908. The press of Ontario. In *A history of Canadian journalism ... 1859–1908*, 160–75. Toronto: n.p.

Wamsley, Kevin B., and Robert S. Kossuth. 2000. Fighting it out in nineteenth-century Upper Canada / Canada West: Masculinities and physical challenges in the tavern. *Journal of Sport History* 27:405–30.

Ware, Carolyn E. 2007. *Cajun women and Mardi Gras: Reading the rules backward.* Urbana: University of Illinois Press.

Warsh, Cheryl Krasnick. 1993. 'John Barleycorn must die': An introduction to the social history of alcohol. In *Drink in Canada: Historical essays*, ed. Cheryl Krasnick Warsh, 3–26. Montreal and Kingston: McGill-Queen's University Press.

Watson, Gordon. 1983. Avonlea Rural Telephone Co. Ltd. In Avonlea Historical Committee, 37–9.

Watson, Jennie. 1987. William McLaughlin family. In *Quest in roots*, 406–7. Brookdale, MB: Brookdale Historical Society.

Watson, Jennie (McLaughlin). 1990. Wm McLaughlin. In *First century of Langford, 1891–1991*, 421–3. Neepawa: Langford Centennial Historical Committee.

Weller, Judith A. n.d. Roman traction systems. Der Humanist. http://www.humanist.de/rome/rts/agriculture.html.

Wells-Barnett, Ida B. 2005. Lynching and the excuse for it. In *Feminist theory: A reader*, 2nd ed., ed. Wendy K. Kolmar and Frances Bartkowski, 117–20. Boston: McGraw-Hill.

Wendel, W. Bradley. 2001. Non-legal regulation of the legal profession: Social norms in professional communities. *Vanderbilt Law Review* 55:1953–2045.

What's On. [2002] ... a stranger comes to town: Historical Film Posters from Saskatchewan. Regina: Dunlop Art Gallery. http://www.dunlopartgallery.org/whatson/page.cgi?key=117 (accessed June 20, 2006).

Whelpton, Calvin, and Eileen Whelpton. 1990. The William Whelpton family. In *First century of Langford, 1891–1991*, 516–17. Neepawa: Langford Centennial Historical Committee.

Whitcomb, Ed. 1982. *A short history of Manitoba.* Stittsville, ON: Canada's Wings.

– 2005. *A short history of Saskatchewan.* Ottawa: From Sea to Sea Enterprises.

White, Hayden. 1973. *Metahistory: The historical imagination in nineteenth-century Europe.* Baltimore: Johns Hopkins University Press.

White, Max E. 1981. Sernatin': A traditional Christmas custom in northeast Georgia. *Southern Folklore Quarterly* 45:89–99.

Wright, J.F.C. 1955. *Saskatchewan: The history of a province.* n.p.: McClelland & Stewart.

Wyatt-Brown, Bertram. 1983. *Southern honor: Ethics and behavior in the Old South.* Oxford: Oxford University Press.

Yamawaki, Niwako. 2007. Rape perception and the function of ambivalent sexism and gender-role traditionality. *Journal of Interpersonal Violence* 22:406–23.

Ziff, Bruce. 2002. Review essay: The 19th-century anti-rent controversy in New York State: Two recent works. *Alberta Law Review* 39:994–1004.

Index

Rimbey, Alberta, 187, 188
Ritchie, James Johnston (Justice), 138, 212n31
Ritchie, Steve, 177
Rochesterville, Ontario, 24, 41, 74
Roseneath, Manitoba, 186
rough music (as denunciatory charivari), 15, 28, 115, 131–2, 142, 176
Rouleau, Saskatchewan, 21, 162
Russell, Benjamin (Justice), 138, 212n32
Rutherford, Paul, 38–39

St Catharines, Ontario, 24
St Thomas, Ontario, 190
saluting (synonym for charivari), 15, 32, 111, 116
Saskatchewan, survival of charivari in, 29, 160–9; Avonlea (site of Babcock charivari). See Avonlea. Bengough, 162; Cardross, 163–4; Congress, 161; Craven, 164; Disley, 162; Eldersley, 163; Florentine, 187; Herbert, 190; Kisbey, 164; Major, 183–4, 189; Milestone, 163; Ogema, 162; Regina, 185; Rouleau, 21, 162; Tisdale, 163; Vantage, 161; Weyburn, 160; Yellow Grass, 163
Schomberg, Ontario, 175, 188
Seaforth, Ontario, 184, 185
serenade (synonym for charivari), 15, 19, 128
sexual activity: focus of pranking, 181, 183–4; interruption by charivari, 162–3, 168, 178, 183
sexual relationships, 4, 14, 16. See also adultery
shamings. See charivaris – denunciatory
shivaree (synonym for charivari), 3, 5, 15, 16, 19
Simcoe, Ontario, 183
skimmington (as denunciatory charivari), 15
slander, distinguished from libel, 137, 138
Snowflake, Manitoba (site of charivari shooting in 1906), 26, 99, 109

sport, 53–6
Springfield, Annapolis County, Nova Scotia (site of Varner-McNayr charivari), 8, 27, 30, 111–43 *passim*, esp. 116–18
'Sullivan's Shivaree,' 177–8, 183, 186
Sussex, New Brunswick, 215n2
symbolic capital, 115, 132

Tanglefoot, 177
Tavistock, Ontario, 183, 187
Taylor, F.G. (Crown attorney), 89
temperance, 58, 73, 77–82, 118, 141. *See also* liquor
Ten Nights in a Barroom and What I Saw There, 58, 80–1
tests. *See under* pranking
theatre, 29
Tisdale, Saskatchewan, 163
Toronto Globe, 8, 25, 26, 31, 35, 95
Toronto Star, 8, 99–100
traditional culture, 13–14, 29. *See also* folklore; oral tradition
traditional genres, 4
transgender, 5, 10, 195n2, 196n8
treat (payment or offering at charivari), 4, 18, 79–80, 81, 182–3. *See also* quête
treating (in taverns), 18, 79
trespass charges, 18
trials. *See* charivari – legal actions resulting from, 18, 19–20, 27
trickery. *See* pranking

Upham, New Brunswick, 185, 186
Upper Musquodoboit, Nova Scotia, 189
Uxbridge, Ontario, 185

vagrancy, 121, 210n26
Vansina, Jan, 12
Vantage, Saskatchewan, 161
Varner-McNayr charivari (Springfield, Annapolis County, Nova Scotia, 1917), 28, 111–43; absence of oral tradition relating to, 129–30; deemed tantamount to libel, 138

THE CANADIAN SOCIAL HISTORY SERIES

Terry Copp,
The Anatomy of Poverty:
The Condition of the Working Class
in Montreal, 1897–1929, 1974.
ISBN 0-7710-2252-2

Alison Prentice,
The School Promoters: Education
and Social Class in Mid-Nineteenth
Century Upper Canada, 1977.
ISBN 0-7710-7181-7

John Herd Thompson,
The Harvests of War:
The Prairie West, 1914–1918, 1978.
ISBN 0-7710-8560-5

Joy Parr, editor,
Childhood and Family in
Canadian History, 1982.
ISBN 0-7710-6938-3

Alison Prentice and
Susan Mann-Trofimenkoff, editors,
The Neglected Majority:
Essays in Canadian Women's History,
Volume 2, 1985.
ISBN 0-7710-8583-4

Ruth Roach Pierson,
'They're Still Women After All':
The Second World War and
Canadian Womanhood, 1986.
ISBN 0-7710-6958-8

Bryan D. Palmer,
The Character of Class Struggle:
Essays in Canadian Working Class
History, 1850–1985, 1986.
ISBN 0-7710-6946-4

Alan Metcalfe,
Canada Learns to Play:
The Emergence of Organized Sport,
1807–1914, 1987.
ISBN 0-7710-5870-5

Marta Danylewycz,
Taking the Veil: An Alternative to
Marriage, Motherhood, and Spinster-
hood in Quebec, 1840–1920, 1987.
ISBN 0-7710-2550-5

Craig Heron,
Working in Steel: The Early Years in
Canada, 1883–1935, 1988.
ISBN 0-7710-4086-5

Wendy Mitchinson and
Janice Dickin McGinnis, editors,
Essays in the History of Canadian
Medicine, 1988.
ISBN 0-7710-6063-7

Joan Sangster,
Dreams of Equality: Women on the
Canadian Left, 1920–1950, 1989.
ISBN 0-7710-7946-X

Angus McLaren,
Our Own Master Race: Eugenics
in Canada, 1885–1945, 1990.
ISBN 0-7710-5544-7

Bruno Ramirez,
On the Move:
French-Canadian and Italian
Migrants in the North Atlantic Econ-
omy, 1860–1914, 1991.
ISBN 0-7710-7283-X

Mariana Valverde,
'The Age of Light, Soap and Water':
Moral Reform in English Canada,
1885–1925, 1991.
ISBN 978-0-8020-9595-4

Bettina Bradbury,
Working Families: Age, Gender, and
Daily Survival in Industrializing
Montreal, 1993.
ISBN 978-0-8020-8689-1

Andrée Lévesque,
Making and Breaking the Rules:
Women in Quebec, 1919–1939, 1994.
ISBN 0-7710-5283-9

Cecilia Danysk,
Hired Hands: Labour and the Devel-
opment of Prairie Agriculture,
1880–1930, 1995.
ISBN 0-7710-2552-1

Kathryn McPherson,
*Bedside Matters: The Transformation
of Canadian Nursing, 1900–1990,*
1996.
ISBN 978-0-8020-8679-2

Edith Burley,
*Servants of the Honourable Com-
pany: Work, Discipline, and Conflict
in the Hudson's Bay Company,
1770–1870,* 1997.
ISBN 0-19-541296-6

Mercedes Steedman,
*Angels of the Workplace: Women and
the Construction of Gender Relations
in the Canadian Clothing Industry,
1890–1940,* 1997.
ISBN 0-19-54308-3

**Angus McLaren and Arlene Tigar
McLaren,** *The Bedroom and the
State: The Changing Practices and
Politics of Contraception and Abor-
tion in Canada, 1880–1997,* 1997.
ISBN 0-19-541318-0

**Kathryn McPherson, Cecilia
Morgan, and Nancy M. Forestell,**
editors, *Gendered Pasts: Historical
Essays in Feminity and Masculinity in
Canada,* 1999.
ISBN 978-0-8020-8690-7

Gillian Creese,
*Contracting Masculinity: Gender,
Class, and Race in a White-Collar
Union, 1944–1994,* 1999.
ISBN 0-19-541454-3

Geoffrey Reaume,
*Remembrance of Patients Past:
Patient Life at the Toronto Hospital
for the Insane, 1870–1940,* 2000.
ISBN 0-19-541538-8

Miriam Wright,
*A Fishery for Modern Times: The
State and the Industrialization of the
Newfoundland Fishery, 1934–1968,*
2001.
ISBN 0-19-541620-1

Judy Fudge and Eric Tucker,
*Labour before the Law: The Regula-
tion of Workers' Collective Action in
Canada, 1900–1948,* 2001.
ISBN 978-0-8020-3793-0

Mark Moss,
*Manliness and Militarism: Educating
Young Boys in Ontario for War,* 2001.
ISBN 0-19-541594-9

Joan Sangster,
*Regulating Girls and Women:
Sexuality, Family, and the Law in
Ontario, 1920–1960,* 2001.
ISBN 0-19-541663-5

**Reinhold Kramer
and Tom Mitchell,**
*Walk Towards the Gallows: The
Tragedy of Hilda Blake, Hanged
1899,* 2002.
ISBN 978-0-8020-9542-8

Mark Kristmanson,
*Plateaus of Freedom: Nationality,
Culture, and State Security in
Canada, 1940–1960,* 2002.
ISBN 0-19-541866-2

Robin Jarvis Brownlie,
*A Fatherly Eye: Indian Agents,
Government Power, and Aboriginal
Resistance in Ontario, 1918–1939,*
2003.
ISBN 0-19-541891-3 (cloth)
ISBN 0-19-541784-4 (paper)

Steve Hewitt,
*Riding to the Rescue: The Transfor-
mation of the RCMP in Alberta and
Saskatchewan, 1914–1939,* 2006.
ISBN 978-0-8020-9021-8 (cloth)
ISBN 978-0-8020-4895-0 (paper)

Robert K. Kristofferson,
*Craft Capitalism: Craftsworkers and
Early Industrialization in Hamilton,
Ontario, 1840–1872,* 2007.
ISBN 978-0-8020-9127-7 (cloth)
ISBN 978-0-8020-9408-7 (paper)

Andrew Parnaby,
Citizen Docker: Making a New Deal on the Vancouver Waterfront, 1919–1939, 2007.
ISBN 978-0-8020-9056-0 (cloth)
ISBN 978-0-8020-9384-4 (paper)

J.I. Little,
Loyalties in Conflict: A Canadian Borderland in War and Rebellion, 1812–1840, 2008.
ISBN 978-0-8020-9773-6 (cloth)
ISBN 978-0-8020-9825-1 (paper)

Pauline Greenhill,
Make the Night Hideous: Four English-Canadian Charivaris, 1881–1940, 2010.
ISBN 978-1-4426-4077-1 (cloth)
ISBN 978-1-4426-1015-6 (paper)